ACE!

Autobiography of a Fighter Pilot World War II

By Melvyn Paisley
With Vicki Paisley

BRANDEN PUBLISHING COMPANY
BOSTON

Library of Congress Cataloging-in-Publication Data

Paisley, Melvyn R., 1924-
    ACE! : autobiography of a fighter pilot, World War II /
by Melvyn Paisley, with Vicki Paisley.
        p. cm.
    Includes bibliographical references and index.
    ISBN 0-8283-1943-x
    1. Paisley, Melvyn, R., 1924-
    2. World War, 1939-1945--Aerial operation, American.
    3. World War, 1939-1945--personal narratives, American.
    4. Fighter pilots--United States--Biography.
    5. United States. Army Air Force--Biography.
       I. Paisley, Vicki. II. Title.
D790.P35 1992
940.54'4973'092--dc20
[B]   92-8971
                                       CIP

BRANDEN PUBLISHING COMPANY Inc.
17 Station Street
Box 843 Brookline Village
Boston, MA 02147

CONTENTS

TO:
Debbie, Frank, Chip & Beau

PREFACE

In the process of writing this story I was drawn into each of the time periods described. As I journeyed through my life's remembrances I attempted to preserve the expressions and feelings which were typical of the times.

It has been said that an autobiography is a book that reveals nothing bad about its writer except his memory. My experience tells me that a clear honest recollection is generally more difficult than creative prose. In any event I struggled to follow the facts as I best recalled them. Most important to me is that the story reflects events as I remember them and how I believe I felt at the time, though not necessarily how I may feel about them today. This book exists because of one person--my co-author and wife, Vicki. She prodded me to write it and then played the part of re-writer and critic, with the intent of driving me toward ear-pleasing prose, opposed to the dry engineering writing style of which I am more accustomed. Her forbearance from the day the idea was conceived to the day of publication was remarkable; she truly became a fire-walker.

I must also give thanks to my friends who stuck with me in this endeavor providing memories, thoughts and constructive criticism. Specifically I would like to thank Admiral Lyle Bull, Darrel Cole, Charlie Fox, Cyndy Karon, Sue Keith, Janet McKim, Jack "Mort" Morton, Colonel Neel Patrick and Ginny Patrick, Sandy and D.J. Ross, Fenton "Red" Royal, General Paul Ollerton, and Colonel Henry Trimble. A special thanks goes to John "the Greek" Peacheos for the many hours he spent in the dusty drawers of the Oregon Historical Society and the Portland Oregonian.

There is probably no better place than here for a belated thanks to the crew of the La Mort that made this record possible. Without the day and night devotion to duty of these non-coms, my Jug and I would not have survived: Crew Chief Stan Michano, Asst. Crew Chief John Conway, Armorer Chuck Higby, Asst. Armorer Ray Hebert and Radio Mechanic Jim Stallings.

The research assistants at Bolling and Maxwell Air Force Bases made possible the detailed accounts of the fighter missions described in this book. They located my group and squadron records, including photographs for the entire time I was on the Continent.

It was with great delight that I uncovered in these records the long lost general orders and a letter of confirmation written by my wingman to verify a heretofore unconfirmed four of the nine aircraft victory record displayed on my P-47, *La Mort*, during her last few months of combat duty.

Five of the nine victories resulted from a single mission on January 1, 1945 in a massive Luftwaffe raid on Allied airfields which involved over 800 German aircraft.

Although scorekeeping was a matter of great pride among fighter pilots, most of the 9th Air Force victories were too numerous to recount. These were the scores of locomotives, tanks, weapons carrier, armored cars and anything else which stood in the way of Allied troops on the ground.

Regardless of the readers' sentiments about the bawdy ballads and marching songs, they are a significant part of the heritage of the Air Force and I include them with no intent to offend.

Finally I trust I have endeared the people who are mentioned and those that are not.

1. Lt. Melvyn R. Paisley climbing out of his P-47
La Mort, after a mission.

INTRODUCTION

Soaring off its target, our P-47 flight finally broke through the wall of flak surrounding the rail yard at Halberstadt. There was good reason for the heavy German defense; the yard was crammed with at least ten locomotives and close to three hundred box cars. I glanced back hurriedly and saw that the two five hundred pound bombs I had just released made a dead hit on a couple of locomotives. Thick black smoke spun into the air and mingled with the flak bursts that surrounded my element leader Ross Gibson and his wingman, who was close behind. Gibson's strike, following mine, was smack in the center of the box car marshaling area, hitting a string of ammo cars. The entire yard and half the city lurched straight out of the earth as his bombs struck. Gibson's wingman, the yard and the city disappeared in the smoke.

As I awakened from my brief slumber, the glow of the massive fireball which haunted my dream, lingered in my eyes like the effects of too direct a view of the sun. But my senses told me that the sun was the last thing one would see from the Nissen hut (a poor man's version of a quonset hut) in which I now lay. In fact, today was just another one of those soggy days in England when native birds best chose not to fly, though our great metal war birds seemed to think they could anyway. After all, God was on our side. Hadn't we proved that by winning the war in Europe just two months before?

I stretched luxuriously in my threadbare bunk which was surprisingly stiff. My hands and feet encroached on my neighbors, though no one complained. We were but a few of the hundreds of men who waited at the Air Transport base, whiling away our time. Our temporary home had the appearance of a huge corrugated steel tube cut in half and placed haphazardly on the cold dank earth. It was comfortable enough, far more comfortable than any of the quarters I had during my last year on the continent. The calendar on the wall had a big X marked conspicuously across the date; it was July twenty-seventh, nineteen hundred and forty-five. Perhaps someone was keeping track of an important event, but for me this was just another day I spent waiting. With time on my hands, I took on the task of writing the story of my life. I was twenty years old and on my way to Japan to help win the war for God's side. But first, I was going home.

Army Air Force pilots were selected for rotation back to the states from Europe after V-E Day based on a point system. I was the first in my class to be rotated, having accumulated the most points as determined by the number of missions flown and decorations received. I left the ranking P-47 ace of the 366th Fighter Group. That was damned heady stuff for a second generation immigrant son of an Oregon logger and a Belgian farm girl.

Writing my life story seemed appropriate at the time; I thought had done it all. But the unit orderly's bark spared me from agonizing another moment over my shortcomings in spelling: "Captain Melvyn Paisley, roll out in two hours for transportation back to the Z.I. or [*Zone of the Interior*]." I grabbed my A-2 leather flight jacket, fifty-mission crush hat and swagger-stick, then hustled to the phone booth. Mom would want to know I was on my way.

Comfortably settling into the journey on the Air Force B-24, I passed the hours with daydreams. Mom's cooking was so near, I could smell the warm apple pie with a tinge of cinnamon. Then there were my buddies, my hot rod and something else which was no more complicated than the familiarity of home. Though we refueled at Greenland and Gander, I remembered surprisingly little about the stops.

Late into the next morning our Liberator bomber made its final approach into what seemed to a fighter pilot like me to be a long runway. I listened lazily to our pilot's communications with the command field when a special bulletin pierced the normally mundane chatter, "A B-25 Mitchell bomber, en route from Bedford Army Air Base to Newark, has just crashed into the seventy-ninth floor of the Empire State Building. All of the plane's occupants are feared dead. An unknown number of civilians are still trapped by blazing fires throughout the building. The explosion of the plane was heard more than a mile away, and debris has reportedly been found as far away as Madison Avenue. The New York City fire department continues at this moment to fight the massive fire which was fueled by an explosion of the bomber's gasoline tanks."

Our plane grew uncomfortably silent. We all knew too much of death.

Through a thick fog below, the Air Transport Command field came into sight. An enthusiastic crowd had gathered to meet us, the likes of which I hadn't seen since I won the 1938 Soap Box Derby back in Portland, Oregon. America was grand!

The gaudy screech of our rubber wheels on the macadam runway reminded me that we were no longer in the land of steel mat fighter landing strips. All at once, a flash bolted through my head. I had left my manu-script on the top bunk in England. And my swaggerstick stood in the corner of the operation phone booth. With a chuckle, I mused how Terry and the Pirates' Hotshot Charlie, who made the swaggerstick famous for Air Corps fighter jocks, would be mortified by my clumsy irreverence.

But there was no sense in looking back. For now I was headed home to Portland.

11 ACE!

After forty-five years, I once again succumbed to the urge to write a story of the period in my life which transitioned me from a logging camp in the wilds of Oregon, through the Depression, the hot rod days of the early '40s, the Great War and finally settling into the working world. Trying to recapture the years lost during the war sent me down several searching paths, including an arduous attempt to sail around the world before stability sent me down the road of a very satisfying career in the aerospace industry. I found myself among friends in the journey and the troubles which befell us seemed to be the price of growing up at the pace the times demanded.

2. Hotshot Charlie, with swaggerstick in hand.

CHAPTER 1

PICKING STONES

Five small faces, stiffened by the ghastly horror, peered from behind the ramshackle door at the rear of the old farmhouse. Not a word was spoken as the children gaped at the limp body of their baby sister who had fallen into the tub of scalding wash water, still sitting on the stone porch. Memories of young Agnes' playful, teasing laugh flashed ominously though the children's minds as my grandmother carefully wrapped the remains of her youngest child in a crocheted blanket. Ghoulishly, the child's scalp hung loosely from her skull. A small swatch of golden hair lay indiscreetly on the clean white wrap. Grandma slumped onto the cold steps and tenderly caressed each fine hair.

The children had been playing only moments before. Laughing and running over the old stone steps, around the wash tub and into the fresh cut field. Grandma was busily doing chores as she most always did, and Agnes was left in the care of the older children, as she most always was. As the oldest, my mother Clara, was surely presumed the most responsible for Agnes' well-being.

It was the hurt on Grandma's face which Mom remembered most vividly about that fateful day. She told me so many times of the despair in Grandma's eyes.

Mom was barely six years old, then, born a Belgian in the year 1900. A headstrong child, old enough to follow her mother's directions, but too young to resist the inevitable distractions. No one blamed Mom, not really.

This wasn't the only child Grandma had lost; no, another died years before in infancy. But perhaps this death caused Grandpa and Grandma to leave their Belgian homeland in search of a better life.

The town in which they lived Scheldewindelka, near Ghent, was much like other small villages scattered throughout the Belgian countryside. An old church stood high on a small rise in the land and a couple of small stores were clustered at the streets' intersection. The little village prospered when the neighboring farms had a good year. But, most of the villagers would lament, life was by and large a struggle.

Economic conditions in the early 1900s were particularly bleak. Small farms could not generate enough cash to support an average family. Survivable farming required large land holdings and large families to work those holdings. And like most of their neighbors, my grandparents could not afford to feed their five children much less acquire more land holdings.

The Canadian homestead act offered hope. "Canada is the land of milk and honey," the promoter said as he stood on the church steps with his hands in the sky, "the place to build your future." Leon and Camille Vermeulen were at first intrigued, then with more deliberation they were convinced. They sold their small farm, packed up their children and their oxen harness and boarded the next train bound for the port of Antwerp.

Grandpa complained bitterly of the conditions on the ship they boarded, but those concerns were never passed on to the children and it was Grandma who preserved the hope.

Crouched low on the ship's port deck, she huddled with her family, their backs against the howling wind. They talked of better times ahead, and the promise of large parcels of farmland offered by the Canadian government. Things were not so bad they had each other. Besides, they expected their new life to be fraught with unsparing hardship. The land was untilled and the towns had not yet grown. But some day, maybe just for the children, life would be better than they had ever imagined.

Many like my grandparents, risked it all, saying without forbiddance "Why not?" It was a devil-may-care courage which possessed them and drove them to do what they were going to do. Others stayed home, in Belgium and continued life as they knew it to be. Their grandchildren would know no other ways. After all, their life was not really so dire, and their futures were not so terribly dismal. "There's simply too much to lose," they rationalized.

Nineteen hundred and seven was the year the Vermeulens settled in Ceylon, Saskatchewan, a tiny little village surrounded by open prairie as far as a crow could fly. Not far from Ceylon was the family's homestead, a wilderness of blowing dust, scrub grass and rocks. Grandpa and Grandma walked every inch of their land, behind a rickety walking plow and a stubborn team of oxen. The kids did what they could to help.

Before the winter's snows came, Grandpa and Grandma built a small wood frame shack with two rooms and a stone basement atop a small rise on their homestead. Obscuring the house in size, was a four-stall barn built for the oxen. My Grandparents had a long debate over building the house of sod or logs. Grandpa argued the more traditional sod house had the advantage of not burning. "Prairie fires are a frightful peril to the crops, the oxen and the houses, too," he warned. But Grandma won the argument, complaining sod was much too dirty, "If you have to work in the soil, you didn't have to live in it. Besides," she added, "prairie fires will move like the wind around the house." And, when the fires came, they did just that. Still, there was little protection from the dirt, which blew with the unceasing wind and which seeped into every crevice.

15 ACE!

The dream of more land and children started to materialize when four more children were born. The family proved up their homestead and exercised their homestead preemption rights for another one hundred sixty acres at three dollars an acre. More families came from Europe and settled the land around the Vermeulen properties. Also many settlers from the eastern part of the continent started moving West. This movement brought farmhands passing through, looking for work stacking grain or hauling bundles to the threshing machines. One of these young farmhands, caused a shocking scandal in my mother's life, the details of which she harbored until her dying day.

The young man flatly refused to marry Mom or maybe Mom flatly refused to marry him. Sadly, but in keeping with the times, their baby daughter was placed for adoption through the church, a dark secret carefully concealed for a lifetime, one too painful for my mother to divulge. There were those who knew, but no one dared betray Mom while she lived. The consequences of enduring her wrath were far too grave. More important their love for her precluded it.

By 1920, the family prospered, building a big new house and barn. Mom was the first child of eleven who left home to work in Ceylon and later Regina, about forty miles up the road. The cash mother made financed even more farm expansion such as machinery, horses and building materials. In the lean years Mom's money helped keep the farm out of hock.

My father, Frank, left his family in Toronto at the age of thirteen and a few years later, somehow came to Regina. It was a Sunday when Dad and Mom first talked at an ice cream social which her church sponsored. Dad approached Mom, having been at the adjacent park with a few roustabout friends, "What about having a drink with us?"

Mom put her bottle of soda pop to her lips and walked away defiantly. One of the other guys pursued her further, too far for Dad who admittedly had his eye on Mom for quite some time. After one punch was thrown, a full-fledged fight broke out. Had it not been for the nasty bruise on Dad's face, it would have been a perfect match -- with Dad walking away hand in hand with Mom.

In 1922 Mom and Dad married and moved west to Vancouver, British Columbia in search of a job for Dad. They lived in a boarding house near the center of town. The landlady was a nosy type who was forever querying Mom on her age. "You're such a tiny thing, you can't be all that old," she remarked as she pried even harder to learn the exact date of Mom and Dad's wedding and the exact age of her newborn son Gordon. Mom knew there was a respectable nine months between the two dates, but she was of the nature to let the old biddy stew.

Soon after Gord's birth, (the name Gordon was reserved for when he misbehaved), Dad took a job as a mechanic on a ship and left Mom and Gord with relatives. Mom cried her eyes out when she read Dad's first letter telling her he had jumped ship in Seattle, Washington where he went to work in the woods as a choker-setter. America was the land of her dreams, but lumberjacks were a frightful bunch. They frequented the saloons near her Vancouver boarding house, and they drank far too freely. A wild, brawling lot, they were. Their philosophy on life was about as uncouth as the yammering lumberjack who sat next to her at the train depot, "Eat'n, drink'n, work'n and screw'n, that's the whole wad, there just ain't anything more to it." Altogether they were a different breed, one Mom would grow to tolerate.

Dad picked up the logging trade rapidly and moved to a better job on the Umpqua River in Oregon. That was when Mom and Gord joined Dad in the woods, stealing across the border as quietly as Dad did months before. Although high climbing was one of the riskiest ways of making a living in the woods, that's what Dad wanted to do. Maybe it was the challenge or maybe it was the money that drove him. For Mom, however it was the danger which bothered her most and the nightmares which frightened her. So many times she wakened to the snap of a safety rope, or the grating rip of a tree which had split unexpectedly as it was being topped.

Not one day passed that the whistle-punk kid didn't sound the whistle signaling an accident had happened. Regardless of what they were doing at the time, the women always quieted when they heard the shrill omen echoing through the tall trees. They knew, more often than not, the accident was fatal. This time. Whose husband was it? They always feared the worst.

I was born right around the time Mom and Dad lived on the Umpqua. The year was 1924, the year of the rat.

Radio was the nation's primary source of entertainment. Most families gathered around their radios at night, listening to the serials and shuffling their feet to the music. America's love for jazz music was at its peak, and George Gershwin's *Fascinating Rhythm* being the number one hit tune.

Going to picture shows was gaining in popularity although there was no such thing as talking movies.

Calvin Coolidge was the subject of most political talk. He ran his re-election campaign on a ticket of "Keep Cool with Coolidge, Safe and Sane Cool-idge," and won. Most politicians were quick to tell their constituents prosperity was within their reach, but most people interpreted that as meaning prosperity was within reach of some of the nation's people-- generally no one they knew.

From a purely dollars and cents perspective, prices were so-so; milk was eleven cents a quart, gas was eleven cents a gallon and new Fords were two hundred sixty -five dollars. Minimum wage was twenty-five cents.

Cars were still a luxury, though surprisingly they were not all that slow. Corum and Boyer (it took two that year) won the Indianapolis 500 with the speed of ninety-eight miles per hour.

Airplanes and flyers were the nation's fascination. The Navy circumnavigated the earth by using a flight of Douglas World Cruisers which cruised at a speed of eighty miles per hour. Two of the original four aircraft landed in Seattle, Washington, their jumping off point, after five months and 26,345 miles of travel having lost one aircraft in Alaska and another at sea north of Scotland.

Altogether, I would say it was a pretty good year, although for Mom and Dad -- their life trudged down the same path.

The Umpqua logging camp was much the same as the life Mom knew before. She worked long, arduous hours in the cookhouse and relied on the neighbors' children to take care of Gord and me. Accidents occurred, just like they did on the farm. My own life was spared in an unexplained twist of fate, not that I was very appreciative at the time. Mom was convinced it was by the grace of God that a neighbor, Dorothy Gallager happened by and snatched me from the path of a moving train stacked full of logs. (Years later she owed my spared soul to my fighting on His side in the War.) All my life, I heard Dorothy say to me, as if I was still that little boy sitting on her lap, "If that brakeman hadn't of slammed on his brakes, we would of been picking up the scraps all the way into the next county." Dad would get annoyed by the visible display of disgusting sentiment, sometimes saying I was much too hard-headed to have suffered any serious harm, had that train run over me after all.

Some of my earliest recollections of childhood are of Gord's and my visits with our mom to the family farm in Canada in the summer of '29 and '35. They were delightful times, which stood out in the more traditionally mundane course of my growing up. For days and days, I explored the endless prairie and all it offered to a mischievous five-year-old anxious to learn the ways of the *privileged*. I taunted the farm animals and explored every outbuilding, including the outdoor privy. Interesting it was. There were two holes in the privy, not one. Lumberjacks never used privies with two holes. I wondered why.

"There's two holes because your Mom had so many brothers and sisters," Grandpa said to me. "Besides, when your mama was your age, she was scared of the coyotes and wouldn't go out alone at night. Grandma would take her by the hand then sit and read the *Monkey Ward* catalog with the lamp. You've probably heard your Grandma call the two-holer her wishing well. When she finds something she wants she rips out the page and plops it into the hole."

Each morning Grandpa gathered everyone in the kitchen and talked about the tasks which needed to be done that day. Although I was too young to make any significant contribution of my own, I listened eagerly for the events in which I could participate or observe -- otherwise referred to by Grandma as "getting in the way". In celebration of our visit, Grandpa *Kloek* (a Dutch nickname meaning strong) told the family he would butcher a pig. Since I knew Sunday mornings were the only time to spare for this activity, I anxiously waited for Sunday to come.

All Grandpa's tools for butchering, scraping, and scalding were neatly arranged on a canvas laid on the flat ground. Once the scene was properly set for making the soap, sausage, head cheese and everything else, Grandpa lunged for a big, old dirty sow, and with the aid of all hands, laid it on its side in front of the barn. In rapid order he struck the squealing pig on the head and slit its throat with a large butcher knife he had sharpened especially for that purpose. The warm red blood spurted all over my bare legs, and turned the caked mud on both the pig and me into a sticky, dark red mass. This left me as something more than just an observer and the sight of the slaughter lingered in my mind long beyond the summer of '29. More immediately, I was sick to my stomach and unable to enjoy the extravagant dinner Grandma so meticulously prepared.

Six years later Mom, Gord and I made the same journey back to the farm. As we traveled along the old gravel road that led from Plentywood, Montana to Ceylon, Saskatchewan, I saw a new barn towering majestically over the open prairie, which brought back fond memories of the one it replaced. The first barn had been destroyed by a twister which roared over the north plains just two years before. Grandma told the story of everyone huddling in the storm cellar listening to the eerie, squealing sounds of the storm and the rattling of the shutters. Dead silence followed and Grandpa raised the wooden doors on the cellar and looked to see what had happened. The eye of the twister spared the house -- not disturbing so much as a shingle, but it whipped through the center of the sturdy old barn, just one hundred yards from the house. Not one board was left standing. The barn was rebuilt only one year before my visit. It was a duplicate of the original, only two stalls shorter. Grandma wasn't so quick as she normally was to explain God's hand in the destruction which had occurred.

The Depression was a constant worry on the farm, much as it was for my parents. The price of wheat dropped to twenty cents a bushel at a time when crops were plagued with drought, army worms and grasshoppers. Though few farmers went hungry, they had little cash to spare. Still, families came from miles around to the Vermeulen dances in the barn loft.

19 ACE!

Everyone knew Grandma and Grandpa had the best barn on the prairie and they knew the Vermeulens loved throwing a good party. Each of mother's seven brothers played an instrument, everything from a banjo and a sax to a fiddle. They were self-trained for self-entertainment and good as most anyone around. With their make-do dance floor and self-made band, Grandma said there was some money to be made. My two aunts and Mom served Nehi pop and Pilsner beer into the night, for a small price of course. I stayed awake as long as I could, but finally succumbed to a satisfying sleep in the back of the hayloft to the beat of *Alexander's Ragtime Band*. If today I had a time machine, I would go back to 1935 and dance a slow waltz with Mom in the loft of that new barn. Mom was a looker and could she ever dance!

Sometime, early in the new morning the party was over and the clear lights hanging in the rafters were disconnected from their windmill battery system. As my mother shuffled me to bed through the starlit night, I heard Aunt Julia tell Mom the night was a great success; they had made a whopping eleven dollars and sixty five cents.

Harvesting on the farm is also a vivid memory. Every year around August, the community joined as a working team. Grandpa offered his twelve teams of Belgium draft horses and all hands on the farm. Gord and I had the job of taking the harvest crew their lunch. We used a simple device, a horse-drawn sled of sorts. The ladies would pile our *stoneboat* with what seemed to be all the food and drinks it would hold and then they'd pile on some more. Huge stacks of bologna sandwiches was the usual fare, each spread with a thin rub of mustard. The men called the sandwiches, *horse cock and grease*, but they ate them all the same. Then there were dozens of metal pots filled with water and fresh coffee. What could be more enjoyable to a kid than bouncing across the fields to the smells of the splashing coffee, bologna and fresh-baked bread.

Mostly Gord and I spent our summer days gathering stones from the dusty fields. Picking up rocks was dirty, back-breaking work, but we were too young to know it. To us it was amusement. On occasion, we gathered buffalo chips which Grandma use as fuel for her cooking. Although picking up chips was easier than picking up rocks, it was no less dirty. We'd gather them one by one and slip them into our gunny sacks. The trick was to pick only the ones which had dried properly, carefully examining them first. Instead we always thought it fun to grab the chips from the back of the moving stoneboat which meant we invariably scooped our hands into a warm paddy the consistency of sticky fudge.

"Phew, God almighty," Grandma would screech as she heated the water for our baths. She'd look disgustingly at our brown bodies, caked with dung. Then she'd rant and rave until the water was hot, all the time cursing the devil and those with similar tendencies. That spectacle alone was worth any discomfort we brought to ourselves through our careless blunders.

Grandma always gave us an extra good scrubbing when we went to the grange building in town to see a talking picture show starring one of our cowboy heros. Tom Mix was our favorite, riding the dusty range and fighting loathsome outlaws. What I didn't understand was how Tom Mix always stayed so clean. Even his hat remained remarkably white in the most fervent of dust storms and gun battles. We were convinced, sure as God made little boys, that Tom Mix didn't take as many baths as we did.

At summer's end, I was saddened to leave the farm. As we drove away on the narrow road to Plentywood, Montana where we would catch the train to Portland, the sun was starting to rise over the hill. The fresh cut wheat stubble reflected the light in a golden haze and the stone pile at the edge of the field stood firm, covered with chaff. I couldn't help wonder when I would return again. When would it be? There was no tomorrow promised, there never was. I stared out the car window, my nose pressed against the glass. My face was still wet with the tears from my final farewell to Grandpa.

3. Ready for the barn dance, Mel's Aunt Julia and Mother Clara.

4. Family visit to the Vermeulen farm, 1929.

5. The Vermeulen farm, 1935.

6. Dorothy Gallager; Mel, Gordon and their mother Clara
at the Umpqua River logging camp.

7. Fully loaded logging train in the Oregon woods.

8. High climbing in the late '20s.

CHAPTER 2

STREET-WISE SAVVY

As the '20s drew to a close the family moved from the logging camp to the city so my brother Gord could start elementary school. We moved to the town of Multnomah, just outside Portland, Oregon, renting what was to be the first of a series of houses that took my brother and me to a variety of schools throughout the Portland area. Everyone we knew rented the house they lived in; struggling all the same to make ends meet on a month-to-month basis.

Having lost my play partner to the Multnomah Elementary School, I looked for new ways to pass the time. Five years old, bursting with raw energy and not one friend in the world, I walked around aimlessly, pouting and kicking at the dirt, convincing myself that Gord had to be having more fun than me.

Gord always took the same path to school, down a narrow dirt road into the railroad gulch and up a steep climb to the school yard. The path was tricky, used as a shortcut by mostly the older boys. One day I followed him, then the next day I did the same. Suddenly a whole new world opened. Captivating and free.

The betrayal came swiftly, however, owed to a pair of brand-new corduroy knickers. Before she'd let me out of the house, Mom carefully snipped the sewn tags from the waistband. The minutes ticked away on the kitchen clock, one after another. At last I was free, and I raced down the path which was still damp from the previous day's showers. Clumsily I tripped over a small stump and fell flat on my face with a violent force. The trees whirled above me as I slid head-first then feet-first down the mud-slick hill, clawing at the few tiny vines which grew in the shade of the trees. At last I was able to wrap one leg around a tree trunk, stopping my descent.

Standing up slowly, I assessed the damage. Not too many scratches. A quick brush-off with my hands took care of the immediate problem and I was on my way again. When I reached the outer edge of the playground, I looked again at the mucky cake of mud which covered every inch of my body, in my hair and in the tear on my corduroy knickers. Dried patches of grime crinkled as I crouched under a huge fir tree and carefully cleared the branches that obstructed my view. This was the place I watched unnoticed as Gord darted into the building at the sound of the first bell.

Suddenly, my hand slipped from the thin branch which supported my weight. The branch cracked loudly and echoed through the woods. An older boy heard the sound then spotted me from the playground, "Hey squirt, what are you doing hiding? You're too young, and too dirty a runt to be near this school."

This was far too great a challenge to go unheeded, so I stood tall (almost three feet short, that is) put a stick on my shoulder, and dared the bully to knock it off. All the while, I stuck out my chin, and looked as mean as I possibly could. I'd been around long enough to know this was the approved way of starting a fight and defending your honor.

A rowdy swarm of boys and girls circled us, at once. There was no way out, no time for second thoughts. Most of the boys had already chosen their favorite to win. My brother stood out in the crowd, not because he was particularly big, but just because he was the only familiar face I could see. He stood rigidly in the back of the crowd, with his lips pursed. His eyes glared at mine and I blurted out tauntingly to my challenger, "If you touch this stick you'll have my brother to answer to."

When the fight was over, both my brother and I were lying side by side on a few moist tufts of grass which had survived on the playing field. Our first fight had ended in a humiliating disaster. Rising slowly off the ground, like a dejected circus clown, I stumbled away from the episode leaving my brother on his fifth day of school to live with it.

Mom was livid, not so much about the fight but the cords. They were beyond repair and Mom was not so quick to put them on me again. Nobody liked knickers anyway; Gord and his friends said they were sissy. "Sissy, Sissy, Sissy," they would taunt. And, if that wasn't enough to endure, the ridiculous bulge of stiff fabric which drooped around my knees, always squeaked when I stomped away.

Mom took a job in a cafe called Nick's, which was named after the owner, a Greek immigrant. Nick kept Mom working through the early years of the Depression (the *Depression* with a capital *D* being an extension of the depression we already knew). Dad came to town on irregular intervals; sometimes he would show up when the weather got too dry and the woods were in danger of fire. Other times, Dad came to town just because it was the day he got paid.

Mom's greatest challenge was to keep Dad out of the Portland card halls, which sucked in loggers like a fresh cow paddy draws flies. At every opportunity she pleaded with Dad to come home with his earnings. "The children have to have new jackets this winter," she'd cry with every bit of convincingness she could muster. "Aw, baloney," Dad would reply gruffly, "you've got money." Then he'd grin and give Mom a brisk kiss on the cheek, "The next paycheck is all yours." Dad wasn't much for listening. Never was. And, from what I could figure, all Dad's logger friends frittered away the nights and their earnings together.

If the subject of money came up in front of me, Mom always said it was "none of my business." And if I wanted something she was unwilling to buy, it was "not good for me," or I "didn't need it." If I persisted, she'd listen no further knowing I would eventually succumb to her reasoning. We had all the essentials, and were more fortunate than most others we knew.

Often I heard talk of Erickson's, a Portland saloon which spanned a whole city block not far from skid road. Mom's voice grew frigid when she talked of the saloon saying it was jammed with drunken loggers and seamen, bellowing, guffawing, belching and quarreling. If she ever thought Dad had been near the place, she would scowl and scold him about the evils of booze and bawds. Sometimes Dad caught me listening, and he'd wink, "Don't you go listening to all that nonsense, I'm just an everyday working stiff doin' what working stiffs do. Your mother's just in one of those moods. Has to give somebody a piece of her mind."

Although Dad more often than not initiated the squabbles with Mom, he abhorred them and did everything he could to escape them once they got going. "Come on Mel, let's go down to Swan Island and look over the airplanes," he'd say. I knew he had virtually no interest in airplanes, but he knew I was always pestering Mom with all sorts of questions about them. The diversion always worked like a charm and with Mom's blessing we would be off to the airport. Swan Island Airport being my favorite diversion of all.

All types of airplanes flew into Swan Island. One I remember better than the others. It was a large three engine plane which seemed to almost hover low over the field as it descended onto the runway. Only the glittering flashes of the sun on its silver body told me it was moving. Dad sped to the terminal so I could get a better look. Every inch of the way I shot out a question, "How does it fly like that? Why does it need three engines? Why is it so big?" Dad's only response was, "They just make them that way." And he must have felt some relief when we reached our destination at the terminal.

I bounded out of the car, heading for the hangar. A mechanic rushed out to stop me, grabbing my arm. "Son, wait until the engines shut off!" I waited impatiently, looking at the largest plane I'd ever seen. The mechanics grip loosened some, but he was still poised to grab me if I ran toward the plane again. "Mighty big isn't it," he said, making some friendly conversation. "It's a Ford Tri-motor, the best flying machine there is." As the engines subsided I touched the wheel which stood taller than me. Nothing could be any more exciting than this.

Dad would drop me off at Nick's for Mom to look after, when he went to the meeting hall where the men talked about labor matters. While Dad was at his meetings, Nick always gave me a huge slice of scrumptious apple pie with a even larger mound of whipped cream. Mom learned how to make apple pie from Nick and I believe to this day she makes the very best there is. Taking a handful of this and a scoop of this, there was never a recipe. It was the feel of the pie crust which told Mom it was right and the all important taste test which confirmed the proper mix for the filling. The unequaled flakiness of her crusts the exquisite taste of the apple fillings and the dozens of long, unbroken curls of apple peels were the testimony to her pie-making ability. Nick said he learned to make pies in Greece, although he'd never admit they were anything but American; "America's best," he said.

Participating in the debates of the Industrial Workers of the World was a favorite pastime of Dad's. It was there where his intellectual gifts were duly recognized, opposed to his brawn. And it was there that all working men became orators with an equal voice -- men who could make things better for their peers.

Still, Dad had trouble agreeing totally with what the Wobblies were trying to do and their methods for doing it. None of their more serious scuffles ever reached his neck of the woods, but word got around. There was always a scandal or two floating around the rumor mill. Some guy got roughed up, maybe another had a bad accident of a questionable nature. Still Dad was a strong supporter of the labor movement, which was just getting off the ground. And, once the A.F.L. came into the woods, Dad's union dues were always paid up, even when we didn't have much money to spare and even long after he stopped working as a lumberjack.

If there was a group of working men known best for their brutal brawls, it was the lumberjacks. Nary a day passed, that somebody's nose wasn't rebuilt. Few would dispute however, that the lumberjacks had a strong worker's code of ethics and Dad was a proponent. Everyone on the job had the responsibility to make everyone else look as good as possible. There was no competing, or trying to outdo each other for a better position and if someone had trouble keeping up, the others would cover. Every man had a right to make a decent living, whether he was weak or strong, capable or incapable.

Dad always talked proudly of the strides workers had made in their everyday working conditions. Unions *had* made a difference. He saw firsthand how the working man's position had improved. But the Depression put a strain on both the worker and the manager.

I began to see the effects of the Depression, when one day a man came into Nick's restaurant and ordered two slices of bread for a nickel. With the catsup and sugar on the counter, the man made a sandwich of sorts out of his bread. That was his lunch, I reckoned. Nick didn't say anything to the man but as the Depression deepened he removed the free sugar and catsup. The whipped cream disappeared, too.

In '32 we moved into the Albina district of Portland, a tough neighborhood by most anyone's standards. I never understood why we moved so often. Maybe we couldn't pay the rent, or maybe Dad just found a better deal somewhere else. Regardless, there were always lots of empty houses then from which to choose.

I often wondered who owned all the houses we lived in. The big buildings in the city, too. I guessed there were people with money somewhere, even in these difficult times. Mostly they were the landlords, the ones dad called idle parasites who he claimed, never worked a day in their lives. They always charged too much and thought we paid too little.

It was in Albina where I first started school, about the same time my parents got their first telephone. Practically every object of any significant value in our house (sentimental value, that is), sat on a crocheted doily. The telephone was no exception, sitting on a table all by itself on a ruffled white doily made by the hands of my Grandmother. Odd looking, the telephone appeared to be a tall black candlestick with a cupped mouthpiece attached to the top. Mom was tickled pink about having the device, though I often wondered why. She used it infrequently, saying so many of her friends hadn't gotten around to getting one. "Women!" Dad scoffed. "Those telephones are too highfalutin for me." No self-respecting logger would use one.

What was it like to talk on the candlestick phone? I didn't rightly know. I dared not touch it.

Then, in my second year of school I made my first friend in life, R.B. Wesley. R.B. was two years older than me, and a whole lot more worldly. Did he have a candlestick phone, the necessary companion of ours? No, R.B. like most of the boys I met, didn't have such a contrivance. "Costs too much," was the simple response R.B. gave in his usual way.

One day R.B. invited me to his house for supper. I sat at the kitchen table, and his Mom served up the food. Gazing down at my plate, I poked the edge of the crisp brown patty with my fork. I decided it looked something like gritty jello which had been fried until the life was out of it, then buried under a blanket of thick syrup. Another poke was necessary.

"Fried mush", R.B. whispered to me. "Bet you like it." After putting a tiny bite into my mouth and half-heartedly swashing it around, I agreed it was good, very good in fact. "I made it from this mornin's leftovers," R.B.'s mom said unabashedly, "the cornmeal we had." It was sweet like candy. Almost as good as the macaroni and cheese my Mom always served.

After supper R.B.'s family and I sat around the table talking for hours. A single bare light bulb lit the shadowy room. As the night crept in, our voices grew low. Suddenly a gigantic moth bashed against the screen door and I lurched from the wooden bench on which I sat. Uninterrupted, R.B.'s pa continued his story in his raspy, deep voice of when his grandfather was a slave. "Owned by a white man," he said. "A po' one, compared to some. Workin' the fields from dawn till dusk. Oh, there weren't no such thing as pay, not fer them." he said. Despite the obvious hardship, R.B.'s pa didn't seem much of a complainer. More important, no one I knew told stories like him.

On the way home, I thought about the tales I'd heard. Maybe they were true, I didn't know much about those things. So many strange visions whirled in my head and I could hardly wait to tell Mom and Dad what I'd heard. Mom and Dad's eyes winced impulsively as they listened patiently to the stories. After I finished, both slipped from the room without saying a word.

One thing that squelched my complaints of not having anything to do, was Mom's rattling off a list of chores to be done. Clean your room, do your homework, take out the garbage. The list was endless. But things were different now that I had a buddy and together R.B. and I battled our common affliction, childhood boredom. R.B. and I got in the habit of taking our lard buckets to the firehouse every day to get a free bucket of milk. On the way home one day, R.B. asked if I had any Pet free show passes. "Yea, I'd heard about the free passes," I admitted looking downward. The Egyptian Theater on Union Avenue gave away free passes for some number of Pet Milk can labels, but we didn't use much canned milk at home. R.B. had a solution to that problem. Before I knew it we were off to the garbage dump to find Pet Milk cans, then we spent the afternoon peeling the labels off the cans.

The next piece of street-wise learning R.B. taught me was to take another kid to the movie show and charge him a nickel. We did just that, for as long as we could get away with it.

It was a crisp fall day when R.B. came to me and said he wanted to surprise his mom and dad by taking home the supper. I was invited, so long as I helped him get what he needed. R.B. wouldn't give me any hints about what it was that I was to do, but he told me Saturday was the big day. Early Saturday morning, before dawn, the two of us walked almost two miles down to the Broadway Bridge crossing the Willamette River. I had never been this far from home before, but R.B. didn't seem to worry much. His confidence boosted mine which was lagging seriously.

We shimmied down the steel trusses to a girder on the underside of the bridge. Then R.B. started crawling out on one of the narrow girders, slick with gooey bird droppings, and told me to follow. He yelled to me, "Don't look down." The river lazily flowed below us, far, far beneath our precarious perch. I crouched low, clutching the nearest girder in both hands and watched. As R.B. crossed to another girder, he stopped and reached his hand into a corner made by two trusses. It appeared as if he grabbed something and stuffed it into his checkered shirt. For the longest time, R.B. crawled all over the bridge's under-structure until his shirt puffed out like a fat lady's. Finally, he motioned me back to the place where we had descended. After we had safely returned to the midst of the noisy bridge traffic, R.B. grinned and showed me what it was that filled his shirt. Nestled between his small, dark chest and his shirt was a wiggly mass of long-legged birds which he called squab. One noisy yellow beak poked through a worn spot below R.B.'s pocket. From above, the pigeons circled us angrily.

On the way home we hitched a ride on the back of a streetcar, something I had never done before. When the streetcar stopped at the bottom of the hill, the conductor got out of the trolley to move the overhead hook-up to another cable. R.B. and I quietly moved to the other side of the trolley so as not to be seen and stood on the step holding onto the outside door handle. R.B.'s voice shook with the moving trolley, "When you see the Sears store, he'll slow down for a turn. That's when we jump off."

Below the Sears store was a shantytown in Sullivan's gulch, better known as Hooversville. I had heard my dad talking about Sullivan's gulch and how Roosevelt would help those workers get back on their feet again. Shaking his head in disgust, Dad said the system was broke and so were the people.

As R.B. and I walked through the makeshift town I stuck close to him since he appeared to know his way around. I saw old people, gray and weary, and children like us who appeared dirty and sad, dressed in mismatched odds and ends. The acrid smells punctuated the anguish which was obvious and so frightening. It seemed the entire population of this neighborhood of sorts, stood in the open, huddled around little fires and crude metal buckets, cooking, washing and keeping warm.

I gaped at the shacks, mostly constructed of wooden packing boxes and scraps of sheet metal. Remnants from the dump, mostly. The roofs were made from uneven slabs of tar paper or anything reasonably flat. I carefully stepped over the crude household paraphernalia which obstructed my path -- broken washtubs, and scraps of furniture. Buzzing flies marked the occasional makeshift chamber pot, which one would otherwise not distinguish from an over-sized tin can. The smell overwhelmed me and I walked in fear of knocking over one of these cans, or stepping on someone's arm or leg stretched across the well-worn path. Here, life's banality was totally exposed. The anguish was unmistakable in everything these people did. I saw it so clearly, though I was an outsider, a mere passerby. I couldn't bring myself to intrude further by peering into the squalid shacks.

On a remote edge of the gulch was a man living alone in a large storage crate; he was the only person in the area lucky enough to have a small garden and a tattered and damp automobile seat on which to sleep. R.B. gave the man a few squabs and it was obvious they knew each other. The grateful man said the slumgullion he had cooking in the small tin can on his open fire would be greatly improved by the squab. Although I agreed with the man, I would have been more resolute if I had been somewhere closer to home.

When we got back to my house, R.B. told me to go ask my mom about my coming to his house for supper. Mom was down working in the cellar, again. On the radio was a familiar tune, the words of which wafted to the basement stairs:

> Oh, we don't eat fruitcake because it has rum,
> And one little bite turns a man to a bum.
> Can you imagine the utter disgrace---
> Of a bum in the gutter with crumbs on his face.

I wasn't supposed to tell anyone what Mom did in the cellar, but R.B. knew. He wrinkled his nose and said you could tell by the smell. That sweet and slightly moldy stench. The more I thought about it, I guessed R.B. was right. The problem was, every once in awhile one of the bottles of pungent brown liquid would burst. No matter how well Mom cleaned up the mess, the smell hung in the cellar and ripened with age. Mom protectively said this was her bread money. Dad called it brew and swigged it as often as he could.

I told Mom about R.B.'s offer and added that he would help me with my homework. Mom always gave her reluctant approval to R.B.'s supper offers, knowing that an offer such as this meant one less mouth to feed. It was 1933, and my parents like most folks were now fully entrapped by the spiraling depression. Food was dear and Mom was practical.

As I left the basement, I slipped a bottle of brew in my bag of school books. If I was to contribute to the meal, I needed to bring something because up to now, I had not laid a hand on a squab.

That evening R.B.'s ma talked a little about her ancestors. She told stories as good as R.B.'s pa and we talked into the night. My favorite was the one about her grandmother, Jessebelle who was a slave on a plantation during the Civil War times. Seems some Union officers took over the plantation and established it as temporary quarters where their men could rest and eat. Jessebelle helped the lady of the house bury all the fancy china and silver under the cotton gin. Then they hid under mountains of sweet potatoes until the soldiers moved on.

"Lawsa mercy, child," R.B.'s ma exclaimed when I told her I didn't know what a sweet potato was. "We gonna have ta git you educated. Not all them taters is white." That was of little concern to me, a tater was a tater; red, yellow or white.

R.B. and I spent all our free time together. We collected little round milk bottle caps which had different pictures from each dairy and sometimes we traded the caps with other boys. A game R.B. taught me to play with the caps allowed us to win more caps. The boy who went first threw his cardboard cap to the sidewalk. His opponent tried to throw his cap so that some part of it covered the first cap thrown. If it did, the first boy lost his cap to the second boy. The trick I learned from R.B. that allowed me to skin my brother was to soak the throwing cap in water and get it pliable like leather, so when I threw it to the ground, it stayed where it hit and didn't bounce around. This was important if you were second to throw your cap. By the time my brother caught on, R.B. and I were no longer collecting caps.

Gord and R.B. were in the same class at school. One day their teacher caught them swinging on the crossbar over the toilet door and they were marched into the principal's office by their earlobes. At the office, Gord got a ruler slapped on his hand but R.B. got a leather strap whacked on his behind. Gord told me the whole story, saying it wasn't fair. I didn't think it was fair either but nobody would do anything about it.

Prohibition ended in '33 and Mom's cellar operation was shut down for good. About the same time she took another job running a boarding-house with our friend Dorothy from the logging camp. Dad went to work as a laborer for the WPA as did a lot of men who needed steady work. The kids used to joke that the WPA meant "We Poke Along," but Dad reminded us we should be grateful for the income. Besides the WPA, some men went to work for the Civilian Conservation Corps. For a dollar a day they planted trees. When Dad talked about the CCC he said there was always someone worse off than you.

In 1935 we moved again to Northeast Portland. Dad worked at Bonneville Dam as a rigger, a skill he picked up in the logging camp. For the first time, stability started to come into our life. The Depression was still on, from what I heard, but that really did not mean so much to me; I didn't know what we were doing without.

It was during these times I met a group of friends that would stay with me throughout my lifetime. We all were in the fifth grade at Gregory Heights School. These were friendships made based on the undefinable quality that makes true friends. We were friends because we liked each other, and for no other reason. There was nothing material we had to offer one another and no favors we had to give. In return for friendship we had only friendship to offer.

We called ourselves the gang because we did most everything together. Altogether we were just rough and tumble kids growing up on our own, at our own pace. No one had much occasion to shepherd us through our trials; that we did for one another.

9. Sullivan's Gulch 1932, Portland's Hooverville and the streetcar on which Mel and R.B. Wesley hopped a ride.

CHAPTER 3

KICKING CANS

As I entered Miss Crissy's fifth grade homeroom class I had the same bout of apprehension that gripped me on each first day of school. Miss Crissy was a big woman, who was stern in appearance and who turned out to be just as stern in her actions. She walked about the room with a metal-edged ruler in her hand which functioned as an extension of her powerful arms. She would thrust the ruler at the blackboard. Then she'd slap it in her hand to make a point, "The Wesco free handwriting method is taught in this school, not the less graceful and archaic Palmer method. You new students will have to catch up with us on this matter." I grimaced as I was the only new student in the class.

Despite the enormous effort Miss Crissy put into helping us "make something of ourselves," the results were surely frustrating if not disappointing. So many day-to-day distractions diverted our energies in so many different directions.

Jack Morton sat directly ahead of me in class. He was about my size, with hair slicked back like Tom Mix and a nose like Dick Tracy. My close proximity to *Mort* and the mischievous relationship which developed between us, soon led me to understand the other uses of the ruler. The rap on the flat of the knuckles was for talking in class, and a spitball would earn an offender the metal edge.

We learned to appreciate that Miss Crissy did not need the principal to settle her class discipline problems. Between her overpowering stature and her unsparing use of the ruler, things were kept well in hand.

The principal's office was a place we tried to avoid in any event, although we were not always successful. Mr. Falding had a hair-trigger temper and never had much interest in listening to excuses, regardless of how honestly they were intended. He was built like a bear and had a well-known reputation for swinging his thick leather strap on boys' little bottoms. Furthermore he believed in conspiracies and would punish all those who were peripherally involved with the same amount of fervor. And if any of the boys became a habitual offender, he would even bring in their parents, though that didn't happen too often. Offenses ranged from talking in class, chewing gum, throwing spitballs, making noise, running in the halls, not putting paper in the waste basket and slamming locker doors. All temptations to which we succumbed regularly, if not openly.

I used my weekends for making a few dollars here and there which I'd spend on all those things Mom and Dad thought unnecessary. Mort's dad let me help in his roofing business, the remains of which had barely survived the crash in '29. Mr. Morton said few people could afford a new roof nowadays, and repair work was the only business he got. Working for Mort's dad meant getting up early on Saturday mornings and riding in his 1928 Chevy truck to some job on the fringes of town. There we'd heat a large bucket of tar to boiling, then haul it by pulley and rope to the rooftop where it was quickly mopped on the flat surface before it cooled. Mort's dad told me about the time one of his workmen was walking across a roof with a bucket in each hand, stepped through some rotten roof boards, and was left straddling a beam with both arms thrust in the boiling tar. I asked for the job on the ground, hauling the buckets to the rooftop using the rope and pulley. It was much later when Mort's dad told me about the time one of the buckets accidently caught on the edge of the building and caused hot tar to pour all over the pulley operator on the ground.

Every summer Mort's mother raised a garden in their backyard. She always planted tomatoes and would let me eat the ripe ones anytime I wanted. I remember this as one of the few times I ever got all I wanted to eat. Mom would never let me get into the icebox to take my fill of anything and if she ever felt the need to lock something, it was the icebox, not the front door to our house. She carefully governed the disposition of every morsel of food which passed through her kitchen.

Mort knew I had a special like for his sister Marion, though I never really told him. One evening when I was leaving his house Mort told Marion to go out on the porch and say goodnight to me. It was through this well-meaning act that I kissed the first girl in my life. It was all very clumsy and not particularly satisfying. Girls could wait.

My introduction to Jack Kendall, another member of the class, was at the school store during our first recess. Jack was taller than most everyone our age and he had sandy-colored hair and a quick smile that was infectious with me. The thing that made Jack different from the other boys, was that he had money when no one else did. He was standing at the candy counter of the school store when we first met, holding several round chocolate covered mints, called *Lucky Bites*. Most of the time the mint had white insides. But, if it happened to be pink, the lucky winner got to choose from a pile of sacks with prizes inside. Jack told me to take a mint and bite into one, generously offering to pay the penny cost. I filled myself with mints with white fillings until one was pink and Jack won his prize. It turned out, Jack had much better candy at home and I was the one to benefit.

The other guys in my gang were not as close to Jack. I suppose it was because his family seemed untouched and perhaps even blessed by the Great Depression which consumed our parents' lives. Jack was the only person I knew whose father had gone to college; in fact, even his grandfather had gone to college. I thought maybe that was the reason they had no worries about money or things they must do without.

Jack's family owned their home plus the two-story Kendall Plumbing and Heating Company downtown. Although I knew little about politics, I heard his family was Republican. That seemed an odd persuasion since all the other families I knew were Democrats. But the main difference I noticed, was the clothes Jack's dad wore. He was always dressed up in a double-breasted suit, starched white shirt and felt hat. If I didn't know what he did for a living, I would have guessed he was in the funeral business, since funerals were the only occasion my dad (or any of the others I knew) wore such attire. However, my dad, even when he got dressed up looked somehow different. Maybe it was the trimly cut hair or the manicured hands which caused Mr. Kendall to look more distinguished. And then there was Mr. Kendall's car. I had never seen one with such a mirror-like shine, and as spotlessly clean. Then right as I got accustomed to it, he bought a new one.

If there was a friendship of mine that might have been tainted by materialistic considerations it was this one, but I don't think so. I liked Jack because he liked me.

I was introduced to Jack Lewis, another member of our ragbag gang through his invitation to come to his house after school and look at his *Big Little Books*. Lew was tall and though he was not thin, he was raw boned and deliberate in his motions. *Big Little Books*, generally the subject of our conversations, were the size of a normal comic strip when they were opened, and a generous four hundred or so pages thick. We collected and swapped them, mostly avoiding spending the dime to purchase them new. After a little negotiation I could make a two *Buck Rogers* for one *Flash Gordon* swap and settle into an afternoon of reading, not particularly scholarly but infinitely more engaging.

One time, Lew negotiated with his mother for me to stay for dinner. I could tell food was scarce on the Lewis table, more scarce than on our own. It wasn't that Lew's father didn't work, he was a postman and had a family of six to feed on what was a regular but minimum wage.

While Lew was negotiating, I was reminded of Sam Levenson's radio program *Can You Top This?* Sam's father set all the children down one evening and told them a guest was coming for dinner. He explained that there was not enough meat for seconds, and when he passed the plate they should say, "No thank you, I have had enough." During the dinner the children followed the instructions to the letter though their father insisted they take seconds. As the dinner came to an end the father said, "We will have ice cream for dessert and all the bad little children who would not take seconds, don't get any."

Lew wasn't so interested in having me eat dinner; what he really wanted was for me to stay to play a couple of new games he'd learned. But with some pleading, his mom reluctantly agreed to the deal. In the interest of getting invited again, I decided I would try not to eat very much.

Kick the Can was the first game Lew taught me. We met some neighbor kids at the street corner where they normally played. Dusk was settling in as we gathered under the dim arc light. Someone placed a tin can at the street intersection on top of the manhole cover. Then we chose *It*, or the loser by a process called *odd finger*, where each player extended either one or two fingers on the signal, Now! If you stuck out one finger when most everyone else had two, you were the loser and were on your way to becoming *It*. When the choice got down to a boy and a girl, the kids told the girl to call either *even* or *odd* when they gave the signal to extend a finger or two. She called *even* and held up one finger and with the boy's one finger, the total was two. She was the winner and he was *It*.

It placed his head against the green mailbox hanging from the light post and covered his eyes while the others hid. "Here I come, ready or not!" *It* yelled. Then he looked for the kids who were hiding and tried to touch one of us before someone kicked the can. *It* got on a boy's tail, as he ran to kick the can. Just before the boy was about to be touched by *It* someone else from the gang moved in and kicked the can saving the guy who was being chased. On the next try *It* caught Lew, then called "Ollie, Ollie, Oxen Free," which meant everyone was to come in for a new game. Lew was the new *It*.

After we played for a while, the game became more and more chaotic with every one running around chasing each other in a good-natured state of pandemonium. Even the glowing arc light above us, suspended on a cross pole, became a part of the game. Lew being the tallest, boosted a tomboy to the level where she could reach the rope holding the light, using the pole climbers' rail spikes driven in opposite sides of the pole. Once she was in position on the light post she waited still until she saw *It* chasing one of her girlfriends. Then she shook the rope hard and broke the mantle, out went the light and that was that.

We learned other games too. Laurel and Hardy introduced us to a game we played either alone, or with others. We'd cut a broom handle in two pieces, one about four inches long and the other about three feet long. The short piece was carved into a torpedo, the shape of a teardrop. Striking the torpedo on the tail-end would make it jump straight up in the air about three feet then we'd try to strike it like a ball. None of us ever got as good as Laurel but of course he probably had a stand-in like Babe Ruth.

One of the biggest problems with this game was trying to find a broom handle. I took all our mothers' brooms out of jeopardy, once I remembered R.B.'s teachings, and we headed to the dump. But broom handles were pretty scarce those days even in the dump. There were lots of Pet labels though, now that they had no value.

My favorite game for two became *mumbly-peg*. For this game a pocketknife and a few wooden matches were all we needed. Lew taught me this game also. He threw his knife by its blade sticking it in the ground. My first try at sticking the knife in the ground by throwing it end over end failed. Being the first one who didn't stick the knife in the ground, I lost the opportunity to start first. Lew placed the point of the knife tip on his fingertip and flipped it outward by the other hand to the ground. It stuck solidly in the ground. He did the same thing from his elbow, shoulder, knee and so on, until the blade fell flat to the ground on the second from last position. It was my turn and on the first position, I failed again. Lew then did the last two positions and won the game. Since Lew was the winner, he had the right to drive a peg (we used a wooden match stick) into the ground with three blows of the knife handle. The first two blows missed the match stick, but on the third it went out of sight. I had to pull the match out of the dirt using only my teeth. Perhaps it was this game which instilled in me some degree of humility in preparation for later life. But mostly the experience taught me to be leery of another guy's game.

There was always marbles, too. We played marbles whenever two or more of us got together. Lew shot with an aggie which everyone considered real class. Since we always said our shooter was protected, his marble was never lost in a game. I used a realie (a sphere made of real marble). In one game we liked to talk about, we agreed we would play for keeps and no doughies were allowed, as usual. Marbles made of clay were fakes or immies and we didn't want any part of them. My gang only allowed steelies, purees (aggies or realies) or glassies. And when we played for keeps, and our shooter was hit, we had to reach into our marble sack and take out a mig for the winner.

We started the game by odd-fingering for the privilege of shooting last. Being last was best since everyone else's shooters were already on the ground. Some kid from a neighboring school won the last shot. I would have disliked him just because he didn't go to my school, but he wasn't a favorite of mine, anyhow. He was always yelling, "Knuckles down!" to me, like I didn't know you had to have your knuckles on the ground when you shoot. He aimed his mig at mine and came close. It was my shot and I measured a spannie (the width of my hand). He was a little beyond, being within one step from my mig. Under the rules, this allowed me to eye-drop from shoulder height. For this privilege, I had to leave my shooter in for one turn, before changing it. I took careful aim with my two-inch steel ball bearing and let go. It was a perfect shot, neatly carving a moon crescent in his once flawless mig and burying it in the soft ground. That was a trick R.B. showed me. My rival would lose a turn for having to dig his mig out of the dirt.

I carefully considered my next move, knowing it would be of little use since it was almost impossible to shoot a steely of that size. I decided on a heist, shooting from the tip of my shoe with my heel firmly planted in the ground and my toe pointed up; but it was useless. Lew had the next shot. When he reached to remove a twig, our rival yelled, "No smoothing." Lew sneered at the kid and snapped, "Why don't you pick up your marbles and go see if the girls will let you play jacks with them." We didn't allow the girls to play marbles and we didn't play jacks.

Wesley Kocker was almost two years older than the rest of us but having spent his early schooling in a country school system he wound up in our class in '37. Koke was even stronger than what his age difference accounted for. He had a scar across his nose but he didn't need it to look tough, he just was. Best of all, he knew how to trap muskrats and drive a car, and while the rest of us were experimenting with four-letter words he had the whole sentence under control. I also give him credit for getting us all thinking about girls.

There was many an hour spent listening to Koke's tales of girl pursuit. This resulted in our gnawing desire to just somehow view a naked breast or snatch a glimpse of pubic hair. As Einstein said, if we put as much thought into science as we put into sex we would have been selling hot dogs on the moon a long time ago.

Although I knew John Peacheos from school, I first became friends with him when we joined the Unity Presbyterian Sunday School so we could be on the church junior basketball team. John was the only child of a first generation Greek father and American mother. He lived over a neighborhood store and barbershop, with his mother running the store and his dad running the barbershop. We called John, *the Greek* or *Greek* for short. He was thinner than one should be, even during the Depression. Still he looked like everything we imagined a Greek to be, with a little hollow in his cheeks, a prominent forehead and a classic nose.

The Greek was absolutely the best kid to go out with on Halloween. He would search for a building site, where we'd get some plaster and cement powder mix. Then he taught us to mix it with some water and scoop the gooey mass into the neighborhood grouch's mail slot. The grouch had concrete mail in the morning -- a sight we only wished we could have seen.

43 ACE!

The Greek's championship prank was to find some dog poop, put it in a brown paper sack and set it on someone's porch. Then he'd light the sack on fire, ring the doorbell and hide within seeing distance. The finale was when the door opened and someone stomped on the smoldering sack with open-toed slippers.

One Saturday morning the Greek dragged Koke and I to his garage to show us a wooden tub he had gotten from a construction site. Though it was used for mixing mortar, the Greek called it his *ship*. We lifted it into a borrowed wagon and tied the wagon to the back of the Greek's bike. Then we headed for the Columbia River. Without much trouble we found a good place to stash it for awhile, not far from the river's shore. The following week the Greek, Koke and I boarded our great ship and set sail on the mighty Columbia with two homemade oars and a couple pieces of hard candy.

Our ship drooped low in the water, and sank even lower as our paddling splashed more water over the tub's rim. We slowly drifted down the river and under the interstate bridge connecting Oregon and Washington. This was a Tom Sawyer adventure at its very best. The world looked even bigger than life itself. It was too bad, however there was little time to enjoy the ride; at least one of us had to scoop the water out of the tub with our hands, continuously. None of us was that good a swimmer and we worried a little about our ship sinking.

As we steered into the Willamette River towards Portland, the current grew stronger and fought mightily to draw us back into the Columbia. Panic was about to consume us and we paddled furiously with the oars and all our available hands. We barely made it to shore before our great ship sank deep into the black silt. If the Greek's mother hadn't come to get us, we would have spent the cool night soaking wet under some tree, happy we did it all the same. Though we didn't get a lecture, the Greek's mom gave us a puzzled look, almost like she seemed distressed with the thought that the only materials God had from which to create men were little boys, like us.

Fenton Royal was a maverick. He had bright red hair and stood out in class as being a pleasant kind of different kid. *Red* would probably have preferred to be a loner but we liked him too much to allow that to happen. He looked strong enough to have things his way, but he would never for a moment let you know it. During morning recess, the gang used to chase Red out of the school and down a steep hill to the Rose City Golf Course. We would throw stones at him until the second recess bell rang, then run for school. Invariably Red wound up tardy. It was hard to keep our faces straight when Miss Crissy whacked the ruler on Red's knuckles.

Sometimes Red would find an old rubber down by the golf course and slip it into one of our pockets, half hanging out. We were the ones who got into trouble, then. Eventually we learned Red was not one to be picked on. Despite everything, we never once fought with each other, and remained the best of friends.

Red had a show-off trick which used to delight us no end. He would catch a neighborhood dog and jack him off. While he was doing it, Red always boasted, "I want to be a dog doctor when I grow up." We joked that the dogs would be much obliged if he did.

Clyde Beaty was our coach, Sunday school teacher and stand-in father. He was our introduction to church fellowship. Also, it was he who unselfishly spent much of his free time taking us on hiking trips and other events. I had more respect for him than any grown-up I knew, outside my mom and dad. He gave us encouragement which not only won basketball games but also won our deepest respect. We listened to Mr. Beaty, and we even stopped our championship Halloween pranks after we got to know him.

The gang decided sometime along the way that meeting under the arc light was not up to our standards. We needed a clubhouse so we set out to find a site. One street below my house was an entire empty block, with enough bushes in one field to allow us to work unobserved. We dug a large square hole and a long ditch leading to it. After absconding with enough lumber from a nearby building site we placed some boards over the areas we dug. Then we covered the boards with dirt as camouflage. We entered the club through the long dark tunnel. I don't remember the clubhouse ever being dry, but that didn't matter. It was a place we called our own.

We armed ourselves with guns made with wooden clothespins, apple boxes and bands of rubber. First we'd cut the shape of a gun out of one end of an apple box. Then, we attached a clothespin to the handle. A rubber band, which was cut from an old inner tube, was stretched over the end of the barrel and held at the handle with the clothespin. A little pressure on the clothespin released the shot. Multiple shot rubber guns were made using several clothespins on the handle and the only thing we had to remember with multiple shot guns was to release the clothespins in the right order so the top rubber band came off first.

We also learned to mechanize our firepower by mounting the rubber guns on our *skate-buses* which were made by nailing a wooden apple box to a three foot section of a two-by-four using salvaged nails from anywhere we could find them. Then we would nail the two halves of a single skate to each end of the two-by-four. Unless we got the nails from somewhere we shouldn't have, they were most always bent and rusty. With these mobile weapons we were prepared to defend the clubhouse at a moment's notice.

One of our sources of cash for materials was to snatch milk bottles now and then, and turn them in to the grocery for a nickel apiece. On one occasion, while we were turning in the milk bottles, the Greek and I kept the store manager busy and Red crawled in on his hands and knees and snitched a bottle of wine. That night in the clubhouse, we drank the wine. It tasted foul, but none of us dared admit as much to our friends. Instead we did our best to cover the taste with some mayonnaise the Greek had stashed in the clubhouse some time before. We'd take a swig of wine then follow it with a scoop of mayonnaise, passing the bottle and spoon from one person to another. It came as no surprise that every one of us got sick to our stomachs before we could get out of the clubhouse.

The gang never missed a single picture show at the Roseway Theater and we did it without money. Once a month we would deliver movie programs for the owner. Programs showing the monthly theater schedule, the three show changes a week, and all the double features on Tuesdays and Fridays were delivered door to door. Picture show passes were earned based on the number of programs delivered. Fortunately our gang always got assigned to the higher density housing areas where we could deliver a lot more programs in the same amount of time. Mr. Lawrence did this for us since many of us had been delivering the programs for so many years.

I can't remember ever missing a show at the Roseway. Mom and Dad also used the free passes when they could find the time. Saturday matinees were the best because the theater would always play some part of a *Flash Gordon* or *Buck Rogers* serial. The plot lasted maybe ten Saturdays. Each Saturday ended in the middle of some suspenseful event, so we were eager to come back the next Saturday and see how the hero got himself out of the cliff-hanger. At intermission, there was a live performance on the stage by a magician or hypnotist, or maybe there was a yo-yo or paddleball contest. One of our gang's members was obliged to win at least one contest to get more passes.

Friday night at the theater was race night. At intermission a short feature of a comical race would be shown, always with ten entrants. The last number on each ticket was your entry in the race, and there was much shouting and urging on of the one you wanted to win. With one out of ten a winner, there was always a cheerful crowd. The prize was a piece in a set of dishes, generally plain but very functional. Because everyone was eager to fill out their dish sets, race-day always drew large crowds. The gang filled out the set for the clubhouse by trading with each other and matching the dishes up with those found in boxes of Quaker Oatmeal.

Our free pass system worked fine until one day Mort and I yielded to an overwhelming temptation, ignoring the call of duty. It was one of those days when we thought a skinny-dip was close to being in heaven. So in the heat of the day we diverted to the swimming hole halfway through the program delivery route. Having never finished our assigned area, we decided to dispose of the undelivered programs in the Columbia slough. Before the night was over a complaint from an irate farmer saying the programs had washed up in his fields, put an end to our career at the Roseway. It was also about this time that a cow stepped into our clubhouse and broke its leg. Someone called the cops who found all our loot, including some street signs which were surely reported as missing a few months before. If our parents had not been so busy earning a living, this might have put an end to the gang.

My grandpa on Dad's side of the family died in 1936 and left Dad five hundred dollars. With the help of this money, Dad bought our first house on 66th Street in northeast Portland for the total price of fifteen hundred dollars. Dad was still working at Bonneville Dam and it was hoped this money would start our slow climb out of the Depression. But then Dad had a bad accident. While rigging a heavy pulley at the top of the dam with his partner, the mishap happened. My dad's partner was leaning into a strong wind, and he slipped and fell off the top of the dam. Dad, caught off guard, followed close behind. His partner held onto the loose pulley block they were rigging, and fell with his legs catching behind a steel ladder imbedded in the dam; he died instantly. Dad released his grip from the pulley falling free to the bottom of the dam and into the water below. Wearing a safety coat he sprung out of the water like a cork released from the bottom of the icy river. Though Dad was much luckier than his partner, he was not uninjured. His back suffered the greatest damage and he would be in an upper body cast for over a year. Dad grumbled that he had endured the most dangerous work of the day as a logger, but he got hurt in this whistle-punk job. The accident was the last of my dad's heavy labor though not the end of his days of hard work. Now we were to live on workmen's compensation while paying off a mortgage.

Another source of income for our family had to be found so my mom, my brother and I took on jobs harvesting the summer crops of the Willamette Valley. We picked everything that grew out of the earth, crawling on our hands and knees to clean the endless rows of strawberry plants and bundling our arms and legs as we mashed through the vines in search of the ripe blackberries. Dad joined us as soon as he was able.

It was strenuous labor from dawn to dusk for the men who worked the fields, pushing always to pick more. The women and children worked equally hard, but their harvest was less and so was the money. Most of the workers at our sides were transients. Some had spent their winters sleeping on the park benches of Portland, panhandlers by necessity, who made the rounds to restaurants in search of half-eaten biscuits or scraps of vegetables.

Some had been homeless since the start of the Depression. Others were relatively new to the life of the down and out.

We were the newcomers, taking on the ways of the transients, living in the fields through the picking season and staying in wooden picker shacks outfitted with a dingy straw mattresses, a tin wash tub and a small cook-stove.

Mom prepared simple meals on the cook-stove, maybe a can of beans or some sauerkraut mixed with a couple wieners. At night the smells from our dinner wafted amongst those of the other shacks and the community outhouse nearby. Mom, Gord and I huddled at night in the one-room shack, fighting the invading cool of the evening, talking and singing songs, while Dad anxiously paced the grounds.

The migrant workers who lived in neighboring shacks and tents rarely had names; instead they were faces from all over the country and voices which were even more distinct. We'd hear them talk in the fields and in the black of night, "Hey Okie, if you see Arkie tell him Tex is looking for him." It seemed the whole Nation's downcast populace was never more than two yards away.

Despite the crowded conditions, keeping order was not the problem one would think it would be. Everyone knew that so much as a quarrel would get you run out of the camp, something most could ill afford. This was my first indubitable exposure to the *crust of the earth*, and I didn't like it for one second. Every night, seeing so many *half-bagged* men so downcast was not an endearing memory to carry back to the school yard.

Having been raised on a farm, my mom accepted this work in stride but Dad had trouble thinking of himself as anything other than the very proud lumberjack I knew him to be, a hard worker who had always provided for his family. To Gord and I, humility was a word we did not yet understand, but to Dad particularly, this work was many steps down the ladder he had already come up. Mom was of the belief that those that live in modesty were the richest, but Dad was born of the nature to seek the top of the pile.

But for now my family lived for the moment, laboring hard to rise above the circumstances in which so many families had fallen. Fighting the gripping demoralization which seized us and the rest of the country.

10. Gregory Heights Elementary School, 1927.

11. The Roseway Theater.

12. Mel's first kiss, Marion Morton.

13. The great plaster tub ride down the Columbia River; Koke and the Greek, 1940.

14. Jack Kendall and Mel, cruising the streets on their bicycles.

CHAPTER 4

DERBY DOWNS AND UPS

Nineteen hundred and thirty-four was the first year of the Greatest Amateur Racing Event in the World. The All American Soap Box Derby was sponsored by local newspapers and Chevrolet dealers of one hundred and fourteen cities around the United States, Hawaii, Canada, and Panama. The International finals were held in Akron, Ohio, the home of the Soap Box Derby. The first prize winner got a four year college scholarship (worth two thousand dollars), and a huge trophy. The second prize winner got a master deluxe Chevrolet coach (worth nine hundred dollars).

My friend Jack Kendall won the local Portland race in '37. His older brother Junior had won in '36, the second year of the race in Portland. Neither of the Kendalls won the National race in Akron. Jack's father would have given his eye teeth to have another chance to win the Akron race, but it wasn't to be with either of his boys, because the rules said a boy could only race in the nationals once.

In the spring of '38 Jack told me if I would like to enter the race, his father would gladly advise me. That was an offer too good to be true. And without hesitation or further thought, I gave Jack an enthusiastic yes, a thousand times yes, then ran off to convince my parents of the decision I had already made.

Jack's dad was the type of adult who made my bones shudder every time I got in the same room with him. In many ways, he seemed so different from the other fathers of our gang, his manner was gruff, and unpredictable. But, despite all my misgivings I wanted to take him up on his offer. This was simply one of those opportunities no reasonable kid would refuse. Immediately, I began to picture myself walking up to Mom and Dad with a college diploma in my hand. What kind of parents wouldn't be impressed by that?

Dad and Mom sat on the putty-colored davenport, patiently listening to my dramatics on coaster cars and college diplomas. "Uh huh," Mom would say, biting her nail and glancing over to Dad. He'd return the glance, responding with his eyes. The quiet was worrisome and drove me to panic. That's when the emotional pleading and negotiating began. Then came the begging. Finally, my folks went along with the idea, and reminded me I would have to figure out how to make the money to buy the wheels and the materials for building the bus. Finding a way to make money was always a problem, just a consequence of the times. Mom and Dad knew that better than me. In the past, my old standby for raising a few dollars was strawberry picking, but now Dad had taken a moonlighting job in Portland and Mom wasn't driving to the fields.

Mort made a lot of spending money cutting lawns, with it having become a business of sorts with him. Still he was obliging enough to take the time to coach me and even find a couple jobs just to get me started and soon I was going door to door selling my services to all the neighbors whose unruly weeds and wild grass required a trim. It was a good cause, the neighbors surely thought, but more important the price was right. That's what I told them anyway.

Lawn cutting paid an average of twenty-five cents a lawn. An occasional fifty-cent job for a well-to-do family, took about a half day to do. Finding jobs became easier. Finding the time to mow the yard was more than a problem; it was close to impossible. A particularly sensitive matter was my finding the time to mow our own yard, a job which rarely paid hard currency. "It's your obligation to the family," Mom scolded, and she never once let me forget it.

The race was only two and a half months away. In that time, about fifty lawns had to be cut, and the bus had to be built and tested. And, since Mr. Kendall wanted me to do all the work on the bus in his basement under his close supervision, I was constrained to Mr. Kendall's schedule. There was, however, one distinct advantage to this arrangement. I had full access to Mrs. Kendall's ice box which was always chocked full of Kool-Aid, popsicles and fudgesicles, treats seldom found at my home. "Yes ma'm, please," I'd gotten that line down, complete with the shy smile and tilt of the head. If I did it just right, Mrs. Kendall would offer me a second fudgesicle.

Fortunately the derby rules never required contestants to count the cost of sustenance in the ten dollar maximum we could spend on the bus. If I added the cost of the popsicles I consumed to the cost of the bus, I surely would have been well over the limit. Mr. Kendall was quite willing to pay the price.

My first task was to design the racing bus, then obtain the materials. The rule book recommended the materials be gathered from around the house, lumber yards, dumps, five-and-ten-cent or hardware stores and wrecking companies. Stressing the importance of distinguishing *second hand* from *old*, the race officials suggested taking plenty of time for this activity. I learned fast that the best materials at the right price were simply not available without some serious scrounging. That's where my training with my old friend R.B. paid off, although something warned me not to mention the particulars to someone like Mr. Kendall who'd probably never been to a dump in his whole life.

Jack's dad insisted on everything being just right and my skills at making this sort of thing just right were nothing that would have impressed the clumsiest of untalented craftsmen. Hour after hour, I worked and reworked all the parts. My dad had never done this type of work and we had no tools around the house with which to practice or do any work on the side. But with my one year of manual training at Gregory Heights, and Mr. Kendall's relentless drive, I built the bus on schedule to Mr. Kendall's discriminating satisfaction.

The bus was designed around the 1938 Pontiac lines. The body of the bus flowed smoothly from the sleek Pontiac front-end shape. The exterior was nice looking, but more important was our agonizing over every detail of the assembly particularly the wheels, axles and the steering mechanism. Although all buses had to use the same six-dollar standard wheels and axles purchased from the local Chevrolet dealer, the rules allowed some reworking of them to achieve maximum performance. This was where Jack's dad thought we could gain an edge. He insisted on my careful balancing of the wheels on a lathe at his plumbing and heating shop. I drilled holes around the edge of the wheel until a hard spin with my hand left the wheel spinning for an incredible seven minutes. Six and one-half minutes was the longest Mr. Kendall had ever gotten a wheel to spin in the past. Bearings were also very critical to the speed of the bus, however any modification of the bearings was strictly forbidden.

Mom picked the color for my bus, which was a metallic gold she had seen on a new Pontiac. Mixing just the right amount of gold flecks in the varnish and brushing the mixture onto the metal sides of the bus smooth enough to please Mr. Kendall was the toughest job of all. Fortunately however, it was the last task and after it was finished I found I had grown to appreciate Mr. Kendall's craftsmanship and perfectionist tendencies. We had a winner on our hands, I was convinced.

The race was just one week away, the day Mom rolled me out of bed at four in the morning. Mr. Kendall hoped to do a pre-race trial run before there was any traffic on the hill on 82nd Street where the race would be held. I jumped on my bike and peddled furiously through the dark, abandoned streets to meet the Kendalls. My bike was foremost on my mind; it was a five dollar purchase I had made from Winchel's Swap Shop the summer before. If only I could win the new shiny red bicycle which was one of the prizes of the race, my bike would be the envy of the gang. A Columbia; it was the best. Imagine, real balloon tires, ones which could be patched with my dad's tire kit. My old relic had narrow little tires without tubes, which were darned near impossible to repair. They were blotched with a myriad of rubber bands which I had stuffed into the holes with glue. It never failed; right when I was sure the tires were fixed for good, they'd leak, leaving me stranded somewhere, too far from home to walk. Mom would swear I only got flats when it was suppertime and she wanted me home.

As I rounded the hill near Jack's home, there were a couple of arc lights which cast eerie shadows in the morning fog. The paper boy was making his rounds when I approached him from behind. He turned quickly to see who I was, and his bike lurched precariously from the weight of the papers jammed into his front basket. His face crinkled in a comical way as he asked why I was out so early. "You could be home in bed, sleeping," he said with great bewilderment. I stopped and told him all about my racer, chattering about every detail. What fun it was talking to him, since I was the only boy he knew who ever built a soap box bus. I tried to act casual, telling him about the lathe and the holes in the wheels, but my pride couldn't be contained. I would have liked to talk some more, but I had to hurry on; Mr. Kendall would not tolerate my being late.

The Kendalls and I lifted the racer onto the back of a pickup truck and headed for the racing hill. Perhaps it was the early hour, but Mr. Kendall didn't seem to share the unabashed euphoria I felt. "Now Melvyn, don't you go telling anyone your time this morning. And you shouldn't talk about the design of your bus, either," he warned with an unusually serious tone. Too late for that, I thought. Still the guilt lingered. Did I say too much to the paperboy? The Kendalls had beaten out the Gibson and Stambaugh boys the two previous years and they both had brothers with racers in the '38 race. This was not something anyone took lightly. I knew this was Mr. Kendall's chance to dominate the race for the third year in a row.

On the day of the race, the 82nd Street hill would be converted into Portland's Derby Downs with an inclined launch ramp. We would not have a ramp for our trial run. However, the Kendalls had made secret pre-race trial runs the two previous years without ramps, so they had those times to check against my pre-race trial time. This comparison would tell us how much work I had to do before the race.

We unloaded the racer just as the bright sun rose above the rooftops. Jack's dad gave me some last minute instructions on handling the steering. "Hold steady on the wheel, don't make any sudden moves, and keep your eyes on the center of the lane." As he planted a firm pat on my back, I felt good about Jack's dad. A slight push simulated the ramp, and I was off, racing down the hill as fast as gravity would pull the bus. After three runs on the 1000-feet track, my average was twenty-eight seconds. Mr. Kendall's eyes sparkled, since this was a better time than either of the Kendall boys had in the two previous years. My new bike was in sight. Could I really do this? I wondered and hoped, and even prayed a little since Mr. Beaty said it might help. When I mentioned Mr. Beatty's suggestion to Dad, he moaned but finally expressed some thought that maybe I should cover all my bases.

The gang was sworn to secrecy as I related the details of my early morning run on the hill. I didn't tell them my time, honoring Mr. Kendall's concern but I embellished the story telling the guys about the fierce tenseness of the early morning race and the stunning grace of the golden racer as it streaked down the hill with the sun splashing off its newly painted sides. "Ho--ly Cow!" Red blurted out after I finished relating all the flashy details. "You just wait until you see those balloon tires, on the Columbia I'm going to win," I told them, detecting for the first time, a twinge of envy.

On Sunday, July 31 a crowd of ten thousand flocked to the city and gathered on both sides of the track on the Portland Derby Downs hill. In a small area set aside for the racers, judges were making special awards for the best paint job, best upholstery, most Soap Boxy and a whole lot of other things. As I stood waiting in the pits, I heard the announcer say over the loud speaker I had won the prize for best streamlined racer. I knew that Pontiac design was a winner.

The marching band stirred the enthusiasm of the crowd with rousing music, lively baton twirlers and a high-stepping majorette. Vendors weaved throughout the boisterous crowd, selling bottles of Coca-Cola and steamed hot dogs. My attention was focused totally on my racer until I saw the skywriting airplanes etching an advertisement in the clear blue sky. I watched as the two planes crossed each others' paths, over and over as they spurted short bursts of whitish blue smoke. Now that's what I called going fast. I wondered, what really makes planes fly? How did they keep from crashing? Could they see us like we could them? The thought of flying generated so many more questions than it answered. How could someone ever learn to fly? How could I learn to fly? The planes chattering engines subsided as they flew away from us, leaving the consequence of their work fading into the sky, "J-E-L-L-O!"

The crowd's attention was riveted to the races as the derby progressed through the series of elimination heats. There were two age groups, Class A was for the thirteen to fifteen year olds and Class B was for the eleven and twelve year olds. I had worked my way up the Class A finals watching the center line and trying hard not to look around for the members of the gang screaming my name. It was now time for the Class A finals. The two best times from this race would race the best time from the Class B finals. The Class A finals was the race for the bike. For me, this was the race to win.

As the ramp dropped, my heart pounded wildly and I could hear the Greek yelling for me in the crowd. I kept my eyes glued to the center of the lane which was the one at the far right. The cheering crowd pressed against the rope at the sidelines next to me to get a better view. Suddenly, I saw a Coke bottle loom onto the track. It was hardly on the track, but it looked menacing. Though I swerved only slightly, it cost me first place in the heat. I came in second and had clocked in for the fourth straight time at 27.3. Jack Stambaugh beat me by six inches with the identical time and the shiny new Columbia bicycle was his.

The final race was next. As the officials moved my bus to the top of the hill, I was in the depths of gloom. The number one prize was gone, could there be any more? Through my choking sadness, I remembered my mother's words, "Remember Mel, you are in it for the fun." It didn't seem like much fun now. My heart deflated until it was as flat as my old bicycle tire, which I in a siege of optimism hadn't bothered to repair. Still something inside me said, "never say die."

All three finalists were lined up on the ramp. This time I drew the inside lane and there was a white highway line in front of my right wheel. Mr. Kendall's voice was firm, "Hold your wheel on the line and don't swerve even if the whole Coca-Cola company gets in front of you." The ramp dropped and we were off. With the crowd cheering, the whole gang whooping and my mother crying, I won the race in a record time of 27.2 beating Stambaugh by the same six inches he beat me in the previous heat. It all seemed like fun again.

I braked hard as the crowd broke through the ropes and closed in on my bus. The drag brake skidded noisily on the roadway, until the bus came to a halt. Through the masses of cheering people, came a car under police escort with the Mayor and Mrs. Kendall. My thoughts were interrupted as, a radio announcer thrust a mike in front of me, "How does it feel champ?" *How does it feel?* What kind of question was that? I had the whole world right here telling me what a great day this was, as though all the days of fretting were behind me. The thing I only dreamed could happen, did happen. Miracles *do* happen to everyday people! But the only response that trickled from my gaping mouth was, "Swell."

Riding back to the top of the hill in the escorted car, I could see the remnants of the skywriters' work blending together in a silky smudge. The crowd which surrounded us was dispersing in all directions. The most glorious moment for me was yet to come as my mom, dad and Gord emerged from the masses to hug their champ. Tears streamed from all our eyes, even my father's although he tried unsuccessfully to wipe them dry before I saw.

Mom took charge of my trophy, conspicuously placing it on the coffee table in the front room on a freshly pressed doily so everyone who came into the house noticed. I suspect the traffic in our house multiplied three-fold during the first month after the derby race, with Mom dusting the trophy every time a speck of dust marred its shiny silver finish. For me, the trophy served as a daily reminder of the upcoming race for the national title.

I left for the nationals in Akron on the eighth of August. Since Mom and Dad couldn't afford to go along, the sponsoring newspaper, the *Oregonian*, sent a reporter on the journey to look after me. The whole gang was at the Portland Train Depot to see us off. There was really quite a fuss over my leaving, and one of my classmates, Lauramae Beatie, gave me a big kiss, not the second one I ever had, though there weren't many between that one and the first. It wasn't until I returned home, that I learned the newspaper had reported "blue-eyed" Lauramae's "affectionate" kiss which she planted on "Portland's ace soap box speed star, a handsome freckled lad." When I read the article, I lost all faith in the news reporters, even questioned the loyalty of Amby, the reporter who had traveled with me. The gang wasn't going to let me forget this one for years, long after the gossipy news clip yellowed in the *Oregonian's* files.

The Portland Rose, as our train was called, had all the things a young kid on his first time away from home could want. I had a berth of my own and meals of whatever and however much I wanted to order. For two whole weeks. No more boiled cabbage, no more canned beets and no more Sal Hepatica; no siree. And, no one telling me what time to go to bed or what I shouldn't eat before mealtime.

The only direction I got was from Amby. Mostly he talked about "bringing home the bacon," a subject of mutual interest. Amby knew I kept up with everything which had to do with flying and airplanes so he advised me not to imitate Wrong Way Flyer Douglas Corrigan at the races. I concluded Amby's advice had little practical merit, but he meant well.

In Boise, Idaho we picked up the Boise local champ, named Eddie. The two of us talked every moment about how we built our bus and how we were each going to win the upcoming race. We told each other everything, except how we were *really* going to win the race; that was a closely held secret. Eddie like myself had never been away from home without his parents and neither of us had ever been on a trip we thought so wonderful. It seemed as though every time the train stopped at a depot, someone met us to say hello and congratulations. Even some Blackfoot Indians came to congratulate us at a brief stop in Pocatello, Idaho. The Indians invited us into their tents which were pitched nearby, then performed some of their traditional dances. We noticed only one of the Indians was barefoot, and Eddie and I decided yeah, he was from the Blackfoot tribe alright.

At Akron, a marching band and shrieking sirens met us at the depot. A welcoming committee took us in long black limousines to the derby headquarters as a boisterous police escort announced our route. The race officials knew how to make one hundred and some odd number of kids happy by decking us out almost immediately in the fancy gear we would wear in the parade on race day. We were also issued special racing clothes, silky racing shirts and pants. The best news of all, was our getting to keep the official chrome helmets stenciled with our home towns and the flashy new gold wrist watches we slept with.

Within a short time, all the local champs got to know one another. One of the fellow home-town winners was Helen Sommerville of Peoria, Illinois. Helen told us she was the only girl ever to win a soap box derby. Because I hadn't seen any girls racing in Portland, I believed her. The Akron officials refused to allow her race in the finals saying the race was for boys only, but she talked them into letting her choose a boy to use her racer. Girls from the local school picketed with T-shirts stenciled with, "Let's have a soap box derby for girls." The girls were not contented for one second with the derby's solution to "Helen's problem."

Though my time in Akron was short, it was extraordinarily extravagant. The big fancy lunches, lavish outdoor excursions, and the luxury of ordering as many milk shakes as I wanted from the Mayflower Hotel room service was everything I imagined of the best of movie scenes. I was spoiled for life. The Depression's still on? No one could have told me about any Depression.

Our first visit to Derby Downs left our mouths agape. Rows and rows of bleachers lined the two thousand foot long track which sloped steeply at the starting line then leveled off. A bright red, white, and blue arch marked the finish line, exactly 1175 downhill feet from the starting line where we stood. We were allowed one untimed trial run that day, so we could get the feel of the hill. . . and the wind rushing against our faces. Thirty miles an hour was considered a good speed for the track, and whatever speed my racer coasted, it felt terrific. This was about as much fun as any kid could stand.

The morning of race day, all contestants assembled on the top of Derby Downs, at Topside where the officials checked and weighed our racers. The rules were strict; the weight of the racer plus that of the contestant could not exceed two hundred and fifty pounds. As I stood on the scales with my racer, I watched nervously as the needle on the scales bounce around the two hundred and fifty pounds mark. It wasn't my racer which weighed more than it did in Portland; I was certain of that. Still it was almost beyond belief that I had gained eight pounds causing the racer and me to squeak through the weigh-in by an uncomfortable four pounds. Another week on room service would have disqualified me for sure.

The celebration opened with a parade led by a military marching band. Following the blaring column of tuba players, were the contestants, wearing our All-American helmets and racing jackets. Although we struggled to hear our marching instructions over the blaring percussion and the cheers, we focused most of our attention on the crowded stands, weaving as we walked and stared into the crowded stands. Intoxicated with childlike awe, we felt wonderful, ready to win the race for our home towns.

It was a splendid sunny day, the band was playing, the Goodyear blimp was hovering above our heads and there were over a hundred thousand people in attendance. The officials rushed us through our heats working hard to keep the racer's energy focused on the derby. I won several heats, racing against two competitors each time. Though victory was still a passing dream, the thrill of the race in Portland was not there. The voices of Mom, Dad, Gord, the Greek, Red, and the rest of the gang, were not in the crowd. My heart just wasn't in it, I knew.

Still, my elimination from the race seemed awful final. No, not unfair, just terminal. My bus was crated, never to be raced again. My derby days were over. All the glory it brought was behind me.

Moments later I was watching the event as a privileged spectator, happy to be there guzzling Coca-Cola and eating Eskimo pies. A kid from Nebraska caused quite a stir when he asked the officials, "Is there anything in the rules which says I have to wear a racing shirt?" The racing officials huddled to discuss the matter, as one man flipped through the pages of the rule book. They shuffled around, all wearing white trousers and shirts, and fancy wing-tipped shoes. No, they finally agreed, there was nothing in the rule book that said contestants had to wear a shirt. Bobby Berger reached to take his off, saying "I've got to pick up three-tenths of a second somewhere and I figure the sleeves on my shirt are acting like sails and holding me back."

In the championship heat, the shirtless Bobby Berger raced against the brother of the 1937 champ, Richard (Dickie) Ballard. It looked like a virtual tie, but the officials at the finish line raised the hand of Bobby's opponent for the victory. Bobby walked off the concrete track onto the unpaved run-out as Dickie was declared the winner by an announcer who had been watching the events on the track. "Wait," a finish-line official gasped, "the photo finish shows Bobby Berger won." With that pronouncement, the reporters, photographers and radio announcers rushed from the jubilant Dickie to the rightful champ. It was a heartbreaking scene, unfair but ultimately fair.

Dickie Ballard, the All-American champ for two and one half minutes stood alone, fighting to hold back the tears. Then he walked over to Bobby and congratulated him warmly. The courage Dickie displayed was stunning.

I didn't know that I could have done the same in his shoes, but I'd like to think I would have. Fortunately, this was not my time to be tested. My throat tightened as I felt the thick lump Dickie surely had lodged in his throat. This was the ultimate act of true sportsmanship, the foundation of the Derby.

Early the next morning, the succession of long black limousines returned a subdued group of champs to the Akron train station for departure to their home towns. Eddie and I spent our last night together on the train drinking milk shakes and talking nonstop about everything which slid though our minds. Eddie departed at Boise, leaving me time to think. High School was foremost in my thoughts; in September I would be a freshman. My old bike would have to last a while longer, but that was okay.

I also thought about Lauramae and her goodbye kiss. It was the real clincher to that incident that nagged me; for it wasn't me who took her home from the depot the day I left for Akron, it was Jack Kendall. Unfortunately I owed it to Jack to find another girl. Sportsmanly conduct was painful indeed.

15. Mel with his brother Gord, Mom and Dad after winning
the 1938 Soap Box Derby in Portland, Oregon.

16. Junior Kendall (1936 Champ) and Jack Kendall (1937 Champ)
pass on their congratulations to Mel.

17. Parade of Champions, Soap Box Derby Akron, Ohio, 1938.

18. Mel is off to a fast start down the right lane
of Akron's Derby Downs, 1938.

19. Bobby Berger from Omaha, Nebraska wins the 1938 Nationals.

20. A crowd of over 100,000 watch the Greatest Amateur Racing Event in the world at Derby Downs, Akron, Ohio, 1938.

CHAPTER 5

HOT RODS AND GIRLS--
SLIPPING OUR CLUTCHES

The Greek and I looked on as Koke prepared to run the one hundred yard dash at Grant High's junior varsity track team tryouts. "Would you look at that," the Greek said. "What's that?" I asked as I looked over to Koke standing on the sidelines. "That girl -- over there! I recognize her from the swimming pool. You wouldn't believe the set of cans she has! Gives me the tremors just thinking about them."

I watched the girl for a few minutes, noticing her letterman's sweater -- a bit heavy for the early fall weather, and her rubber-soled saddle shoes. She was pretty in a craggy sort of way, but I didn't see what the Greek got all that excited about. Koke interrupted my thoughts. "I made it!" he yelled as he ran to us, splattering mud from the track with each stride. "The pole vault's next, Greek," Koke said. "You'd better quit gawking at that flutterbump and get over there. And look out for the mud, it's really slick."

When the Greek hesitated Koke glanced at the girl again and chuckled, "Just think about all the time you've been wasting looking at those pictures in that doctor's book you squirreled away in the clubhouse. You've worn the pages slick, it's about time you showed a proper interest. Take my advice, quit choking your fox and lay your hand on the real stuff."

The Greek grunted within his eyes still fixed on the girl. Koke nudged him. "Maybe you should try out for the football team, get next to one of those cheerleaders. I thought about doing that myself. Besides, wouldn't it be great to take on Gord and the Kendall's over at Benson High? I bet we could show 'em how to play football. Guess you'll be too busy for that Mel, working and all. You don't know what you're missing."

"Not this time Koke. Pop at the garage asked me to help him fix cars on the weekend and I'm already working at the grocery store during the week. I'll leave it up to you and the Greek to keep the girls happy." I was going to be busy during my High School years, as were the other gang members, but with a little more prompting from Koke, skirts and cars became our new gnaw replacing clubhouses and bicycles.

About this time the Depression was showing signs of easing and things were looking up in general for my family. The greatest relief in Mom's mind came when she learned President Roosevelt had signed a bill allowing anyone who came into the U.S. illegally some years before to automatically become citizens if they could prove their date of entry. To be an American, a legal one that is, fulfilled Mom's greatest dream.

We moved again, and for the first time I had a room of my own. My bedroom was the unfinished attic of our house which had all the privacy a guy could want. I was proud of the room and lining the ceiling and walls with cardboard boxes and showing it off to all my friends. Mort showed me how to build a crystal set, made from a coil, a cat whisker wire, a crystal and a head set. I laid in bed for hours listening to the tales of the Lone Ranger and his faithful friend, Tonto.

However, building model airplanes was my favorite pastime, cutting little pieces of soft balsa wood, gluing them together, doping the skin over the frame, and then carefully painting the proper markings on the canvas with a fine paint brush or toothpick. Most of the planes I built were suspended off the attic roof, dangling over my mattress and swinging with every faint movement of air. In my daydreams, they came alive. The pilots with all their reckless courage shot through the air, diving, rolling and carving a perfect loop. They flashed through the clear blue skies with a silk scarf trailing behind; they ripped through the blackened clouds with the rain tearing at their goggles. More often than not, I'd fall asleep to the rain on the attic roof, with my headset still on, wondering if Jimmy Allen returned safely to his field.

There was one other significant distraction at my family's new house. Across the street lived a very cute girl who looked like Venus to me, and with a lot of prompting from Koke, I started the pursuit of my first love. By the end of the first school year, I had shed my bicycle and Virginia and I were walking to and from school, me carrying her books and holding one of her hands. We'd sit on her porch until dark most every night, talking and quietly smooching when no one was around. Sometimes Virginia's grandmother would catch us setting around and chase me off. "You're going to get the piles boy, setting on that cold porch like that," she warned. That seemed such a small price to pay.

Koke coached me along in the relationship. But with all Koke's advice on what to say, I never could lay a hand on Virginia's firm rounded breasts. Fortunately, the Greek came to my rescue. He knew Virginia's next door neighbor, Jean, and in confidence he told her about my difficulties. Jean was a real pal, telling Virginia, "Don't you worry, a little of this sort of thing is all right." And with this lead-in, I proceeded to pursue my attempt and with final success laid my hand on the first breast in my life. Ah, this was much better than the first kiss.

At the school yard, Koke told me about the next step. I was eager to get started, but my dog Gilmore -- named after everyone's favorite gasoline -- always sat with us and put his nose right where I was trying to put my hand. With these clumsy attempts to carry my endeavor further, I finally got run off the porch for good.

The Greek never got far at all with Jean. She complained and she squirmed, then she slapped his hand. It seemed she was an advisor only.

After both the Greek and I met with such disappointments, we decided some firsthand observation was required. Koke's advice was helpful all right, but things were not going as well as we would have liked. The Greek had an idea. I agreed to meet him one evening whereupon I resurrected my faithful bike and pedaled furiously to his house. In my rush I forgot to put the clip on my leg to keep my pants from catching in the bike chain and my bike came to a tortured halt as my pant leg creased in the blackened chain. "*Drat!*" I said to myself as I yanked the chain off its tracks and ripped my cords in the process. Now I would have to give them to Mom for mending and I knew she would wash them. Cords were never supposed to be washed. This was my best pair with several hard-earned layers of grease I had gotten from repairing my bike and helping at Pop's garage. Oh well, that was just bad luck, hopefully not a prelude of our evening to come.

As I came to the store, I noticed the house next door had a scarlet fever quarantine sign on the door. My imagination cautioned me that it may have crept across the yard to where I was about to walk. My steps grew lighter and about then, the Greek stuck his head out of the window and yelled down that he was on his way. I was spared from the thoughts of catching scarlet fever and I was also spared from screaming his name from the curb, which his parents hated more than sin.

The Greek's great plan was to wait until dark then sneak behind Gregory Heights and watch the spooners on the Rose City Golf Course road, where Red used to find the rubbers. If we were real lucky we could get a little education on technique.

We had a couple of hours to kill before dusk, and the Greek had a little money in his pocket. He said he had worked at his mom's store that day, and had enough money for us to have a root beer contest. We bicycled to Davis Drug Store and plopped down at the marble-topped soda fountain. The Greek yelled to the soda jerk, "Two black cows, and keep 'em coming." We sat and drank the root beer floats and read the magazines on the rack, calling it a draw at four each. It always amazed me that root beer floats were half the size of milk shakes but in a milk shake contest we could drink more, as many as four to five, depending on whether or not we had just eaten supper.

We would have sat around some more but Mr. Davis complained of our reading his magazines, and told us to put them back, immediately. As we turned to the magazine rack away from Mr. Davis, the Greek opened the magazine in his hand, put a mouthful of puke in the center and set it on the rack. The Greek had this puke routine down pat and would occasionally aim it at the screen door of some grump at Halloween. This semi-controllable stomach infliction was also responsible for almost getting him thrown off the pole vault team since he often puked if he hit the ground too hard after a vault.

It was time to move on to the golf course road anyway. There was a full moon and we thought the conditions were exceptional. Everyone should be in the mood and it looked like we would be able to see perfectly. We hid our bikes down the road a ways, then positioned ourselves on a dirt bank about six feet above the road. At last, a souped-up '37 Ford sedan passed and came to a stop. The burbling of the engine subsided, the lights went out, and the radio came on. The sounds of *Oh, Give Me Something to Remember You By*, wafted through the trees and the Greek rolled his eyes to the provocative words. Soon, the driver stepped out of the front seat, took off his pants and crawled in the back seat. The girl did the same -- got in the back seat that is. "Keeno!" the Greek exclaimed. But, the Greek and I decided that this approach called for a relationship which we did not have with any girls we knew.

So, we waited to be sure the act was taking place as the heavy iron rocked on its stiff springs. Then we slipped down the bank to the car and jumped up and down on the polished chrome bumper. The guy exploded from the rear seat. We thought for sure the act of disengagement was more tricky and would give us a greater lead than what we had. We ran full speed to our bikes, feeling all four root beers sloshing in our stomachs. Just as we lunged for our bikes and tore off, a large rock hit my back fender. No harm was done. My bike had many a dent but none made by such a glorious event. We heard the guy scream far behind us, "I'll get you, you red-haired s.o.b."

The Greek and I mused later that the guy couldn't have possibly seen what color our hair was and besides, neither of us had red hair. Could it be that Red had beaten us to this new sport? He was crazy enough to do it. For a long time, we talked about our exploits of that evening deciding we didn't learn a whole lot about technique, but what we really needed was to think more about how to get a rod.

Koke was old enough to have a driver's license and convinced me the two of us should buy a car together. I sold my soap box bus, bought my mother a set of crystal perfume bottles for her birthday and put the rest of the proceeds into a rod with Koke. We found a Model T -- an old car even then, for only fifteen dollars. The engine was in dire need of attention, but it would make it home. I didn't have a license yet, but that wasn't so important; Koke drove most of the time.

While having a Model T was quite an accomplishment, buying gas and oil was a whole different problem. When we had money, we didn't need gas and when we didn't have money, we needed gas. More often than not, we were out of money and out of gas. Our methods to solve this problem met with some difficulty. One night, Lew, Mort, the Greek and I went out on a midnight requisition as Koke sat in the car in a friend's driveway out of gas, again.

Just a block away we found a parked car in a dark alley and after looking around for anyone watching, we opened the gas cap and slid one end of the siphon into the car's tank. Quietly we slipped the other end of the siphon into the large square five gallon can we kept stored in the trunk. As the can started to fill, the sides flexed and boomed like a bass drummer in the school band.

We spread out in every direction, like drops of oil plopped in a bucket of water. Half a block away the Greek and I climbed a trellis onto a roof. Nervously we sat and watched as the cops surveyed the scene.

The next day Koke returned to our car with a can of gasoline and the cops nabbed him. He flaunted his letterman sweater and successfully pleaded no participation. Then two weeks later Koke and I tore the rear end out of the T on a country road and we sold it for three dollars and fifty cents. My short-lived independence vanished and I was back on my bike.

Mort and I used to jump the tailgate step on the Sandy Boulevard. streetcar riding free down to the Y.M.C.A. We decided Charles Atlas had to be on the right track to attract girls. Body building would inspire any girl to commit passionate indiscretions according to the advertisements we had read. Well anyway, it was worth a try. Unfortunately I tried to get results much too fast. I loaded the barbells with all the weight I could find, then snapped the weight to my knees. So far so good. Then I snapped the weight to my neck and dropped it onto my shoulders, all the while losing my balance. I spun around like a half-conscious boxer, trying to keep from dropping the whole mass on my feet, then I slammed into the mat backwards, breaking both wrists.

A lady doctor with an office in her house not far from the Y put both my arms in a cast. It took me a couple hours to build up enough courage to trudge home to my mom and show her my bandaged limbs which looked like two legs of an albino elephant crossed on my chest. For six weeks I wasn't able to do so much as button my own fly. To me, that was just another girl-driven adventure gone wrong. Mom was livid and the guys rolled on the floor laughing and scratching. They roared, "Now, you can't even play with yourself." Mom fumed each passing day that she dressed me, and fed me and bathed me. "I hope you've learned your lesson," she said with smoldering exasperation every chance she got. But I hadn't; the desire for girls remained.

Football games were the only avenues outside our classes to meet girls, and besides they were a good excuse to get the gang together. In 1940, Grant High School had a mythical National Championship play-off game with a visiting team from Ohio. On the night of the game the gang joined to cheer our team onto victory. With our team captain, Don Hoff, weighing in at two hundred and forty pounds and two brutes named Beers and Morrison as our running backs, we had a good chance to win even as the underdog.

On the way to the game some of the guys from the gang and I each snitched a pair of girl's panties off some backyard clotheslines. At the pep rally session we rushed the cheerleaders and came away waving the panties. This was not all that bad of an act we thought, but that's also about as close as any of us got to getting into the girls' drawers.

The game started off with the entire stadium singing God Bless America and pledging allegiance to the flag. Normally this was a formality which most of us could do in our sleep, having sang the anthem and said the pledge every day of our school life. This time was different. There was still some confusion on whether we should extend our arms to the flag as we normally did during the pledge. Many of us had received instructions to leave our right arm crossed over our hearts during the entire pledge since the straight arm looked too similar to the Nazi salute to Adolf Hitler. Others were instructed to use a salute which resembled that used by the U.S. military. The war was closing in on us, our parents talked about it, and we saw the newsreels every time we went to the movies. But for now the game was foremost on our minds.

The Grant Generals lost the game 20 to 12 and downtown Portland became a riot of fun. The crowd tore down the goal posts and accidently ran one through a streetcar on the downtown Broadway Street run. The gang joined at Jolly Joan's, a downtown hamburger hangout where I owed everyone a hamburger for losing the race to the goal post. Unfortunately, I didn't have enough money on me to pay and if only I'd been faster on my feet I would have been spared from what I had to do.

Finishing my hamburger ahead of everyone, I apologized for having to leave early and said I would pay for everything on the way out the door. I left the guys with instructions to wave to the cashier once I got with her to settle the bill. Then I told the cashier the guys waving would pay for my burger and rushed out. I knew the guys would be annoyed but we all were at one time or another short of money.

I didn't remember until I got home that the panties I snitched were still in the pocket of my cords so I stuck them in the glove compartment of Dad's car. My intention was to take them out in the morning and put them in my locker at school. As I came home from school that next day, I saw my mother cornering my dad with a broom handle waving these young girl's panties and yelling accusingly, "What were you out with, some cracker-assed wench?" To this day, I haven't said a word about those panties.

Working for the local grocery after school allowed me to buy my first wholly owned car. For sixty dollars I bought a 1930 Model A Ford roadster. This was the start of a lifetime love affair with automobiles.

My Model A was spartan, essentially a square box on wheels. An old Detroit production car void of imagination or guts. It lacked upholstery, other than an old blanket the owner threw in the deal. The windshield swipes were missing, and it only had a couple instruments on the dash. I suspected the speedometer was reasonably accurate but the gas gauge was unreliable. But in all, she had a lot of potential.

About the same time every one of the gang was trying to get rods also. Mort got a 1931 Chevrolet roadster, Red got a 1930 Model A four-banger with a rag top just like mine and Koke already had his 1928 Chevrolet coupe. Both Lew and the Greek lost the battle to their folks and had to make do in our rumble seats. Jack had the *maybe sometime* use of his folk's Buick sedan straight off the production line.

Lew ran away from home over this car issue, and lived in the Greek's garage until the Greek's mother spotted Lew one morning and gave him the word. Then Lew hid in a filling station and soda shop where we hung out, but in a few days he decided to return home to his mom's bean sandwiches, a specialty of hers.

With the cars we finally drew in the girls. Elaine was the first girl I got all that serious about. Mort's girl was Charleen and there wasn't much we didn't do together.

I met Elaine when she was a carhop at a drive-in. Carhops and cheerleaders were the *creme de la creme* of the high school girls. Football players seemed to go for the cheerleaders, but hot rodders went for the car-hops. Both groups of girls were appealing from the standpoint of looks but carhops had the advantage of working odd hours which was a built-in excuse for a late Friday run, to places like Blue Lake or Jantzen Beach famous for their jukebox music.

There were three drive-ins we frequented. Yaw's Top-notch, in our high school district, had the best hamburgers in town if not the whole world. Tik Tok was closer to town and that's where we went to look over the hot rod competition and the girls from all over the area. Jim Dandy's was the place that sort of belonged to the gang and was on the northeast side of town, out toward Blue Lake. If anyone wanted to challenge us to a drag they knew where to come, just like we knew the favorite hangouts of every other gang.

Football games never lost their charm as a gathering place for girls and pursuers of girls. Our hot rods, polished to a slick Simonize sheen were the bait we used to lure one or another young girl into our clutches. Jamboree Football night particularly, was known for drawing out all the girls from everywhere in town. Eight teams rallied at the Multnomah Stadium, with each team playing only a quarter. The remaining quarters of the game were played as the season progressed. No one came for the football, it wasn't all that interesting. We used the event to start off the weekend fun.

The Jamboree night of our junior year, we all wound up at the Blue Lake Chateau. Unlike most other places, the Chateau had two jukeboxes offering plenty of choices. Everyone showed up including Junior Kendall and Gord and their gang from Benson High, a lot of bobby-soxers with mismatched shoes from Jefferson High and our whole gang, plus many other kids I didn't know. The cycle crowd from Jefferson was also there. They were known for stirring up trouble; one guy's dad was on the Portland police force and had hushed things more than once. It looked like it would be a swinging night.

The dance floor was full. I plunked a nickel into the jukebox and started jitterbugging with Elaine to Glenn Miller's *Little Brown Jug*, singing the chorus:

Ha! ha! ha! you and me,
Little Brown Jug, don't I love thee!
Ha! ha! ha! you and me.
Little Brown Jug, don't I love thee!

Suddenly, a guy as big as a moose stepped up to me and tried to cut in on my dance. Junior saw the whole thing and urged me to tell the guy to "Kiss off."

A noisy crowd gathered around and everyone was egging me on, so I took advantage of the guys from Benson standing at my side. They were all football players, two years older than me and a lot bigger. I pushed the guy a little although I was slightly nervous about what might happen remembering all too well my first fight under the protection of my brother. This time the guy backed right off making me look like a hero. But he did not forget our encounter.

About two weeks later the same guy cornered me in front of the Sandy Jug just after I had ordered my usual shake and burger. He leaned his elbows through the openings where my A's side curtains should have been and for the first time I got a good look at his bulging shoulders and meaty forearms. He looked even bigger than I remembered. This was the time to develop my negotiating skills, so I told him I would drag with him to settle the dispute. No one with two ounces of sense would fight this iron-fisted gorilla. He accepted my offer and I was relieved, the plan worked like a charm. His new hopped up '32 Ford would leave my A in the dust, and if it didn't I promised to see that it did. This was not the day for me to lay down some rubber. Our argument was settled that simply.

One night I borrowed Dad's '39 Ford when my car was torn down for another adjustment to the engine. It was the first and last time Dad let me use his car. I took Elaine to Jim Dandy's for an after school snack, and with a little strutting and bragging scared up a race with a rival who had his own '38 Ford, a real gow-job that had been out before. "What do you think that old goat of yours will do all out," I said to the '38 as I tipped my gow hat off my forehead. "Better'n that steam roller you're driving," he retorted. Since none of us had ever been in a position to take him on, I didn't know what he had under his hood. Just from looking at the gleaming body and listening to his blubbering pipes I knew the engine probably wasn't stock.

But, tonight I had an opportunity to prune him in the name of my gang. Just for the glory, we said, since we never placed bets on drag races. In California the big boys had started betting their car titles on the races, but fortunately these pink slip races never caught on in Portland.

We squealed out of the parking lot, shooting gravel in every direction then we roared down the highway toward Blue Lake. The streets were quiet as they usually were after dark; our primary concern was falling into a deep rut since most everyone's cars had been lowered to reduce the drag. When we got to our favorite location, the gang and some friends of my opponent quickly blocked off a mile of the highway, positioning two cars facing into the street at the finish line.

My opponent and I lined up quickly at the starting point. There was no time to spare, since we had to finish the race and clear the area before the cops arrived. For good luck, my white gow cap sat between Elaine and me. If I was driving a roadster, it would have been on my head, but it wasn't cool to have it on in a closed car.

Revving our engines, my opponent and I watched carefully for the starter to wave his t-shirt, our makeshift flag. I could hear the throaty burbling of my opponent's well-tuned engine. Down came the flag, and we popped our clutches and stomped on the gas in unison, squealing our wheels and laying a thick coat of rubber on the road as our rods shot ahead. Our adrenaline surged and smoke curled upwards in the shadow of the lights. We knew the ecstasy of such a love-making episode with our cars. I looked over to my opponent, studying his confident face and anticipating his next move.

We wound up tight in low, still neither one of us was ahead. I knew then, the only way for me to take the lead was to *goon shift*, so I pressed on the gear shift, and leaned toward second gear. The gear shift locked into position by the pressure of the gears. Then, I immediately hit the clutch. Anticipating the squeal of tires that this would bring from my Model A, I grinned confidently at my opponent. But, I missed second gear, breaking off a tooth which wedged itself alongside the gearbox. The whole bottom of the transmission blew out and I came to a jolting halt while my opponent slid to an easy victory.

The innards of my dad's car hung from the undercarriage like a greasy gutted chicken. Drag races always had exciting endings win or lose, but this scared the hell out of me. What was I going to tell my dad?

Fortunately no cops came, and I got one of the guys to tow Dad's car to the house. No one was willing to stay and support the story I planned to tell.

Dad was in bed, breathing a raucous snore. He was now working a steady job and would be getting up early to go to work in the morning. I stood quietly at the side of his bed, generating the courage to tell him what had happened and worrying how he would take the news. He was capable of becoming fairly violent, which was a carryover from his logging days. I still remembered some of his fights in the logging camp; in fact his twice-broken nose served as a reminder of those times.

I poked lightly on Dad's shoulder and after I heard a moan, I told him the story with staged calmness. "Dad, you won't believe what happened to your car. I shifted when I was pulling away from a stoplight and the transmission seemed to act up so I had it towed home." In the ensuing silence, I felt compelled to ramble on. By then, my mom was awake and told me to go to bed. She saw the pressure building. I walked away wondering if Dad believed the story.

A friend of Lew's, named Sam, had a cabin up by Mount Hood and we used to go there in droves. The cabin had an enclosed loft which the older guys used for their amorous affairs, but only the gang members knew that the cord dangling from the kitchen ceiling with the apple on it, went through a hole in the ceiling and was tied to the bottom of the bed springs. Whenever we saw that bobbing apple we howled like wild wolves.

Sam was able to keep the place policed up enough that his mother let us use it throughout our high school years. One Friday evening Mort took Elaine and Charleen in his roadster to Sam's cabin. I was to meet them later, after I got off at the grocery store where I worked. With the back of his car loaded with several glass jars of grain alcohol and grapefruit juice -- a mixture which was tasteless but would scramble your brains, he started towards Mt. Hood.

Mort always *stood on the head*, as we called it. He simply didn't know how to drive without stomping on the throttle. As he rounded a curve on Powell Valley Road heading into the town of Gresham, Mort slid on the gravel broadsiding a telephone pole and essentially slicing his car in half.

On my way out to Sam's cabin, I spotted the remains of Mort's car being drug onto the bed of a tow truck. A police officer (they were police officers when they were helping us) told me they were on the way to the hospital, so I followed them. When we got to the hospital, Mort was sitting outside Elaine's room. He was in good shape but a peek through the door window told me she was not.

After a brief discussion with the doctor, we all agreed it was up to Mort and me to go see Elaine and Charleen's parents. Our message was, "they will be fine." All three passengers had been thrown from the car, and the girls looked worse than they really were. There were many questions asked about minors having liquor and was Mort drinking but all that passed without too much of a problem.

Mort was cited for reckless driving and the cops noted the violation on the back of his license. He, like me, had already filled the back of the license with notations so the cops were writing on the edge. Fortunately however, we were never stopped for drunken driving. We didn't drink a whole lot -- just couldn't drink the only gut-rot we could afford, and do all the things we wanted to do.

In the late fall all the hotrodders of Portland met at Long Beach, Washington for the Gypsy Tour. This was the opportunity to find out what everyone's car would do all out, going as fast as we dared and making as much noise as we could. The tour was an annual event for both the hotrodders and the cycle boys on their big Harleys and Indians. We used it to test the handiwork we did on our irons, taking full advantage of the sponsor's first-rate instrumentation for clocking top speed. Mort and I started out for the beach late at night, short of sleep.

Mort never had the problem I had staying awake so we agreed he would tailgate me and my A in his newly acquired '34 Ford roadster. We called this drafting where the partial vacuum behind my car pulled Mort's roadster along, with hardly a need for gas. But the real reason Mort was tailgating me was so he could slip up and bump me when I started to doze off and wander. As we came down the winding road into Long Beach, Mort sloughed off on his bumping duty and I fell asleep and rolled the car over on a turn. My friend and passenger, Wahoo tumbled out one side and I went out the other. Wahoo was a tough Indian and it didn't surprise me that he wasn't scratched; fortunately I suffered no serious injuries either. Happily the tour was for guys only and the girls were safely at home. My pride was rattled, but we picked up the loose pieces of metal and proceeded to the beach in my A with its splintered windshield, and scrunched up sides.

The fastest time was run by Emmy Payne's four-port Riley modified '32 B roadster four-banger, at one hundred and twenty miles per hour. Not a bad soup-up job for a car rated at a top speed of sixty. On his last run as the wet sand shot from his tires, he blew a rod through the side of the block and it lay smoldering on the beach. That was the hottest rod we'd ever seen, but with a little tinkering we knew Emmy would have her back on the road again, running faster than ever.

We drove into Portland feeling everything we had done that weekend. As I approached 82nd Street and Sandy Blvd. to drop off Wahoo, I heard the newspaper boy call out, "Extra, Extra, read all about it, Japs Bomb Pearl Harbor!" That was the last Gypsy Tour we would see for a long time. "You just watch," I told Wahoo, "we're going to teach those yellow-bellied devils a lesson they'll never forget."

The Depression was just a memory now. Suddenly there was more work than workers. My whole family applied for a job at the Oregon Shipyard. "Land a 'goshen," Mom exclaimed to the interviewer. "You want me to be a welder?" "That's right ma'm. You can do it, I know you can. This lady here will teach you everything you need to know. She'll tell you, there's some pretty tight places on these ships of ours and we need someone your size to squeeze into them. It's the double bottoms -- there's not much room between the two layers." Mom was unconvinced at first, looking at the husky woman who stood in front of her. But two days later Mom was a trainee, busily welding deck plates on a liberty ship. At first I didn't believe her, but she came home with all the slag burns to prove it. Dad took a job as a head rigger, a trade he carried over from the woods and his days at Bonneville Dam. Gord became a choker-setter and I worked the graveyard shift as a helper on a rolling mill while going to high school during the day.

Koke was the first to leave for the service, joining the submarine force of the Navy. Lew went next, still bitter over losing the battle with his parents over a car. He too, went to see the world with the Navy.

For the first time I could ever remember, my family and I had money, cold hard cash. Mom and Dad could walk into a store and lay down the green bills for appliances or car parts which we in the past had saved up for months to buy. I was fascinated by the phenomenal access to money, but Mom was still cautious. "I don't trust those banks of ours one bit," she said emphatically. "No, not me, I learned my lesson already." I never paid much notice to her prophesy of an impending Depression since she'd been predicting a return to the hard times for so many years. But I finally realized why the cookie jar was always filled to the brim. Under the false bottom halfway up the side of the jar was a load of silver dollars she had carefully cleaned and placed there.

With my earnings I bought a '35 Ford coupe, built a bed in its trunk and made an entrance from the front end so I didn't have to leave the car to crawl into the back. The most exclusive speed shop in town agreed to soup it up, putting everything one could put on a stock V8 to eke every bit of power I could out of it. In addition, I did some other modifications to the body, including the installation of a dual exhaust system with chrome extensions, Porter mufflers which gave it the sound of a growling motor boat, ripple disk hubcaps, rear skirts, sealed hood panels, a chrome dash, and fine mohair upholstery. The last task -- if there is ever a last task on a hot rod, was putting on six coats of hand-rubbed black lacquer after having spent many hours sand papering and smoothing. Now I could challenge any rod at Jim Dandy's with my head held high.

A friend of mine who had the classiest 1932 Chrysler roadster in town talked me into buying a zoot suit. He assured me the girls loved their *reat pleats* and *drape shape*. Every jitterbugger needed one.

Zoot suits were remarkable primarily because they mocked all the normal body contours. The top of the trousers reached to the top of the shirt pockets and the legs tapered from fullness down to narrow little cuffs around the ankles. The knee-length jacket had extraordinarily wide lapels, heavily padded shoulders and a stream of buttons running down the sleeve. With this abomination, it was important to add all the right accessories. I wore a bright-colored matching knit tie and suspenders, and a key chain which slumped below my knees. Of course, I topped it off with a Pork Hat sporting an eight inch brim and a pair of English brogue shoes. What a get-up for negotiating a drag at the drive-in.

The haircut was important also. I let my hair grow long enough to comb it around behind like the tail-end of a duck. The cut was called a *D.A.*, short for *duck's ass*. Mom and Dad threatened to trade me in for any other kid on the street, however, it all seemed to work as Elaine and I stumbled through my first adventure in the back of the coupe. Alas, as I envisioned pearly white thighs and dewy beaver, it was all over before I knew it. The lecture from Koke on semen retention was all for naught.

I borrowed Dean's car one night while mine was getting a new set of racing heads. While cruising Sandy Blvd. in Dean's iron, a prowl car coming from the opposite direction flashed his spotlight at me. "Step on it!" my friend sitting beside me urged, "You can prune him. This rod'll go at least ninety -- Dean put everything he could in her." I thought to myself, the back of my driver's license was more than full, and I can't afford to get another ticket. I squirmed in the seat for a moment, then my passenger gave me all the confidence I needed. "We can go to my house, put the car in my garage," he exclaimed with an impish grin. "That cop'll never know what happened." That's when the chase started.

My tires squealed as I made a run for the hill by the golf course, down into the flat by the railroad yard. "Right turn," my friend screamed into my ear, and we fishtailed around the corner losing control for a second. "They're gaining on you. Take a left, quick! Traffic! Look out!" I churned my way through the chaotic maze of traffic, as the cars scattered and blasted their horns. "Right turn," he said and I careened around the corner. "Nuts! More traffic! Quick take a right. Don't worry about the stop sign. He's a block behind you." I didn't like barrelling though stop signs but fortunately there weren't any cars. "Go! Go!," he yelled. "He's gaining. Drat! Another cop car! We gotta do something fast!" With the next instruction, my erstwhile friend guided me smack into a dead-end street. Three flashing and screaming patrol cars followed, blocking the only exit. As I stood with my hands against the car, the Black Maria rolled up, and I was hauled to the slammer.

"Empty your pockets," the cop demanded at the station. He snatched my wallet and sifted through its contents one item at a time. My special rubber with the *French Tickler* went into the wastebasket without comment. Next, the cop took a couple of risque pictures I had, and slipped them in his desk. I never saw them again, but was confident he would. Defiantly, I told him I was a juvenile and he couldn't keep me in jail over night. Not saying a word, he lifted the telephone receiver and called the number he found on my dad's business card in my wallet and related the details to him. Dad mused, "A night in the cooler wouldn't hurt him." The experience was disheartening to say the least.

The brutish guy in the next cell was in for manslaughter. All night long he shrieked, "I didn't do it, I didn't do it, besides I didn't mean to!" My dad was right, a night in the cooler didn't hurt me, it taught me a lesson. Morning brought the incessant sounds of an automatic-flushing toilet which never stopped swirling as I forced down a bowl of cold, lumpy mush. I vowed never again.

A few days later I saw the movie *Wake Island* with Brian Donlevy, showing the island being lost to the Japs. This drama added to a speech by a Hubbard, Oregon boy named Marion Carl convinced me it was time to serve my country. Marion was a major in the Marine Corps and had become a fighter pilot ace. I was impressed as he spoke to our high school, standing so proud in full uniform and saluting the flag as we sang *God Bless America*.

I had been thinking about going into the service ever since I had heard the news of Pearl Harbor. From the start joining the military seemed like something exciting to do and then it grew into something that I just had to do. It angered me that my country had been attacked and the news was getting worse. I wanted to prove to the Japs and the Krauts that they had taken on a force they never should have. A young able-bodied man had an obligation to join the military or he owed it to everyone to explain why he didn't. To me, the word *patriot* took on meaning for the first time.

The next day I enlisted in the Army Air Corps. I was accepted into the cadet program August 14, 1942, but had to wait for my eighteenth birthday before I could report.

For as long as I could remember, I had an urge to fly. It was Jack who first showed me how to make the balsa-wood airplane models which hung in my bedroom. While I never could make models as good as Jack, I was proud of them all the same. My favorite was a model of a Fokker Tri-wing, like the Red Baron flew. Another favorite was the Spad flown by Frank Luke, the great balloon buster who was an ace in WWI. His picture was on the model box, as was his story on flying. He was a hero, a knight of the sky. There was no greater distinction in my mind. Now I had the opportunity to fly and I would do everything it took to make the grade.

I had to report for duty before my senior year was over. The government had a special program, however, which allowed those of us who had not yet graduated to receive a graduation certificate and that was what I planned to do. My brother joined the regular army and later applied for the cadet program, the only option for someone his age. Unfortunately, Gord's application got caught up in the bureaucracy when the Army learned he was not a citizen of the United States. Years before, when my parents got their citizenship straightened out, Gord's had fallen through the crack and by the time he got naturalized through the simple process of joining the service and filing the appropriate papers, the program had passed him by. His assignment was as a baker for the Army in Europe.

One piece of unfinished business remained for me. I had not yet appeared in court for the chase episode. Fortunately Dad convinced the judge to drop the charges because I had signed up for the service. However, I lost my license.

The gang was about gone. Jack left for the Navy, and Red and Mort left for the Army. The Greek was classified as a 1-C for being in an essential job. From the start, he wanted to join the service worse than anyone, but he knew the stomach which gave him so much trouble on the pole vault team surely would have kept him from passing the physical. Being classified 1-C was disturbing to many, particularly a patriot like him who was spoiling for a scrap with the enemy.

Occasionally I would still slip behind the wheel, sneaking my car out of the garage when no one was home. Dad caught me throwing gravel all over Jim Dandy's one night starting out on a drag race. Dads weren't supposed to know about Jim Dandy's and I didn't think mine knew either. Anyway soon after that my car wound up on blocks in the garage of a Gregory Heights classmate.

A week before leaving for the Air Corps I was at a party with my friend Dean and his girl Polly Green. Dean had been drinking too much, so I took his car and Polly home. That night I learned that one can't rely on a girl to keep her secrets and it came as no surprise that Dean never let me use his car again. Polly always claimed someone else told Dean about our coming out of the woods carrying the rumble seat cushion.

When I left for the service, the only remaining gang member was the Greek. Mom put another blue star on the white silken banner which hung in our window; my brother's was already there. She would pray daily that the stars would not turn gold.

As I packed a few necessities, I recalled General Arnold's plea for recruits, "Send me the hotrodders off the streets and I'll have an Air Corps that will bury the enemy." I was raring to go.

21. 1940 version of a '36 Ford Coupe, about as good as they get.

22. A pre-war version of every kid's favorite,
a hopped-up '32 Ford Roadster.

23. Dragging for the glory.

24. Negotiating a drag race at the local drive-in
with gow hats donned.

25. The '35 Ford Mel stored for the duration.

26. Mel's mom and dad during the wartime shipyard days.

CHAPTER 6

THE BASICS

The train ride to Fresno, California for Basic Training (B.T.) was a far cry from my days of glory on the Portland Rose. The crowd which formed around the platform the day I left was muted in an unnatural sort of way. Mom and Dad stood solemnly at my side with anxious smiles forced on their stiff faces. I gave Mom an awkward hug and waited a moment with Dad, looking for some sign of what he might like me to do. He reached out his hand and said with a steady voice, "See if you fly those airplanes any better than you drive." Then he murmured the more conventional "good luck," as his lips quivered.

The platform was filled with guys no different from myself. Most were teenagers, naive and willing, with smooth faces conspicuously marred by an occasional pimple. Few of us were old enough to know fear, or the full dimension of the journey on which we were about to embark.

Still we quieted uncharacteristically as the sergeant called our names, and we dutifully formed a crooked line with our bags at our sides. What a motley crew we were, sitting, standing and slouching in our best pairs of worn-out corduroy trousers and over-sized sweaters. Not one zoot suit was in the bunch; everyone either had the good sense or good advice to leave all remnants of those behind.

Mom and Dad waved as I boarded the troop train. Though they didn't speak, their message was clear. Their little boy was leaving them for good; he'd return a man in everyone's eyes but theirs. He *would be* one of the lucky ones who returned. He simply had to be. In all my childhood years, I had never seen my parents pause long enough to be so maudlin. And as uncomfortable as it was, I shared their sentiments.

At the end of our journey, we were met by other trains with hundreds of more guys. A tough-talking sergeant took charge immediately and tried to make order of the chaos, demanding we line up in alphabetical order. We shuffled about and pointed ourselves in the general direction of the booming voice, but still the mass of incoming recruits looked strikingly similar to the throwaway vegetables at a Sunday morning farmer's market.

Within a matter of hours, starting with the letter A and ending with the letter Z, the Air Corps gave us the look of sameness. We stood in line, waiting while the sergeant looked us over. The A's filed out of the line and into a building, which caused a vague stir. It was on that cue, that the sergeant underwent a frightening metamorphosis, becoming an enraged bull who bellowed, "Shaddup! I don't want to hear a word out of this line! You! Whadaya doing lookin' around, you lookin' for your mama? All eyes front and center? I talk, you listen! You hear that, you raggedy-ass bunch of suckers!" All of a sudden, the sergeant had our full attention and we wanted more than anything to be the next name called. The abuse persisted and I was convinced the sergeant was a bona fide maniac. We were no damn good, and he wanted to be sure we knew that.

At last we came to the P's and with a couple quick swipes of the electric clippers, my D.A. was replaced with a jagged crew cut which looked like all the other fifty-second haircuts on base. By the time we lined up again, we were all dressed in olive drab, down to the underwear and handkerchief. No one had to guess anymore where the Lucky Strike green went; it was all on us. Most of our personal effects, civilian clothing and nonregulation gear were mailed home, along with the standard Air Corps safe-arrival letter addressed to our moms. We were in the United States Army now and there was someone to remind us of that fact every second of the day.

We now looked like books on a wellordered library shelf. My new buddies would be the guys standing at my sides, sharing similar letters of the alphabet. They, like me, were selected for this program because of something the Air Corps called physical soundness and mental attitude, which prepared us for whatever was to come. We made friends with each other the way you would in a pool hall or bar, talking a little, telling a few stories, then warming up to those few who seemed the most agreeable. It seemed as though some guys made a dedicated effort *not* to get along, but the Army made it impossible to be a loner in the public facility we shared. They forced a togetherness on us, the likes of which few had ever seen before.

We were crammed into olive-drab barracks which had no interior doors and little more than the basic amenities. At the rear of the barracks were the toilet facilities, which openly confronted any pretenses anyone wished to harbor. Everything was exposed: urinals, commodes, wash basins and showers. I walked into the latrine my first morning, waited my turn to get a basin and stared into the polished steel mirror. The room and its bustling mass of humanity was shockingly distorted by the mirror, and the view was equally repugnant when I turned to look at it directly. There we were, strangers in various stages of undress; shaving, pissing and crapping in the biggest ten-holer I had ever seen. What a sight it was to see the homely-looking line-up on the open-air commodes, all the guys I would come to know, sitting in all their glory on their thrones; some readers, some talkers and some thinkers. There was no privacy and therefore there was no privacy violated.

Most of us quickly developed a whole new vocabulary of four-letter words to prove we had been around and were now *men*. The Southerners had their own down-home version of swearing, which they pronounced as five letter word equivalents, *shiat*, *fawck*, *daime* for starters. These profanities were reserved mostly for the barracks and would vanish from our vocabularies when we were any other place with civilians, especially parents and girls we were trying to impress.

From the first day forward, the drill sergeant set out to prove none of us were good enough to be a cadet. We kept looking around for airplanes but what we saw was two months of hills and fields full of dust, marching and singing to the rough bark of the sergeant:

> Hup, tup, threep, four,
> Sound off, sound off.
> Well, I wish all the ladies
> Were bricks in a pile,
> And I was a mason--
> I'd lay 'em all in style.
> Hey, Bobba Reeba,
> Hey, Bobba Reeba,
> Hup, tup, threep, four,
> Sound off. Sound off.

Six hours each day the Sarge yelled at us, "Right flank, harch! Column right, harch! I can't hear you!! LOUDER! MAKE THIS BUILDING SHAKE!" We half-yelled and half-sang until our voices were hoarse. Later, we'd have to clean up the lyrics the Sarge taught us, once we became cadets.

In the dark of the night, hours before sunrise we faintly heard the trumpet call over the loud speaker. Then the Sarge's booming voice broke our trance, "Okay men, out of those fart sacks! Drop your cocks and grab your socks! You have twenty minutes to fall out! Move it!" That meant we had twenty minutes exactly to get washed, showered and whatever else we needed to do, in our community latrine where everyone else wanted to do the same thing at the same time. Then we scrambled out to roll-call formation in the semi-darkness.

The barracks were spotless, the traditional mother-in-law's white-glove spotless, and the Sarge organized G. I. parties to keep them that way. We snaked around on the floor on our hands and knees with a hard bristle horse brush and a foul-smelling bar of naphtha soap, scrubbing everything until it was as clean as a surgeon's operating room. "This is chicken shit," we complained to each other. "What's this have to do with becoming a pilot?" After a couple hours we settled out some, joking about the chicken shit. "You know what that white stuff in chicken shit is? Well, that's chicken shit, too." Everything we did was chicken shit, or at least that was what it appeared to be at the time.

The sarge wiped his bleached white glove on the soles of our extra pair of boots, or anything else which looked like it might not have had the attention it required. Any G.I. who got the Sarge's gloves dirty was in for a merciless tongue-lashing or more K.P. Get caught with a dull shine on your boots, and you suffered the same fate. The sarge yelled as we stood in a brace, looking disgustingly at our feet, "I want to see the reflection of the barracks light bulb on the surface of your boots. Everyone understand?" By now we knew the Sarge's questions generally required an enthusiastic "Yes, sir!" and that's what we gave him.

We sat around for hours, trying to put a shine on our boots every which way. Finally an ex-ground-pounder sergeant going through the flight program with us agreed to show us how to polish the boots for a package of cigarettes, having learned the secret while working in his uncle's shoe factory in New England. We watched the laborious process. "Take a cloth like this, pull it over your index finger. Dab it in the warm water you have in your shoe-polish can lid, then dab it in the shoe polish. Grind it in like this, covering no more area than maybe the size of the dime." In unison we tried it ourselves and after we finished, the boots projected a fine ebony luster, fit for any inspection. Unfortunately, after one tromp through the dirt and we started over again. Just more chicken shit.

Order was the Army's obsession, nothing was to be out of place. Dirty clothes had their place in our olive-drab laundry bag and did not go on the floor. If any of us wondered what happened to the magic system most of us had at home where our dirty socks and underwear disappeared from the floor then reappeared clean the same day in our chest-of-drawers; it was gone. The equivalent of *Mom* was nowhere to be found.

Likewise there was nothing which equaled Mom's cooking for whatever we remembered it to be. We didn't eat anymore. We chowed down in the chow hall which had all the pleasantness of a community latrine with an obnoxious sergeant presiding over the ritual. Like most guys our age, we were generally too famished to complain much about the quality, but being on spud call was what we really detested. More K.P., more chicken shit.

Physical Training (P.T. as it was called) proved that tooling around in a hot rod and chasing girls didn't keep us in able physical shape. We suspected the sergeant had orders to keep us from roaming the base at night so he did everything he could to ensure we dropped -- not crawled -- into our bunks when he commanded us to do so.

The obstacle course was every P.T. instructor's answer to his deep-seated, morbid desire to free the world of low-life recruits. My instructor came on like gangbusters and persisted with a dedication and vengeance known only to the most hardened of criminals. He started with chin-ups, push-ups, sit-ups and deep-knee bends, enough to get most of us gasping for breath and wishing someone would put us out of our misery. Unfortunately, there was always some college athlete in the crowd who made us all look bad.

The course which followed purged any residual sign of life from our tortured bodies. It was hand-over-hand across the mud hole, over the wall, up the rope climb and then, *on the double*, back to the exercise field. I think it was a toss-up whether the rope climb or the wall was the most taxing. I'd say it's the rope climb, probably because I could manage to scale the wall, though I couldn't do it with a whole lot of speed or grace. The knots on the rope did me in the first time, and I would be forever leery of them. I got behind that day on the course and I slipped down the rope as though it was a firemen's pole. The knots battered my balls a half dozen times before I could slow my downward plunge. I writhed in pain at the foot of the rope, in a heap as the sergeant yelled a colorful array of expletives and threats. Gathering strength, I lifted my body and thought of something Koke once said, "Any woman who thinks childbirth is the most painful thing in the world has never been kicked in the balls." If I would have had the strength or courage, perhaps the sergeant would have learned the same lesson. But no one wanted to wash out of the program over something this foolish and I gritted my teeth to keep from saying something I would later regret.

"Alright men, assume positions for the duck walk!" the sarge shouted, looking straight at me. I dropped immediately into a full knee-bend position and placed my hands on my hips, with my torso straight and my head held high. On the command of "Quack," I quacked and waddled forward, then on command I turned to the left. I, along with the entire class, waddled like ducks around the parade field for fifteen agonizing minutes. The torture wasn't over there.

"Ten hut, hit a brace!" the sergeant shouted. We forcefully straightened our warped backs, thrust out our chests and tucked in our chins. No one dared exhibit the excruciating pain they felt in their backs and when the sarge was convinced that no one would, he howled "Dismissed," which signaled another day of P.T. was past. Our barracks blended into the night and there was complete silence ten minutes after the sarge announced the last piss call. Tomorrow was the base-wide sporting competition, another grand opportunity for premeditated abuse of recruits.

Through the endless inspections, drills and exercise we could see a unity of purpose, most markedly in the evolution of discipline. We hated the sergeant to the end, and then we loved him for all he had done for us. He started us down a fast track where the urgency of the war would not allow the luxury of time or dissent.

From B.T. we were dispatched for College Training, a new program designed to overcome any trainee deficiencies in academics when the Air Corps dropped its two-year college requirement in their effort to meet the war demand for pilots. It was at this point, when I first learned the way of the military, that a friend made often became a friend lost, at least for some interim period of time. Many of the friends I made in Basic were assigned to different detachments. Some, I would meet again.

My group, Detachment 18, went to Missoula, Montana. We were mostly the M, N, O and Ps from Basic. However, a few odd letters slipped into the group, almost like someone made a mistake and put a few library books back on the shelf improperly.

The purpose of College Training was to sharpen us up on the scholastic skills peculiar to aviation. In two months the Air Corps tried to teach us everything we needed to know about English, history, geography and math. They even grilled us on the use of a slide rule. The emphasis, however was on physics and what it had to do with airplane flight. Our first day we learned that the pressure of the air flow over a surface, such as an airplane wing, was inversely proportional to the velocity. That was a mouthful, further explained as meaning an airfoil has less pressure on top when it moves through an air mass. These *simple* laws of physics, they said, are what make wings and propellers work. And although the connection of physics and flying seemed very remote then, at least we had started talking about flying and airplanes.

The education level of the group varied. Some were at the high school graduate level, some were close to being at the high school graduate level, but not quite there, and others had a little college. The Air Corps did their best to get us all to the point where we could understand the principles of flight and the physics of combustion engines. There was no goofing off here, especially for the *not quite* high school graduate crowd.

Between classes we drilled, and drilled some more, always working on discipline. The upperclassmen dedicated themselves to harassing us. They ran in packs, like wolves descending upon their targets. "Halt and freeze! Grab a brace!" they'd yell. Then as we stood, chins tucked to our necks, they'd pick apart our uniforms, calling us a slovenly bunch of mongrels or whatever other clever phrase came to mind. Sarge was never far behind with his accusing wrath, "Rack 'em back! Alright, march! Watch those arm swings. Six inches forward, six inches back. Six inches, you hear?" We marched everywhere, to the mess hall, to classes, and even to church on Sundays. We became a team although the sergeant usually complained it was a sloppy one.

For the first time in our short careers with the Army, we were addressed as *Mister*, and it was here where we were expected to act as gentlemen, in addition to being good soldiers. Table manners suddenly became important. Like most everyone, I got caught having two hands on the table at once. A grievous sin for officers, who should know better. And thanks to the indignation of an upperclassman, the next meal I ate was a square one, sitting upright in a brace on the front of my chair, eyes straight ahead. "You, Mister. Eyes front and center," the upperclassman yelled. I raised my fork full of food vertically from the plate then moved it towards my mouth on a level plane. I repeated the sequence on the fork's way back to the plate for a second bite. The upperclassmen had a knack for making meals far worse than they should have been.

Chow time was important to us, but of infinitely more interest was the promise of our first flight in the Taylor Craft aircraft which sat conspicuously on the nearby field. We wouldn't get to do anything with the aircraft ourselves, however. The Air Corps just wanted to see if any of us were the type who would puke up our guts in a tight turn. They wanted to know our inclinations, up front, before they invested too much time and effort.

Most of us had never been in a plane, and had no idea what to expect. The instructor ignored my obvious awe. "Jump in the back seat," he yelled, as he shoved a small package into my face. "Here's a bag. If you puke in the plane, you clean it up. And if you get so much as one drop on me, you wash out of this program. You hear that, Mister!!!" We sped down the dirt runway and lifted into the sky. Then came the test. The first loops brought my stomach to my throat as we careened to the ground. There were more loops, and success was almost in his hands (or down his backside) as we climbed again, did a couple of rolls, then plummeted in a spin at a speed I'd never felt before. As I stepped from the plane with an ashen face, I dreamed of looking this guy up after the war and putting one of the Greek's burning sacks on his porch.

Mail call was either a pleasure or disappointment, depending if you or your buddies got mail. We'd gather around the sergeant listening for the call of our names. Mom was pretty good about writing, much better than me, and she couldn't have known our joy when she sent cookies or candy. Packages were exciting for everyone. I ripped open the first one I got with everyone hovering over me. At the first exposure of a toll house cookie nestled in the wax paper, a frenzy of greedy hands plunged into the box.

Seconds later, the torn wax paper was all that was left. But Mom sent a five dollar bill and a letter too, telling me the news:

Portland, Oregon
June 10, 1943

Dear Mel,

I must rush to get this letter into the mail box tonight so the mailman can get it first thing in the morning. I'm working the swing shift now, at the shipyard. I thought it would be a problem working so late, but it's not so bad. There are a lot of girls going home the same time.

We're getting along okay. Your Dad's out trying to get a new tire right now. We had a flat the other night when we were coming home from the shipyard. One of those retreads you know. You'd never seen anything like it, the tread peeled off like an orange. Dad doesn't have a ration ticket and no one seems to be very helpful. But we'll get one somehow, just don't know what we'll have to pay for it. Enough said about that. You probably don't want to hear about all these problems.   Hope you are fine. I've enclosed five dollars, I know you can use it.

I will close -- need to collect my scrap paper for Mr. Rogers' boy. He's a paper trooper, says he wants to become a corporal this month and is short some 100 pounds of paper.

Love,
Mom and Dad

After a month, a new class came in. This gave my group an opportunity to practice a little hazing of sorts. We had suffered so much humiliation from those who came before us, it was now our turn to make life miserable for the new recruits. Standing in a brace for upperclassmen every time they walked down a hall and eating square meals at chow time got old fast for most recruits. It was discipline, however, and we'd pass off the tradition enthusiastically with only the best of intentions.

Our first leave came almost before we could put any real thought in what we wanted to do. Elaine made my planning easy because she wanted to come for a visit. It was somewhat of a status symbol if your girl thought so much of you she came to see you, assuming she was reasonably pretty, that is. In a way I was happy about her visit. She was good-looking and bright, but there was something which bothered me.

One of the old gang members had dropped a real bombshell on me in a note he wrote while he was on leave in Portland. He said Elaine was running around with another guy, though it was no one I knew. I could not help spring the allegation on Elaine before she left. She cried, and it was such a scene, but the relationship was over. I rationalized cadets didn't have time for that sort of stuff anyhow. Some said it even affected a guy's eyesight. Besides, who wanted to get a Dear John letter when they were worrying about fighting a war.

My class left Missoula after two months and moved on to Santa Ana Army Air Base in California (better known as SAAAB) for Classification and Pre-Flight Training. This time the atmosphere of the train ride was at an all-time low. It reminded me of being in a cattle car with bunks stacked row after row, car after car, three high. We took turns in the bunks and the rest of the time we were shoulder to shoulder, with guys we hardly knew who were forever singing, humming, whistling, talking, smacking bubble gum, belching or whatever.

As the classes came in from all the Western region College Training Detachments, all the names were mixed in a giant pool and we were realigned again by alphabet. The order was now Paisley, Patapoff, Pfifer, etc. We saw a ten percent washout at Fresno and twenty percent at Missoula. Washout paranoia had infected us all by now, and I knew I would have to work hard to stay in the program.

Santa Ana was a huge sprawling base with endless rows of woodframe barracks and buildings. A few tar paper buildings were stuck in between to accommodate the overflow. Of grave concern, however, was the fact that there was not one airplane in sight, not even a runway. Just more barking sergeants.

The real threat at Santa Ana, however, was the classification officer. It was his job to assign us to navigator, bombardier, or pilot training schools, and he continued to remind us if Santa Ana wasn't our cup of tea, he could arrange to have our asses thrown off the base in an hour, and we could find ourselves helping the Marines take Tarawa. No one seemed to know how the classification system worked. We took some tests, even had a private interview with a psychologist to determine if we had any hang-ups. "Do you like girls?" he asked. "How long has it been since you last wet the bed?" Although some of the answers were obvious, others we couldn't do anything about, like the test for hand-eye coordination. The sergeant giving the test yelled at everyone, but it was the final analysis which really counted. We wondered how much the Air Corps cared about our saying we had a personal preference to be a pilot. Or how much weight they gave to meeting their quota. No one knew how they made their decisions and we were threatened daily with the unknown. Everyone wanted to go to pilot training and the thought that any of us might have to be a navigator or bombardier was devastating. Who wanted to be a navigator for some cocky pilot or wind up having the Nazis take potshots at them while they hovered over some bombsight dropping their loads?

A rumor floated around that a dose of clap would be enough to get a guy thrown off the list for pilot training. We never knew if it was true, but we worried about *everything*.

The flight physical or 6-4 was a serious concern for everyone. I went to it sweaty-palmed like most of the guys I knew, knowing that if my body didn't pass the test, I would wash out of the program. There was nothing I could do beforehand which would change the results.

For what seemed an eternity, I was shuffled through the maze of examination rooms, by the call of my name. First came the eye tests, which had a reputation for washing out more cadets than anything else. In all, twelve vision tests were administered, including color, distance vision, near vision, accommodation and others. I felt good about those.

Next we were introduced to the flight surgeon, a bespectacled guy with a spindly beak of a nose. Most disturbing was his habit of speaking in grunts, especially since few of us had undergone such extensive physical scrutiny before. He poked, inspected and judged each human specimen which stood before him, stark naked. And he maintained a stiff poker face when he rammed his finger up our backsides, then lifted our balls roughly while we tried to cough, two procedures for which I had an instinctive aversion. He gave few clues as to what transpired within his mind, and his final assessment was altogether a mystery.

After the Doc checked us over head to toe, we were shuffled to various other rooms where we gurgled, coughed, spat and urinated on the command of various corpsmen. Like the Doc's assessment, the lab results would take time.

At last the Air Corps came to a decision and we were called to a traditionally public ceremony where our destinies would be privately announced. It was a formal ceremony with all the drama and suspense to rip our nerves to shreds. Would we be pilots, bombardiers or navigators? The answer was held in the hand of the classification officer sitting in front of us at a wooden table. One by one he called us to his table, where he revealed the answer to our pleas. My hand trembled as I reached for the white card and flipped it over. Pilot, it said. I was going to be a pilot. A Pilot!! That was one more hurdle passed.

In the normal rush, I didn't have time to let my parents know, but in its typical manner the Air Corps took care of that for me. The base commander sent Mom a letter:

"2 Aug 43

Dear Mrs. Paisley,

It is with great pleasure that I notify you that your son, Melvyn R. Paisley, has been selected by the Classification Board for Pilot training in the United States Army Air Forces. I congratulate both you and him on this achievement.

He will soon be transferred to one of the Army Air Forces West Coast Training Center elementary flying schools and will then begin his flight training. The course of instruction which he will pursue throughout the flying schools is thorough, intensive and the best that our Country can give to him for his future duties and responsibilities as a member of the Army Air Forces."

The third paragraph laid on the praise a bit thick, something I knew Dad would particularly appreciate:

"In either war or peace, a Pilot occupies a position that requires sound judgment, a keen and alert mind, a sound body and the ability to perfectly coordinate mind and body in the flying of the airplane..."

Of course the commander stamped the outside of the envelope with a notice "good news." Our moms all fretted about us constantly and the commander didn't want to frighten them unnecessarily.

Most of us were now cadets, also called *gadgets* and occasionally called *dodos*. First off, we were issued new uniforms which were a slight improvement over the normal G. I. issue. They were similar to commissioned officer greens, with our rank insignia, a round black cloth patch with crossed airplane propeller and wings sewn on the right sleeve. Our officer's hat was covered with a dark blue braid, and the emblem was a crossed propeller and wings. Another bonus was the fifty percent flight pay, which boosted our salary to seventy five dollars per month. And just in case we needed it, we were given one thousand dollars worth of free life insurance.

In Santa Ana's Pre-flight Training we were to spend two months on the basics of military customs and courtesies, aerodynamics, code, engine technology, and fire arms. On top of that we also got more drill. Discipline was the watchword. The Sarge demanded that we make our beds so tight a dime would pop back six inches when dropped from a foot -- an impossible task, of course, one that didn't matter to him. When a planned inspection was before a weekend, some guys would make their beds the night before, then sleep on the floor. It was darned difficult getting everything done in the morning and some would do most anything to ensure their weekend pass, even risk a bed check.

Everything we owned was jammed neatly in a small foot locker which looked like everyone else's. The sergeant checked our lockers every day without notice. There was only one acceptable order for its contents; socks were rolled as prescribed and uniforms were folded just so. Shoes were placed in pairs, toes in on the floor. Any screw-up would earn you gigs or demerits, enough gigs and you lost out on a weekend pass, not that there were many of those. Worse yet, too many gigs could get you washed out of the program.

There was dust everywhere in our desert home, but the inspector of the barracks ordered that dust was to be nowhere. When a Santa Ana blew across the fields, we picked up every last particle by hand. Either the Air Corps didn't know the vacuum sweeper had been invented yet or didn't care, and if the inspector found so much as a speck, he gigged everyone who was even partially responsible.

Each week we had to wipe our gig record clean by doing extra laps at P.T. or walking them off on the parade grounds early in the morning or late at night. The bounds of the sergeant's imagination was the only limit to the undesirable things a guy could be asked to do to clean his slate, always on his own time, of course.

Entertainment was hard to come by, and I suspect that's why we spent so much time reading the base paper, called *Cadet*. It always had great stories on flying but most of us flipped to the comics first. Our favorite comic strip character was Miss Lace of *Male Call*, who was constantly being pursued by two conniving Army privates. The luscious Miss Lace would say to one of the boys, "Oh, General [she always called them General], when you're flying around with those won--derful hands of yours, you really must be careful where you land." When, oh when, would we meet someone like that?

Six weeks after we came to Santa Ana, we were finally granted our first open post, which lasted from three o'clock Saturday afternoon until three o'clock Sunday afternoon. The beach was only fifteen miles away, and we hadn't even seen it yet, much less laid a hand on the fine sand or the cocoa-tanned girls we talked so much about. The day before our leave the squadron flight surgeon gave us the stern lecture, "Now you will all go into Long Beach tomorrow after the morning drill, *if* you look good enough to the Commandant." Then he flipped on his slide projector and gave us the approved Army V.D. propaganda speech. It went something like this: "When you walk down the pier at Long Beach you can almost hear the applause, clap, clap, clap, and that's what you will get boys, clap. So remember, those gorgeous young girls can really fix you up."

He showed us a couple of slides, forewarning, "Here is what your dick will look like in two weeks with the clap." The picture was very graphic and very grisly. We guessed someone had put a .45-caliber slug through the head of the guy's prick. The picture of the gooey mass of flesh was so dramatic, it was etched in our brains. We all went looking anyhow. Still the lecture may have worked after all, because looking was all we really dared to do.

The bottom line was, leave was never what it was cracked up to be. We had to worry about anything we might do which could wash us out of the program. Even the joy of telling the guys how we might have done in town was not worth the risk of getting a dose. I always thought the guys who talked about their good times were just trying to make the rest of us jealous. Maybe they did, and maybe they didn't do what they said they did. But we still had a twinge of yearning.

As corny as it may sound, going to church was always the tactic I took for planning my outside entertainment. Invariably I would get invited to some girl's home for dinner. There wasn't the thrill, but a good meal was hard to come by. Also it was great to have a regular whom I could count on when we went into town for dancing and all the less risky endeavors. Thus I avoided the dreaded CLAP.

At Santa Ana we earned our pistol target qualification in a course aptly named, *Kill or Be Killed*. A beefy, ragged-along-the-edges Marine sergeant gave us the course at Camp Pendleton. Shooting a .45 automatic pistol accurately was a hopeless task, we learned. It was like putting a basketball in the net from the full length of the court, which was all just luck. We did the best we could, hoping never, ever to have to rely on them.

The sergeant drilled us on standing guard around a jungle airfield. He bellowed at us, "The enemy will slip up behind you and wrap his arm around your throat. The second you reach to grab his arm, leaving your side exposed, he's gonna open you up with a knife. Let me tell you men, that's not what you should do! Instead, reach behind, squeeze his balls as tight as you can and drop your full weight. Take my word for it, he'll release his grip." I had every confidence he would, especially if this guy did the dropping. We all harbored in the backs of our minds the thought that surely no pilot would have to stand guard duty in some jungle. But the truth was, at the rate students were washing out, this training just might come in handy for some.

Before I left Santa Ana, Mort wrote and told me his sister Marion married our football star, Lionel Beers, who had joined the Marines. Marion and Lionel were at Camp Pendleton, and I had a chance to see them before I left. Lionel and I sat on a bench and reminisced about the Grant-Waite game, where he did the blocking for two impressive crowd--wrenching touchdowns for the Generals.

Then I turned to look at Marion, who still had her wonderful girlish smile. My first kiss had slipped away from me, but I rationalized Marion looked better with him than with me anyway. As we parted, Lionel told me I had shed my zoot suit just in time. The city declared it a misdemeanor to wear one in L.A. after a few riots, which were precipitated by a dispute between the Chicano zooters and some sailors looking for women.

It was interesting to me that the sounds of Camp Pendleton were much the same as my base. Though it was Sunday, the men were drilling, marching on the hard, dry land which never stayed idle enough to grow so much as a patch of clover. Like us, they half-sang and half-yelled, irreverent songs as they marched. The words were different from the songs we sang, still they had the same undefinable quality. Once you heard them, you couldn't tear them off your mind:

> Be kind to your web-footed friend,
> For a duck may be somebody's mother,
> He lives in the creek by the swamp,
> Where the weather is always damp;
> Now you may think this is the end;
> Well it is!

The dead silence following this lyric carried me to the gate of Camp Pendleton and all the way back to Santa Ana.

The two months we spent at Santa Ana, studying, drilling and being grounded seemed like an eternity. But at last the majority of our class was dispatched to Primary Flight School. It was a joyous day for those of us who barely squeaked through the exams; ten percent of our buddies had failed to make the grade.

CHAPTER 7

FLYING BY THE SEATS OF OUR PANTS

I drew a position at the Mira Loma Flight Academy at Oxnard, California. Seven months in the service, and at last I was going to fly.

The school at Oxnard was a civilian owned and operated flight school, as were many other Primary schools. According to rumors it had a good reputation, not for being tough or easy like some, but for having maid service, of all things. Although we never saw any maids (other than the cadets doing their regular housekeeping chores), we still thought we were fortunate having not drawn one of the military schools. Many said the pilots at the military schools were bitter about being stuck teaching while the battle was raging without them. Everyone wondered how and why a supposedly proficient pilot got left on the homefront.

Mira Loma, in addition to Cal-Aero at Ontario, California, was owned by a Major Moseley, who was a retired army officer. The grounds overlooked the Pacific Ocean between Oxnard and Ventura, which was surely the most glamorous setting for any Primary school in the country. We lived in small cottages with two men per room, fine accommodations for most any circumstance. The coarse blade grass was neatly clipped and flowers lined the buildings. Real flowers, thriving in the gorgeous sun. My roommate was Cadet Patapoff and in two short months we had to help each other struggle through our initiation into flying.

First off, we were issued flying gear -- a blue gabardine flight suit, leather helmet, parachute and the coveted A-2 leather flight jacket. Now we had the total look of a pilot, which meant we were at last cadets. Nearly thirty-five percent of our buddies had already washed out because of weak stomachs, weak eyes, weak heads or the clap.

The Air Corps seemed to do everything in its power to make its cadets want to be successful in its pilot training program. That was surely one of the reasons for the fancy uniform and all the flight gear. It wasn't just the fancy gear, though, which made us want to stay; we also knew if we washed out, it was back into the regular army. Back to the grimy life as a *dogface*. We had all been exposed to enough of that in our short careers with the service.

Fortunately, we had now reached the point in our training where the real washout was behind us, and our goal of being pilots was within reach. From here on out, about the only thing which would send us back to the regular army was a serious breech of discipline or lack of flying proficiency. There would be a few more washouts, but we'd lose even more to flying accidents.

At Oxnard, our instructors introduced us to a new task in ground school called aircraft recognition. They set up a projector in the front of the class, then used it to flash silhouettes of various enemy and friendly aircraft onto a screen. For endless hours, the operator repeated in a monotonous tone, "Ready . . . now!" That was our cue to jot down the type of the aircraft. Then the operator showed other aircraft from different approach angles. Just as we became reasonably proficient at identifying the aircraft silhouettes, the operator decreased the time of the projected image until our brains registered it, but our eyes seemingly could not see it. The task became more difficult and the instructors became more testy, "Damn it, use your eyes, men! What do you want to do, shoot down one of our own aircraft? How would you like it if one of your buddies blasted you clean out of the sky?" We winced; the key was total concentration. Total control over your eyes and brain, and total coordination. We knew this was important, life or death important, and we tried hard to succeed. We also recognized this was the first time our instructors brought up the subject of enemy aircraft, which meant we were getting closer and closer to actual combat.

Civilian instructors came on the base every morning from all around the area. Instructors were hard to find, since most of the qualified pilots were fighting the war. As a result, the instructors were everything but pilots in real life. Two were actors who drove up from Hollywood each day in a 1941 Cadillac convertible which had a coal gas converter in the back to avoid the gas rationing problem. Patric Knowles and Robert Cummings; we'd seen so many of their movies and never thought there would be a day we would see them in person. Both Patapoff and I hoped to get assigned to one of them.

Instead Patapoff and I wound up with an older man, who we guessed to be about forty years of age, and who was losing his hair as well as his waistline. It turned out this guy was probably the best instructor at the school. He was a tough, obnoxious bastard, but he was smooth and had enough patience to endure most of the mistakes we made. Our plane was a PT-17, a Stearman open-cockpit biplane built by Boeing Airplane Company, one we considered a real humdinger of a plane. As I was introduced to the Stearman by my instructor, I stood in front of it with all my flight gear. The airplane was so massive and overwhelming, I hardly thought it possible to fly it alone. It was two hundred and twenty-five horsepower and it looked like all mustang.

The instructor, Mr. Oakes (we called him John when he wasn't around), slipped into the front seat. "Wind 'er up," he yelled. I grabbed hold of the starting crank with both hands, slowly winding the flywheel. Mr. Oakes engaged the wheel to the engine, and the engine fired, then roared.

Quickly crawling up into the back seat I connected the one-way Gosport tubes the instructor would use for communicating with me. We taxied down the runway in a series of S turns meant to give me visibility in the forward direction. Then we stopped abruptly at a forty-five degree angle to the runway.

As we paused at the end of the runway, the instructor ordered me to start through the checklist, which was not particularly lengthy. Nearing the end of the list, I checked the magnetos, then shouted, "Seat belt on and locked." And, we sped down the runway.

The wind blew at my face like the time I drove Emmy Payne's A-V8 at the Gypsy tour. I always loved a rag-top because you could feel the speed. Emmy used to say, "I don't need a speedometer; I can tell how fast I'm going by the wind." I was sure we were going faster than I had ever been before. Then the plane took on a lightness and started to leave the ground.

As he did some simple maneuvers, my instructor leaned into the turns and told me, "Everything about flying should be natural. Don't force your movements. A good flyer flies by the seat of his pants. Everything should become second nature." Likening the seat of the pants reaction to what it takes to successfully pull your car out of a skid, he said the mechanics of each action must disappear from your mind and only the feel should govern your actions. "Now, I know your dad probably told you not to drive faster than you can think, but in an airplane you have to. Instincts are what you'll need for combat flying, and you'd better get them down pat." On this first flight I was bombarded with philosophy, precepts, procedures and most of all the thrill of flying in that open cockpit. I'm afraid I was looking everywhere and seeing nothing, but I felt so much. From that moment on, I was hooked on flying.

The instructor circled the field and made several touch and go landings. On the third pass at the runway, he told me to take over the stick and take a shot at landing. First I had great trouble holding altitude in the pattern around the field. The plane jerked in the sky and the wind gave, as I knew the ground wouldn't. But after a few touch and goes of my own, I felt the instructor ease the pressure on his stick as he followed me through every move.

Each night after cramming in our night studies, Patapoff and I stayed up until lights out talking about the day's flying. We'd say but not complain, what a tough bastard John was for an instructor. Then we wondered aloud how we did. First Patapoff would worry how he did that day, then I would convince him things surely went well. Then I'd invariably say to Patapoff, "Damn it, I really flubbed the dub today. It was that lazy-8, I just can't get it right." Patapoff would sooth my washout paranoia "Mel, you did okay, I'm sure. You know there's one thing John will always do, that is tell you in the worst terms if you did anything wrong." That was the way of the Army.

In just ten hours of flight time, we each had to solo. If it looked like a cadet needed longer, then he would have to take a check ride so the Air Corps could determine if he had some sort of fundamental problem. There was so much to learn. Our lumbering and graceless movements had to be replaced by a smooth naturalness, a transition which bestowed both ecstasy and survival.

One day the instructor launched off on a series of acrobatics. He demonstrated what a remarkable airplane the Stearman was for inside and outside loops, chandelles, Immelmanns, slow rolls, barrel rolls, snap rolls and on and on, including some maneuvers for which he knew no names. Because of the Stearman's bi-wing construction, we could do maneuvers most planes couldn't withstand. Mr. Oakes did them all, and when we finished the flight for the day he said, "Today I wanted you to get the feel for those maneuvers. Tomorrow it's your turn." Later that night I talked things over with Patapoff. There was little consolation in what he said, or how much more I read on the subject. By now, I knew no one could learn how to fly from a book or from talking about it, any more than they could learn football that way. You had to experience it. Toss the ball, make the tackles and make some mistakes. Though I accepted trial and error as the only way to learn, the consequences were terrifying.

As we slowly worked our way up to altitude in the bright morning sun, I was thinking of the many things which we had done the day before and was trying hard to make every turn proper and well coordinated. Mr. Oakes talked me through each maneuver. Going into a stall was the most fundamental of air maneuvers and was the most important. When an airplane stalls, it quits flying; the lift is not great enough to keep it in the air. That's enough to get the attention of a novice like me.

Nervously I responded to his every instruction "Back off on the throttle slowly. Lift the nose and as the plane gives a slight shudder, drop the nose and give it some throttle. That will get you flying again. Not bad, but try to keep the wings level even though you are losing airspeed, otherwise you'll go into a spin." I did it, but it didn't feel that good and the thought of going into a spin didn't make me feel good either. "Okay, do the same thing, and I'll talk you into a spin." I didn't have to wait long for that, and I heard Mr. Oakes calm voice through the rubber Gosport tube, "Now, you are about to stall. Give it hard rudder on the left." The plane's nose dropped and we started spinning slowly, each turn getting faster and faster and tighter. The ground was a spinning green and brown blur.

I concentrated hard on Mr. Oakes' words, which were now more forceful, "Remember from ground school, count the turns, one, two, three."

I wasn't sure how many times I had gone around, I'd lost count. "Now hard right rudder and let the plane come back to life. Slowly pull back on the stick as the spin stops." I noticed John backed off the throttle more than I did and I didn't even feel it with all the action going on. "Remember, keep off the throttle. Power just tightens up the spin." I was elated; this was really exciting. It wasn't as hard as I thought it would be. I had augured a hole in the sky and there wasn't so much as a trace, but I could see it in my memory like I had spun down through a sky full of white clouds.

My adrenaline was pumping full blast as I tried to duplicate each of the instructor's maneuvers. Going through a half loop and rolling out at the top into an Immelmann, I controlled the plane into straight and level flight with the horizon and the wings making three parallel lines. What would I do without a horizon? Controlled maneuvers felt good, but the stall and snap roll particularly would take a little more time to get where I could do them by the seat of my pants.

After I did my second or third jagged snap roll, the instructor abruptly said, "Take this bird in for a landing." As I taxied the plane into the ramp for storage, I knew for some reason we were quitting early. I had just finished a shortened flight, giving me a total of three and a half hours to date. Normally I had another half hour to go for the day, but I thought it was best not to ask the reason.

"Don't park the plane," Mr. Oakes said, "I want you to taxi to the end of the runway again." What had I done? I wondered. Were the Immelmanns too loose, or the loops too sloppy? Maybe that landing was not as good as I thought?

As I turned the plane to a forty-five degree angle at the end of the runway, Mr. Oakes said to me, "Remember, set the brakes, use your head, maintain your altitude in the pattern, and hold it steady on the landing." Then he crawled out of the plane, onto the uneven concrete. This day I would solo!

I pointed the plane down the runway, and built up speed. The wind smacked against my face and the plane's tail lifted gracefully off the ground. Backing off a little on the stick, then adjusting again adding a little pressure, the ascent was almost perfect. A little more pressure, I thought. Hold it steady, you are swerving a little. A little more pressure and I lifted from the earth, flying, on my own for the first time ever. The whole sky was mine. My instructor became a mere speck in the beautiful scene below. The sun was just going down as I crossed the beach to make my turn onto the downwind leg. I knew at that moment, nothing would stop me from becoming a pilot. Girls and cars would have to wait. I had something more important to do.

After we learned each new series of flying skills, we underwent a check flight by a military instructor. There was no cramming for the dreaded test. When you crawled into the instructor's *wash tub*, either you were a flier, or you were not. If you weren't -- you washed out, and you became a member of the *other* service. We had seen some washouts in Primary. Most were shuffled off the base the moment they got the bad news -- before they could talk to their buddies. The Air Corps hated rumors they didn't start themselves and this was one way to keep the sour grapes from spoiling the whole barrel. With us not knowing all the circumstances, we worried about washing out, just as the Air Corps would have wanted.

The object was to keep going, learn as much as you could, and not make any mistakes. Check pilots seemed to be most unhappy with their position in life and they all seemed to resent what you were trying to do and where you might be going. We got the feeling they wondered why it wasn't them who were training for combat. Their attitudes, which they wore on their sleeves, made for a rough ride every time.

Each test was a milestone; check off coordinated flight, check off precision turns, check off holding altitude and proper position in the landing pattern and lastly check off acrobatics. We knew what we had to do to get where we were going.

Two short months later, our Primary Training drew to a close. I had taken only one weekend leave, and that was for the USO dance where we joined with the Cal-Aero school. Since this was such a special event, I went into Ventura and got the first shave I ever had in a barbershop. The barber enjoyed catering to young cadets, even though he had to tell me to quit moving my face like I was giving myself a shave. We enjoyed talking, then he gave me a ticket to see the Hit Parade broadcast in Hollywood starring Frank Sinatra.

When Frank walked on stage wearing a big bow tie, I was startled to see him as such a skinny little kid who looked not much older than myself. But *The Voice* was truly magnificent and if it was possible, he sounded even better than he did at Blue Lake on the jukebox. Every girl in the audience shrieked at the top of her lungs, causing the fillings in my teeth to vibrate wildly. Frankie was their idol, to the consternation of many adults who felt his efforts should have been concentrated on winning the War.

At the dance that night in the plush Los Angeles Biltmore Hotel, most of the guys spent their time swapping stories about flying. The USO girls, even though we outnumbered them by two to one, struggled hard to get a dance out of us. One of the more outspoken girls blurted out to Patapoff, "It doesn't make any difference, we understand you guys aren't much action anyway. You've been flying on your backs so much, it's all in your head!" We ignored that too.

As the night drew to a close, we were flying with our hands all over the table. "Shrooom!" I sounded as I twisted the flat of my hand across the tabletop, dropping into a loop. My wingman's hand hissed through the smoky air, following my every move. In the background, a song played which seemed so fitting. It was Glenn Miller's *In the Mood*.

A week later I left for Basic Flight school at Marana, Arizona with seventy hours of flying time under my belt. I had soloed in near record time without a near miss or an accident, and Patapoff and I were still in the program. There was nothing in the world which could compare to that feeling of accomplishment, but we still recognized we had a long way to go on the path to getting our wings.

The field at Marana was not at all like Mira Loma, and here we were reminded we were in the Army. There was more marching and singing, "Hup two three four, sound off, sound off, off we go into the wild blue yonder, flying high into the sun!" Also there was forever a shavetail second looey giving us a, "Suck in your gut, Mister!!", "Grab a Brace!" or "Reach for the Ground!" Almost as if they knew where we'd come from, they'd scream, "This isn't any country club, you know." Dusty shoe soles got us a gig. Six gigs and we ran around the airfield carrying our parachute on our backsides, banging at our legs the whole way. What a pathetic sight it was, watching our friends running around the airfield in the late hours of the evening. Even more pitiful was my joining them.

At Marana we flew the BT-13 Vultee basic trainer, a safe and forgiving airplane which was ideally suited for our introduction to instrument and night flying. It was said the BT-13 took off, flew and landed at the same speed, which made for a very uninteresting flight. That meant the thrill of the open cockpit was behind us. However, the BT-13 had radio gear, which was something new. The radio was a toy at first, and little more. We all had our favorite little jokes, like someone shrieking to the tower, "I'm on the final approach with only one engine, clear the field!" Of course there were only single engine airplanes at Marana.

The cadets assumed no one else knew who was talking on the radio, and the anonymity gave everyone a little added courage to say whatever came to mind. Lots of stories passed around on what someone had said. One story went like this: It seems an airplane was coming into Marana and called for clearance to be the next to land. A cadet called out to a plane crowding in, "What's wrong with you! You have your head up? Can't you see that I'm ahead of you?" The first pilot replied, "Do you know who this is?" The cadet shot back, "No." And the first pilot said, "This is General

Wright!" Then the cadet said somewhat sheepishly, "Well you know who this is?" The general said, "No." and the cadet replied, "Thank God!"

One of the most difficult things for me was code, and Marana was our introduction to using Morse code to ride a radio beam. In our cross-country flight we flew over what was largely desert, mountains and unmarked, undefinable brush and mesquite fields. It was all too easy to get lost and that was something no one needed on their record. The large towns like Phoenix and Tucson had radio beacons which would guide us into, out of, or around the cities. They also broadcast a fan beam on which one could orient himself by reading the quadrant call letter and the beam identification sent out in code. Like most other rookie pilots I was spared by these radio aids from making that embarrassing call, "I am uncertain of my position and could use some guidance." That was a polite way of saying *I'm lost*, but it was no less embarrassing.

Soon we learned the value of the relief tube, too. This was the greatest of inventions from a cross-country pilot's point of view. It was also one of the simplest of inventions, made of a rubber tube extending from the cockpit to the outside. It had a small funnel on the using end and we all liked to complain of how small the funnel was. But the truth of the matter was, it worked. The only problem being, when an airplane rolled over in some acrobatics maneuver, besides getting all the dust off the floor you got the residue from the tube.

The BT-13 was not a good airplane for acrobatics and we did little of that in Basic Training. However, unlike the Stearman, the BT-13 would almost land itself. The gear was fixed, like the Stearman, and few other planes would take a harder landing, better than the pilot. If you stalled it too high on a landing it could drop from twenty feet out of the sky without so much as a complaint or bruise. Fortunately it also lacked the tendency to ground-loop like the Stearman. For all it was, the BT-13 was not as much fun to fly as the PT-17, but this was the time to pick up a whole lot of other skills which were necessary while not all that exciting.

We got a good start on instrument flying at Marana and put in hours upon hours polishing our flying skills. Here we were also introduced to night flying, which wasn't anything like flying during the day. In the black of night, we found our normal instincts withered to the point of worthlessness. Shadows hid the switches which we could find only by memory and touch. Below, darkness blanketed the variations in the earth and all that was familiar. Lights were our only beacons, but to us each light looked so much like all the others. Distant street lights looked like stars and stars looked like street lights. Our own glowing exhausts looked like exploding rockets. Add all this to the lights of the small towns and the aura of the glow from Tucson and it took on the appearance of the display on a pin ball machine after we'd had a few too many drinks.

While flying over the desert one unusually starless night, every mountain looked like it was above me. This was one of those nights I had convinced myself I would crash into some rock sticking out of the ground, unless I concentrated one hundred percent. My muscles were tense, and my actions were stilted. Maybe I was even frightened, though there was some sort of unwritten code for cadets against admitting these inadequacies. Then it happened. While reaching across the controls to adjust the radio, I accidently flipped the switch for the cockpit light. The inside of the canopy lit up like a florescent fishbowl reflecting into my eyes. What little orientation I had, vanished in a flash.

Scrambling, I flipped off the light switch, and more darkness than I had known before consumed me. The mountains were still there, my wits told me, but damn it, where were they? My instincts drew a blank. While I had learned the important technique of flying by the seat of my pants, this was not the time to do it. Night flight, like instrument flight, could confuse your senses and you had to discipline yourself to use only your instruments. Fortunately, the many months of intensive training took over. My radio compass guided me back to the safety of the Marana Tower, and the old faithful needle-ball-airspeed instruments kept me from going into some unforgiving maneuver. Another night, I was safely back on the base after having spent what seemed an eternity in the black vacuum.

At Marana, the alphabet alignment came into play again. This time I was in a squadron with Paul Ollerton and Russell Oplinger. I knew almost from the start these two guys would become life-long friends. How lucky we were to have fate, and Uncle Sam, throw us together. Paul was from Tempe, Arizona, which was not all that far away, and Op was from the fertile farm land of Decatur, Illinois. Both had an easy unassuming way about them. Paul was a hair taller than me and had an appearance of Hotshot Charlie with a head just a little large for his farm-boy frame. Op had a way about him which reflected a better education and upbringing than most of us had.

Paul had a school chum named Parry, who was also assigned to our squadron and whose dad owned a bar in Tempe, Arizona. The eighty-mile drive from Marana to what became our favorite bar offered little more than barren desert. It looked the same whether we were sober or not, or whether it was night or day. Paul would tell me I should sell my hot rod, which I was always bragging about, and buy some of that land. I scoffed; twenty-five cents an acre seemed like such a horrendous amount for a pile of sand and a smattering of prickly cacti.

What little free time we had was spent in Parry's dad's bar. Drinks were always on the house. But, fortunate for all, there wasn't much free time. It was becoming more and more apparent, the way to stay alive was to work at becoming the best damned pilot we could be. That took time and more intense concentration than we ever thought we were capable of achieving.

Our next hurdle was to get into an advanced school for fighter pilots. Many students went to multi-engine schools, because of the large demand for transport and bomber pilots. I wanted no part of that. The thought of being a chauffeur for a load of cargo was not at all appealing.

But again, the final decision was up to the Air Corps, which said it would take into account such things as their requirements, the aptitude of the student, the student's physique (husky pilots were needed to handle the bombers), the results of another psychological test, and the student's preference. We suspected the Air Corps' decision had more to do with what they needed at the time than anything else.

27. The PT-17 Stearman. It all started here.

28. Ready to solo.

29. Flying by the seats of our pants.

CHAPTER 8

FIGHTERS AND PART-TIME LOVERS

As the assignment list was posted on the headquarters bulletin board we all ran to read our fate. After some struggling, I elbowed my way to the front and quickly scanned the list. There was my name; I made it! I would go to Advanced Single-engine Flight School at Luke, just seventeen dusty but sunshiny miles from Phoenix, Arizona.

Patapoff drew the multi-engine school at Livermore, California. He said it was what he wanted, though none of us understood how that could possibly be. Someone had to do it, he told us, then wandered away. Paul and Op made it into Luke with me and our goal was to stick together all the way to combat.

Cadets flowed into Luke Field by bus, train and truck convoy. We were fortunate; Parry borrowed his dad's car which allowed us to report in style. The four of us pulled up to the base headquarters looking none the worse for wear after stopping for a free one at our favorite bar. Like Marana, the base was built on a barren patch of land, generally devoid of any vegetation which would serve to keep the dust down. But the base had a proud heritage, as it was named after Frank Luke, the WW I ace who was a local Phoenix boy. Our excitement was hardly contained as we saw on the strip what seemed like hundreds of AT-6s and P-40s. We had arrived!

The AT-6 was *the* airplane to fly in Advanced Training. We first talked of its capabilities at Primary and everyone said it was the best. It had the same laminar flow-wing design as the P-51 Mustang, the fastest propeller fighter ever built, which was now earning a tremendous reputation in the European theater.

The P-40 was our first introduction to fighters. It was *the* plane General Chennault's American Volunteer Group flew for the Chinese in their struggle against the Japanese invaders. Long before, the screen version of Robert Scott's book, *God is My Copilot*, made the plane famous to all movie-goers, like myself.

At the first opportunity, we hustled to the flight line to look over the planes. An AT-6 sat on the apron, the crew chief just having cranked up the inertia wheel and stepped back to let the pilot engage the engine. With one loud cough it started and wound up with a throaty roar. Then the roaring growl of the engine subsided some. We clasped our hands over our ears blocking out the noise, which was far louder than Mort's dad's old Cadillac when we started it without a muffler. The pilot taxied the plane to the end of the runway, then paused as he checked the mags. Then he gave the AT-6 full throttle and raced down the strip. Within seconds, the plane lifted off the ground and the wheels drew up into the body like a metal bird tucking away its feet. To think we would be doing this soon. Could it really be true?

There were four hundred cadets in the Luke class of 44-D who were assigned to ten squadrons. Paul, Op and I were assigned to squadron 5. Also, in my squadron was Jim Luke, nephew of Frank Luke. I had remembered making Frank Luke's Spad as a model airplane not so many years before. My friend Ted Cauthorn from Grant High was also at Luke, I'd heard, and I quickly found him in squadron 2. In addition, we met some new friends there, including the Ross brothers, Sandy and D.J. They went through some sort of experimental training program, attending Cal-Aero for Primary and then Basic. There was a plan for them to stay and do Advanced at the same facility, but that fell through, and to our good fortune they joined us at Luke.

Sandy and D.J. were from California and their snappy, worldly ways told us they weren't from the backwoods. D.J. was shorter than me, but was husky and looked as healthy as the California sun could make anyone. Sandy had the good looks of a young Don Ameche and had a wife only a good-looking guy like him could snag. Wives were an exception; there were only three married guys in our class.

We all came to Advanced Training with about one hundred and thirty-five hours flying time and would pick up another ninety hours before graduation. It would take an accident caused by pilot error or a real breach of code to get you washed out of the program at this stage. But there was still the threat that some minor flight infraction could get you sent off to navigator or bombardier school.

One of the more interesting ground school activities at Luke was skeet shooting, a luxury few civilians could enjoy, since shot gun shells were no longer available for sport. Each cadet spent about two cases of twelve gauge shells, practicing over and over. The practice taught us how to lead a target at different closing angles. This was the very same skill we would use when closing in on an enemy plane in combat.

Before we got to Luke, we had put in five hours of Link trainer time at Marana Army Air Field, Arizona. We put in another ten hours at Luke. Every hour would improve the instrument flying we did in the AT-6 under a hood. Link trainers, while not particularly exciting, improved our capability and confidence to methodically adhere to what the instruments said to do.

I put in my time, struggling with the machine and doing my best to fight the debilitating tedium which the Link was well-known for causing. As I sat under the hood the instructor reminded, "Don't let the plane fly you,

you fly it. Never let the instruments get ahead of you. If you want a one needle width rate of turn, make the instrument hold at one needle width. A climb of five hundred feet a minute doesn't mean you should climb maybe five hundred and twenty-five feet per minute. Be precise."

The Link did not give its pilot a *seat of the pants* feeling, and maybe that was as intended. That kind of flying had no place here and would only get you in trouble. A few near misses in the Link would help anyone shake the urge to ignore the instruments and respond to his senses.

Like most, I crashed on more than one occasion. There were no sound effects, no crashing noises, and the only pain I felt was my gut reaction to the instructor's jarring voice, "You just crashed your airplane, cadet. You're dead meat. Now get out of my sight." The instructor let my subsequent insecurity simmer for twenty-four hours and the next day he demanded I arise from the dead, and crawl under the hood for another round in the world of make believe.

I found flying in clear weather, using instruments in combination with my senses, actually improved my seat of the pants flying. With time and a lot of practice I became part of the machine, discovering the thrill of flying when the airplane became an extension of my body.

Instrument instructors always sat in the front seat of the AT-6 with various tricks stowed under their hats to throw off the cadets flying the plane on instruments from the back seat. If a trick worked on one student, it would never work a second time on him or any other students. The lesson was always too well learned, and the victim always passed the word onto his buddies.

My instructor pulled the shenanigan where he dropped his glove in the aircraft and asked me to retrieve it. While my attention was diverted for an instant, he placed the aircraft in a slight diving turn, then he told me to take over. I noticed the small change in the instrument readings, but took no action. The instructor warned me, "You are losing altitude." I pulled back on the stick and the aircraft reeled into a tightening spiral; it was diving straight for the ground. Our altitude was still decreasing as I continued to watch the altimeter unwind. Pulling back harder, the spiral became a vicious spin. I knew we were on a course to certain disaster and being under the hood as I was, in a tail spin, made a drag race seem like the cat's pajamas. My instructor's voice remained calm, and since we still had enough altitude, he talked me through a recovery saving me from the ultimate embarrassment of him taking over the stick.

More time in the Link trainer prevented this insanity. The Link also allowed us to hone the more mundane skills like beam-riding, procedure let-downs, and procedure turns which allowed us to land the AT-6 while under the hood. Soon I was making the approach for our landing under the hood with the instructor taking over just before touch down. Being able to pilot an airplane from a point in space to a known spot on the earth while on instruments is truly a great achievement. Most of all it requires strict discipline, which the Air Corps teaches you through forced obedience in every action you take in daily life.

It was nightfall before I generally had a chance to talk to Op about our days, our mistakes and our victories. I flopped onto my bunk when I heard Op's voice. "Mel, you missed mail call today. You must be dreaming about graduation or something like that. Got a letter for you. Sorry it doesn't smell sweet enough to be from a girl."

I opened the letter and recognized immediately it was from my Mom:

> "Portland, Oregon
> February 10, 1944

Dear Mel-

It was good to hear from you. I don't know what to call you now, however. Should I address my letters to Lieutenant Paisley, now that you are about to graduate from flying school?

I hope you are well. We are doing fine. Dad surprised me yesterday with two pair of nylon stockings for my birthday (a little late). I don't have the slightest idea where he might have gotten them. I bet he had to pay close to five dollars a pair, but I'm not going to complain. I never could wear that make-up on my legs like the younger girls and I'm getting bored with wearing slacks all the time. Now maybe I can talk your dad into taking me out to a dance.

I heard from the farm, Grandma said my younger brother Herman is in the service in England. You said that is where you might go, so maybe you can look him up.

We look forward to seeing you when you come home on leave. Be sure to let me know ahead of time so I can bake a pie.

> Love,
> Mom and Dad

P.S. Dad says thanks a million for the Zippo lighter, he was running out of matches for his cigars and was on the brink of panic. You know Dad and how he feels about those awful things."

That single letter and the reminder of my impending graduation was enough to lift my spirits in preparation for the next day.

My first cross-country out of Luke was a magnificent experience which started in the late afternoon and ended late at night. I covered a good part of southern Arizona, flying to the Colorado River, back to Castle Rock, along the Black Mesa and back to Camelback Mountain, a remote ridge north of Phoenix. The sky was clear and by nightfall the stars were out. Flying across the desert was such a delight, I eased back in the cockpit and let the plane fly itself. I crabbed into the wind just the right amount. And only now and then, did I trim the plane to compensate for the change in the center of gravity caused by the decreasing fuel level. I switched the radio channel from the tower to the Palladium in Hollywood and I flew to the easy tunes of Woody Herman, dreaming about being back at Blue Lake.

Training and discipline gaps became evident as we shifted from the trainers to the fighters. One cadet made the mistake of pulling up the landing gear instead of the flaps while the plane was still on the ground. We all looked on as the aircraft unceremoniously flopped to the ground and the prop chewed at the runway. It would take more than a top-rate check ride to save that guy from becoming a bombardier or navigator. Another story went around the field until it became an established fact. It seems a cadet brought a P-40 in with the wheels up. When asked by the instructor why he didn't heed the tower's warning that his wheels were up, he replied, "I couldn't hear the tower because some horn in the cockpit was too loud." The plane was equipped with a horn warning device to let you know your wheels were up.

The first day I flew the P-40 Warhawk fighter was awesome, everything I dreamed it would be. The aircraft I flew still had the testimonials of its recent combat days with a fierce-looking sharks' mouth painted on each side of the air intake on the front of the fuselage. The drab camouflage paint and the obviously hasty repairs to the aircraft body were other reminders of the plane's battle history. Most poignant was the smell of grease and sweat which permeated the cockpit.

I took a deep breath of the stale air and strapped myself in a little tighter than normal. This was not going to be just another day flying. As I started the engine, the deafening roar blasted my ears and dulled my concentration for a second. I was alone, there was no one to catch the little mistakes one often makes when flying a new aircraft -- mistakes which could lead to a disaster. My mind shifted to the extensive checklist, which was far more extensive than those of other aircraft I had flown. At last I blasted down the runway, then soared into the blue sky.

The pre-flight instructions raced through my head, "This airplane can climb into an Immelmann from the straight and level. You won't have to dive to get enough airspeed like you do in the AT-6. You've got all the power you need. However, you must be sure you have enough altitude for this maneuver."

I practiced a few stalls, then leveled off and attained maximum cruising speed. It felt good. Then hauling back on the stick, I whipped the plane into a half loop with the intent of rolling out at the top. This was a maneuver the ground instructor said the Flying Tigers used to shake the zeros off their tail. As I approached the top of the loop in an inverted position, the plane started to stall. Damn, I knew then, I had pulled through the maneuver too slowly. DAMN!!! Upside down, then tail down, the plane plummeted from the sky. Faster and faster. I was horrified! God, I didn't want to bore a hole into the ground. Then I came to my senses and shoved the nose down and picked up some airspeed. The P-40 responded beautifully, much like the Stearman.

Three mistakes is what it took to get the maneuver right. Three times stalling at the top of the loop. Three times kissing death. Then it all seemed so easy. I simply had to pull through the loop a little faster and have the grit to try it again, once I failed.

As I approached the field to land, I encountered a slight crosswind which concerned me since I knew the P-40 had a greater tendency than most to groundloop. Fortunately my experience in the Stearman taught me how to avoid doing an often destructive pirouette upon landing. Dropping a wing into the wind, I slipped into the field against the wind heading straight down the runway. Just before touch-down I lifted the wing and equalized the foot pressure on the rudders. "Stay alive on the rudder, don't let the plane start to wander even slightly," the instructor had said. It would take a lot more practice in the P-40 to feel comfortable.

Approaching our gunnery range at Gila Bend for the first time from the sky reminded me of what I always envisioned as the end of the universe. As far as the eye could see was hot sand and rocks, a haven for nothing but rattlesnakes. We blasted into the area in trail, each AT-6 doing a 360 degree turn in series, then screamed one by one into the field leveling our wings just as we touched down.

In one hour we would return to the sky for gunnery practice. Our target was the towed sleeve or sock on a modified AT-6 which had the back seat reversed. From the back seat, the spool operator extended a cable with the white canvas sleeve, maybe twenty-five feet long, on the end. We would follow the lead AT-6 and make passes at the sock, coming in from behind and shooting bullets and tracers. The trick was to continuously reduce your angle, then break away at a minimal angle so you didn't get the tow plane in your line of fire.

The bullets of each AT-6 making a pass were painted a different color so we could determine how many hits we made on the sock. As expected, the two guys in the tow plane had about as bad of an assignment as one could get, and all anyone else had to do to get the spool operator's job was make a hole in the side of the tow plane with his color bullet. If Uncle Sam knew he was insuring the lives of spool operators, we never would have been given free life insurance.

Flight gunnery practice was the first time I used my airplane as a weapon. I rolled my airplane close to the sleeve, looking into the florescent gun sight in front of me, which appeared to dangle in space. I closed in on the sleeve, reducing the lead. It felt comfortable, having spent so many shells on the skeet shooting range. The trick was to keep the plane in a coordinated flight, since any skidding or sliding around would cause the projectiles to fly in all different directions. At last I was in range and everything looked good. The sleeve was in the gun sight with just the right lead. I pressed the trigger and for the first time felt the exhilaration of firing .30 caliber ammunition from my plane. This was as close to the real thing as we were going to get in the States.

Ground targets were more fun because we could see our ammo hit the dirt around the target. Everyone had their own target,2gallwhich meant we had something to brag about as we sat around the gunnery shack at night in the only calm known to Gila Bend. Locking in on a ground target is almost hypnotizing and it was easy to fool yourself into sticking your nose right through the target. We knew we had to get close to the target in order to hit the bull's eye, however we had to leave time to pull out. In a way, ground gunnery was like a hot-rodder's game of chicken -- a drag race towards a brick wall where you don't want to slam on the brakes until you know you won the dare, but you know you have to stop or swerve away before it's too late.

If pilots were killed at Luke, it was most often the consequence of ground gunnery practice. We always said they were the ones who lacked the skill, the determination or the luck. If it had to happen, maybe it was better these men were killed then, than later in combat when they were likely to take someone with them. Maybe that was true. Just maybe.

The two months at Luke passed quickly. Behind us were many good Saturdays at *our* bar in Tempe and at the Westward Ho Hotel in Phoenix. A rumor took on some substance that the Air Corps no longer would wash us out for getting the clap since we were so close to graduation. That was one rumor we hastily accepted as fact, then started actively pursuing the risk. Some guys worried about the girl they would be going home to on leave, but I didn't have that problem. So before I knew it Parry had me lined up with a gal wearing a low scooped-neck blouse at a time when all the others were wearing baggy sweaters that reached to their chins.

The last leave before graduation I talked Parry's friend into taking me home to meet her dad. *Dad* met me at the front porch and although he greeted me proper enough, I wasn't prepared for the fact that he looked like one of Pancho Villa's lieutenants. It was his expression which troubled me most. I never saw it, but I knew he had a big stiletto somewhere on him. That night my newfound friend and I sat privately on her porch swing exchanging kisses and touches. When I thought the time was right I slipped my pants down to my knees. Just when I was about to apply all my meager hard-earned technique and pent-up desire, I heard some footsteps. Heavy footsteps. Someone was coming. With visions of my standing in the courtyard in front of Pancho Villa's firing squad, or with that pig sticker in my ribs, I leaped up pulling on my pants at the same instant. "Oh my God!" I shrieked under my breath. My G.I. belt buckle had slid through the slats in the wooden porch swing and I was stuck in a very compromising position. I got a good feel for what it was that made those muskrats which Koke used to catch in the traps chew off their legs to get away. Although the noise turned out to be a false alarm, that was the end of the attempt, and I found my way back to Luke ready to go back to Portland to find a nice young girl.

With two hundred and twenty-five flight hours under our belt, including ten hours of night flight, ten hours instrument time and fifteen hours in the Link trainer, we really thought we knew what we were doing. To date however, six cadets had been killed in our class, all blamed on pilot error. We didn't know if there was any truth to the Air Corps' report that we were losing more pilots in training than we would lose in combat. We really didn't want to think much about it.

Every time a cadet plowed into the ground gunnery target or runway, we all sobered a bit. Still, our cockiness was dampened only slightly. We *had* to think we were better. We were too good to fall to such error. That was our means for survival and we were going to be the ones who survived.

Some cadets bought new officer uniforms at the Post Exchange, but not me. I was going home on leave after graduation looking fit to kill. For a few dollars more a tailor in Phoenix decked me out in custom *pinks and greens* and a new camel hair overcoat. The custom-made clothes probably all came out of the same warehouse as the ready-made ones on the base, but they somehow felt different. And the hat, it was the same, but now it had that all-important fifty-mission crush, giving all who wore it the rakish look of a seasoned veteran. Oh, I felt like a million dollars and it was springtime in Portland. I could just see the girls coming out in force, wooing the cadets in their smart new uniforms.

On graduation day we marched to the parade grounds to receive our wings. It was pouring rain -- for the first time in four years. As we proudly stood in a rigid brace, the wet soaked through our new tailor-made uniforms and dripped off the ends of our noses. For the last time, we marched in cadence and sang the bawdy ditties which haunted our thoughts night and day. We wouldn't sing these songs as officers unless it was for old time's sake over a drink at the officers' club. On this last day our shoes squished with every beat:

123 ACE!

Sound off!
One! Two!
Sound off!
Three! Four!
Cadence count
One! Two! Three! Four!
One! Two!----Three! Four!

Eeney meeney miney mo,
Let's go back and count some mo'.

We will march to beat the band,
And we'll never bite the hand.

The Fifth Squadron it is the best,
They always pass the Colonel's test.

The First Squadron is just like Krauts,
They're all afflicted with the gout.

I had a good home but I left,
        YOU'RE RIGHT!
You had a good home but you left,
        YOU'RE RIGHT!

As we passed into the review area all four hundred cadets sang the favorite of us all:

Many's the night I spent with Minnie the Mermaid
Down at the bottom of the sea.
Minnie lost her morals, down there among the corals;
Gee, but she was mighty nice to me.

Now, many's the night with the pale moonlight,
Down on her seaweed bungalow;
Ashes to ashes, dust to dust,
Two twin beds and only one of them mussed.

Now you can easily see, she's not my mother,
Because my mother is forty-nine.
And you can easily see she's not my sister,

Because I wouldn't show my sister such a hell-uv-a good time.
And you can easily see she's not my sweetie,
Because my sweetie's too refined;
She's just a peach of a kid, she never knew what she did;
She's just a personal friend of mine.

A few married guys, like Sandy Ross, had their wives pin their wings to their uniforms. Most of us did it ourselves. This was the greatest day of our lives. We were now full-fledged pilots and officers and gentlemen to boot. But, in a small way we acted a little like kids attending the high school graduation many of us missed.

Most of us graduated as second lieutenants with our spanking new gold bars on our shoulders. Sandy graduated as a flight officer, or a *blue bar*. No one knew why some of us became second lieutenants and others became flight officers. I think he must have had more fun. Or maybe that was just a penalty of marriage in this crazy war.

Graduating the same day were ten squadrons of U.S. fighter pilots plus one Chinese squadron trained to carry on the tradition set by the Flying Tigers. None of the Chinese could speak English, but we saw the pride on their faces as they marched to their own songs going to and from the flight line. The Chinese Air Force would be gratified for the return of these fine flying officers to fight our common enemy.

The washout rate at Luke was low. There was a time in the early days of the war when the Canadians swept up the washouts for their own Eagle Squadron, but the Air Corps finally saw the real capabilities of the washouts when the Canadians used them in the battle of Britain. That's when the Air Corps accepted the Navy policy that once a pilot made it to Advanced Training, they would do everything they could to keep him in the program. They had too much invested in these men. And they didn't plan on throwing away their investment if the guy breaks some minor rule or maybe ground-loops with a hangover.

Ted Cauthorn and I got assigned to Harding Field at Baton Rouge from Luke. Before we had to report, we got two weeks leave plus a week travel time. Ted and I went home to Portland as two shining new shavetail lieutenants.

Dad met me at the train and handed me my old car keys and a freshly minted driver's license sans the writing on the back. He must have found a judge partial to young servicemen. Though he was still a little goosy about letting me drive his car, he went all out to make those two weeks memorable. He said to me as he handed me the keys to my car, "I hope a year in the Air Corps has settled you down, and remember the new wartime speed limit is thirty-five miles per hour." It was probably not all that notice-able, but I had mellowed some by then.

The Greek and I got together and I told him a few embellished flying stories, but things at home were somehow different. People were really serious about the war; patriotism was the only way to describe it. And, I realized after fourteen months of marching to military band music, I too was a true patriot. My life was dedicated to winning the war for my country.

I went to Mort's house to visit his folks, although it was too early for tomatoes. Mort's kid sister, Lois, greeted me. *Hubba-hubba*, she wasn't the scraggly little girl I remembered! and before I left the house I murmured to her, "Wait for me, I'll be back." As she looked into my eyes I felt for the first time how potent an officer's uniform and a pair of wings really were.

While carousing around Portland, Ted and I met a couple of girls close to our own ages. Ted and Wheel (Yvonne Wheeler), besides having fun got real serious. Helen and I had fun and got serious just for the week. We romped and did the swing all over Portland. Our uniforms were the required wear for on duty and off, and we couldn't have been more proud of them. Being a serviceman represented a lot of sacrifice and people seemed to know we had been missing some fun while we were in training. They all wanted to buy us a drink and sit around and talk.

It was great going to Seaside, walking the beach and talking about what we had been doing. Probably it was more interesting for Ted and me to re-live our days in training than for the girls to hear it. But they were good listeners, or more likely good pretenders. At the end of the day, Helen and I were on the sand with a motel blanket and a bottle of grapefruit juice, some grain alcohol and a lot of talk. It was too cold to spend the night outside, but how I would have liked to wake to the warm sun with the sand glued to our bodies. I couldn't help but see Elaine after my trip to the beach, but we both realized that it was an old affair long past. Just a memory of my first girl.

Ted and I arrived in Baton Rouge and set girls aside for awhile. Flying -- serious flying -- was why we were there. Harding Field was the introduction base to transition us into the fighter we would fly in combat, which was the P-47 Thunderbolt. We put in a month of ground school on the airplane and got introduced to New Orleans.

For the first time I was introduced to the disarmingly smooth talk of the Southerners which was so foreign to Westerners. Also, we came across a lot more *colored* people than we had seen on the Western bases. Unfortunately, the folks labeled as *colored* and the Southerners mixed like molasses and water. Appalling, was the only way I could describe the treatment of nonwhites by the Southerners. Though the Air Corps pleaded for men to serve their country, the Corps made it known through its actions that if your skin wasn't light enough, you were unsuitable for training as a pilot at Harding, and this uppity attitude permeated throughout the ranks. I had never been exposed to such deep-seated prejudice and it was all so disturbing that I tended to stay close to the guys I knew from the more familiar West.

Ted and I sampled all the New Orleans culinary specialties, including red beans and barbecued shrimp. This wasn't anything like the pot roast, cooked dead or the meat loaf ala Quaker Oats we were raised on. In New Orleans we also discovered the Ramos Gin Fizz at the Monte Leone Hotel, which burbled delightfully in our mouths and slipped down our gullets so smoothly. We studied the bartender's technique so we could duplicate the tantalizing drink. Then we floated to the point of silliness to the tunes of Benny Goodman.

New Orleans' Bourbon Street was tempting to all our senses. The music was soulful and the atmosphere was sinfully overwhelming to a bunch of small town boys, like us. Although we couldn't stay away, we knew better than to over-indulge in the wickedness. So we observed and sampled cautiously.

The local girls and lots more camp-followers flocked to the school in Baton Rouge. I don't know what it was, but there was something about pilots that drew girls like bees to honey. There were all types from everywhere in the country, all ages too. We'd never seen so many willing women tempting us away from the Air Corps training program.

After a month, we were transferred to transition school at the Abilene Army Air Base in Texas where Op and Paul joined us, having completed their Transition in the Far West. In Texas, we got our first introduction to the P-47 C razor back, which had a canopy extending to the vertical stabilizer. The Thunderbolt was such a formidable mass of metal. It was seven tons of shear power with a sixteen-foot-diameter, four-bladed propeller. Its eight .50-caliber machine guns could fire seventy-two hundred rounds a minute, and it was capable of carrying two thousand pounds of bombs and anti-tank rockets. It was considered to be a match for the German's best, the FW-190, at low altitude and had a definite edge at altitudes of fifteen thousand feet and above.

In ground school we learned the capabilities of the airplane and the ordnance it carried. The normal load out of bombs was a five hundred pounder under each wing and a belly tank in the center to extend the range. Another option was to put a thousand pounder on the belly and two three-tube rocket launchers on the wings. We would have the opportunity to try them all in ordnance lay-down training.

A couple of days into the program, we practiced taxiing around a bit. The plane we used for this exercise was painted with broad red and white stripes that a half-blind goon couldn't miss from a couple miles away. Everyone knew this paint job said, "All stay clear, the guy driving this thing hasn't flown it yet."

A week later, I had my first flight in the massive P-47. Being a single seat airplane, I was on my own from the start. The thought reminded me of my first experience in the P-40, which still was as fresh in my mind as the day it happened. As I taxied out, I read off the check list, which was more like a small book. Pulling on the bucket seat to force it as high as it would go, I sat high on top of my parachute. The flight instructor grumbled about my taking this elevated position because I lost the maximum protection of the armor plate which covered the back of the seat. But the high position gave me the visibility I wanted for taxiing, landing and, more important, for combat maneuvers. It felt right and I vowed to use this position from this flight on.

As I pulled into my forty-five degree position on the end of the runway, I looked for planes which were incoming or on the runway. I didn't see any planes in my way and requested permission for take off, "Abilene Tower P-47 in take-off position. Request clearance for take-off runway 270." The tower responded and I gave them the standard, "Roger tower, Wilco and out!" Only the new guys had to get tower clearance. The old pros taxied to the runway, pointing their nose straight down the runway for takeoff. If the sky was clear, they gave it full throttle, like they did in combat. Rookies were somewhat more cautious, for good reason from what I saw.

As I slowly pushed the throttle forward, the two thousand horsepower Pratt and Whitney engine whirled the prop through the air. The plane responded magnificently, picking up speed one would think impossible for something of this size. As it lifted slowly off the ground with fifteen degrees of flaps down, there was a low heavy rolling sound, almost as though the plane groaned at its own weight.

Once airborne, I was engrossed in the task of trimming the rudder just so, and lifting the wheels. Sitting high in my seat I could see the ground sinking away, when a blunt object struck a fierce blow on my forehead. Stars flashed before my eyes, and blood oozed down my goggles and over my mouth. I looked around the cockpit, stupefied. The canopy had come unlocked and raced down its tracks striking me with its handle. Maybe it was never locked, I thought. Fortunately, my leather helmet cushioned the blow enough to keep me from being knocked out immediately. I was lucky this time, but I needed to get on the ground before I passed out.

"Abilene tower, P-47 just departing field. Permission to return to the field. Emergency landing!" The tower gave me permission to do a quick three hundred and sixty degrees turn into the field. I struggled to stay alert as I prepared for the final approach and landing. Easy, now. I was almost on the ground, when the tower operator snapped, "Get your wheels down!" "What happened to the warning horn?" I gasped. Thank heaven for the tower operator!

After taxing to the loading area, I was pulled from the cockpit by the crew chief who shuffled me into the ambulance for a trip to the hospital and a couple stitches. Op met me in the emergency room, "Take a bow, Mel! That was quite a maiden flight! You won't forget it, that's for sure." I was too scared to be as embarrassed as I should have been. Maybe even for a second, the infantry looked pretty good to me. If I would have gone down, the accident investigators never would have figured out what happened. Just another dumb pilot error, they would have surmised.

After we had a couple weeks in the P-47 we began to understand some of its peculiarities. A Republic Aircraft factory test pilot showed us what the airplane really could and could not do. The books never said it all. There were always a few more tricks a gutsy test pilot had learned, which could save your ass in a tight combat situation.

The test pilot flew a P-47 D with a bubble canopy. This was probably the airplane we would fly in combat. I watched him carefully as he accelerated under full power using water injection to cool the cylinders. The increased power allowed the plane to climb steeply away from the field in almost no time. But the test pilot warned: the maneuver was for war emergency purposes only and was good for about ten minutes maximum, before the engine started to get into real trouble.

Op, Paul, Ted and I watched in awe nudging each other and passing off unusually serious remarks about every detail of the performance. We still tended to make a shallow climb out of the field, feeling a little nervous about the whole thing. The test pilot got to thirty thousand feet in short order, rolled the plane over into a split-S and then dropped straight down to the center of the field. Through this maneuver he demonstrated the much talked about feat of taking the Thunderbolt past the speed of sound.

We could hear the voice of the test pilot as he spoke to us on the squawk box talking us through each move. "The stick is still responsive and I am gaining speed. The stick is now starting a violent oscillation. Now the vibration has stopped and the stick is frozen in place; I cannot move it. The airplane has entered the realm of compressibility, nearing the speed of sound. The only way out of this maneuver is to turn the elevator trim tab control and the airplane will slowly recover from the dive. You must have patience here." The ground rapidly closed on the airplane as we heard the very sound of the demonstration. Holy shit! this was downright spooky!

The P-47 climbed again to over twenty thousand feet, then started into a shallow dive. The pilot's words crackled on the loud speaker, "I am now going to pull the nose of the plane straight up into a hammerhead stall." Our instructor told us not to do this maneuver because the plane could tumble and the nose and tail would swap ends all the way to the ground. Under this condition, the controls are totally ineffective. The test pilot recovered from numerous hammerhead stalls, giving us detailed instructions on how to do it.

His last feat of the day was to buzz the runway at fifty feet with the wings vertical to the ground flying straight and level. There was obviously no lift from the wing, keeping the aircraft in the air. The test pilot explained the propeller and the Pratt and Whitney 2800 engine alone were capable of keeping the aircraft from falling out of the sky. At the conclusion of the demonstration, the head instructor warned us that the maneuvers we saw were not ones we should attempt on our own. Not one of us could wait to get up the next day and try them all.

Our first bomb practice in the P-47 took on a heavy gloom after someone plowed into the target area. However, the training program forged on and our flight of four approached the target area in an echelon formation. An instructor pilot watched from the air and gave us each a *do better* speech after we pressed the target. This program was new and we were the first class to take it. The P-47's value as a ground support airplane was just being recognized.

I was the third plane in my flight to drop down on the target. As my wing lined up with the target bull's-eye, I did a hard wingover at ten thousand feet and put the dot in the center of the gun sight, right on the target which was a large bull's-eye painted on the sand far below me. My Jug balked as I fought to keep its nose to the ground, planning to release my bombs when the sight circle was equal to the size of the ring. That was the minimum altitude for the drop, also the best assurance for success. The first plane's bomb exploded in the distance; it was way off target and the dust was rising some distance off to the North, slightly masking one edge of the bull's-eye. The second plane held off, and I waited some more, wanting to drop my load after his. My time, however, was running out quickly, and my plane bucked as it accelerated and became extremely difficult to hold on target. I was skidding and sliding all over slick sky and I fought harder to maintain the nose-down position. The bull's-eye got larger and larger and still I didn't see the second impact. I couldn't hold much longer. Then I saw the second bomb drop, even farther from the bull than the first. It was outside the circle all together.

My plan was to hold a little longer and get a little closer. Now! I yanked the release for my bomb, and the plane gave a slight rise on the nose. Immediately I hauled back on the stick and felt the Gs smash me into my seat as I racked the plane around and up to the blue sky. The brown, sandy ground was behind me. Looking back at what had to be triumphant success, I saw the bomb was only close to the bull's-eye. I would have to get a lot more practice in on this if I planned on doing any serious damage to any Jerry tanks.

Formation flying was another skill which took hours and hours of practice to get right. Living through a good scare speeded the learning process. We flew in flight formations of four aircraft starting in Basic Training, then, got more serious in Advanced. Our formations got tighter over time, but the real difference was our learning to fly tight formation while going up through clouds, something which was not that easy to find in Texas. This practice not only instilled discipline and skill into our flying, but more important it was a crucial capability for combat. Climbing through clouds in formation meant we lost no time joining up again on top; we knew where our wingman was. This was critical because the enemy might just be sitting on top of the clouds ready to fight.

Our flight leader was an instructor when we were first introduced to formation flying in the P-47. Starting, the leader had a wingman on his left and element leader on his right with tail-end charlie on the wing of the element leader. Over and over we would hear, "Okay, number four get in closer. Pull it up number three. . ." This was not as easy as it looked at the start. The trick was to do just one thing--keep your eye on the wing of the plane you were flying on. Hold your position and pay no attention to anything else. It was throttle and controls, throttle and controls -- plus the seat of your pants. Formation flying on the wing of another plane was the only time when we had to fly through weather on instinct. The flight leader was always on instruments forging the path and everyone else was flying on him.

In a turn the element leader would change positions with the leader's wingman to keep charlie from getting in a difficult flying position. In echelon the flight was all on the right or left of the flight leader. Any out-of-position maneuver would be amplified down the line to charlie, with a forceful whipping action.

Heading into weather for the first time, I was flying the element lead as we entered the cloud cover in echelon formation. The turbulent wash coming off the wing of the plane I was flying wing on forced me to continuously react. I shoved my throttle from one end of the quadrant to the other, over-compensating, then correcting, then over-compensating again. The flight leader's voice over the radio broke the tension, "Let's keep it a little loose. It's a little bumpy in here; keep three feet between your wing tips." The strain didn't let up and we held our positions, just barely. Going through clouds, the leader never made turns large enough to call for a change in position between his wingman and the element lead. But the way his wingman was bouncing around, I thought he might be doing it to us this time.

Soon the cascading of each mismovement broke up the flight and we were all on our own in the cottony muck. This was the worst of situations; we knew we were somewhere close together, but we couldn't see one another and all of us were forced to go on instruments immediately. Discipline was what counted now more than ever. We couldn't worry about what was in front of us. Now we had to keep our eyes on the instruments since instinct would only serve to get us killed. Fortunately, our flying needle-ball-airspeed got us all back down below the overcast where we could again see one another. We needed to work harder on this skill. It was back to flying in clear weather with our wing tips a yard apart and with our lead going through every conceivable maneuver. Practice was what it would take. Flying in the worst of weather in formation would have to become second nature.

We were often assigned areas where two of us could practice our dogfighting skills, which we knew would be something which might save us someday. From the start of our training at Luke, the emphasis was to be aggressive, push the attack, and watch out for your buddy. A major part of our time was spent on two element flying, which was perfected by General Chennault for the Flying Tigers. Chennault did away with what had been a three element flight used by the Air Corps in the late '30s. Two planes were all you really needed. The first plane presses the attack and the second plane protects the leader's tail and leaves him free from other defensive concerns. This strategy led to many two-on-one maneuvers, developed individually by two team members which were designed to box up an enemy and restrict his avenues of escape.

One day Ted and I drew each other for this duty and implemented a plan we dreamed up at the officers' club one night. We would fly to the edge of our combat area, then feign engine trouble so we had to let down at the W.A.S.P. base. The Women's Airforce Service Pilots organization trained women to fly first line combat airplanes so they could ferry planes within the U.S. and overseas. The closest base was in Sweetwater, Texas, right close to our assigned dogfight territory. I touched down at Avenger Field, on the outskirts of Sweetwater with *engine trouble* and Ted's excuse was to stay with me to be sure the W.A.S.P. maintenance crew did what they should.

We made arrangements to have the airplane looked at and then had lunch in the cadets' chow hall. We told the girls enough stories about flying those *great big* airplanes to establish ourselves with them and that took care of what we did with our free time for the rest of our stay in Texas.

About the time we were finishing flight school, Helen, from my last Portland leave, decided her interest was for more than a week. She hopped the train and appeared at the base in Abilene. I saw that she got checked into a motel in town. The only problem was, I didn't have enough time to be attentive to her, between my flying duties and keeping up with the gals in Sweetwater.

The guys always had a knack for sensing a gal who was not attached. One Saturday night at the officers' club, a ground-pounder captain visiting the base made a pass at Helen. Ted saw that I was too shit-faced to defend Helen's honor and decided to do it for me. It turned out that Ted wasn't in much better shape than me. When I got out the back door of the club to see the fight, Ted was swinging in every direction while trying to hand me his wristwatch. For some reason he seemed to be more concerned about his watch than anything else. Considering his condition, Ted fought valiantly and in all I'd say he did a fine job of protecting my tail. Or was he looking after his own tail, I wondered. Helen and Ted were awfully friendly. But no, I shouldn't have those thoughts; Ted was an officer and a gentleman. I thanked him for taking care of whatever he was taking care of for me, and Helen boarded the train for Portland the next day.

We left Abilene ready to take on Hitler and Mussolini, or was it Jack Oakie and Charlie Chaplin? The Thunderbolt was not flying in Japan, so we all knew from the start, we were going to Europe. And we were elated, because that's where all the action was.

Everyone in my squadron would leave for England with four hundred flying hours and an instrument card. Fortunately, Ted got orders too, though he was under threat of a court martial for giving the lover-boy captain a shiner. For six dollars and fifty cents a month, I signed up for my ten thousand dollars of life insurance provided by Uncle Sam. One hundred dollars a month was to be put away in the bank in Portland, so I could get a new rod when I got home. With the last task completed, of signing my Last Will and Testament, I was raring to go.

We had only lost one pilot in Transition. That was George Peterson from Oregon, who had graduated in squadron 5 with me at Luke. For a while, I thought I would be the one who would have to escort him home, an honorable task but a sad one. Because my orders were already cut for England I breathed a guilt-laden sigh of relief, having been excused from the burden. Death was something foreign to most of us, and we did what we could to keep it that way.

30. "Okay Number Three -- Close it Up!"
Learning formation flying in an AT-6.

31. Looking for the nightlife in New Orleans, Lt. Ted Cauthorn and Mel.

32. "Fair warning -- Don't get near this airplane!
The pilot hasn't flown it before."
Taxi training before our first P-47 Flight.

CHAPTER 9

ACROSS THE POND

Camp Kilmer, New Jersey was our mustering area for transport across the North Atlantic. There we were ankle deep in oozing red clay, undergoing our last round of showdown inspections. When we weren't in a stiff brace in front to some testy major, we were getting more orientation briefs, physical checkups and inoculations. Despite the increasingly more vivid rumors of impending combat, most of us were grateful to leave the known perils of Kilmer.

Our embarkation point was New York City, where we boarded a crowded troop ship. One by one we dragged our bags up the gangplank onto the ship, with my classmates from Abilene all being assigned to the same deck. Bunks were stacked four high, bodies were everywhere, and functioning showers were nowhere. Thirteen days of elbowing the swarm of sweaty men and the slow rocking of the ocean made most of us want to puke as no plane had. Even the chow hit an all time low, consisting solely of field rations, a concoction of dried eggs, an occasional tin of Spam, dried milk, and stale tropical chocolate that wouldn't melt no matter how long you gnawed on it.

Some of us would have gladly traded the Wing cigarettes we were given for something of more use. Unfortunately it was rare that anyone was willing to give up their two sheets of toilet paper, considered the only other item of any significant value included in the rations. The reason was the tension, I suspect. The obvious surge in the usage of both cigarettes and toilet paper was surely the most telling barometer of the tension which mounted with each passing day.

Making landfall at the port of Liverpool, we saw England for the first time the way train riders see towns in the States. The worst was what we saw first and what we believed it all to be. The garbage was piled to our armpits on the docks and the buildings were decrepit and sooty. Even the people looked dowdy, in drab clothes in the drab weather. No one heralded our arrival.

From Liverpool we traveled by train to Stoke-on-Trent and then by bus to Shrewsbury. We completed our journey at the Royal Air Force (R.A.F.) field at Atcham, not far from Shrewsbury. The R.A.F. field was never designed to accommodate the thousands of servicemen who descended upon it. Neither the toilet facilities nor the hot water could keep up with the onslaught. Our only relief was to take off into the countryside on one of the bicycles supplied to us for transportation. The bikes were just a notch better than the one I had discarded some years before, since balloon tires had not yet made it across the great pond.

What I saw of the English countryside was not what I remembered in the light-hearted movie *Mrs. Miniver,* in which Greer Garson and Walter Pigeon played the leading roles. The tranquil English fields were abuzz with a steady cavalcade of G.I.s on cycles and low-flying fighters. The freshly painted white picket fences of the movie were nowhere to be seen, but there were more permanent stone fences everywhere, reflecting a certain coldness and timeworn acceptance of boundaries. The people wore clothes which one may have guessed was the civilian uniform of the day; the styles were not identical though they lacked variation and color. The lively British humor we anticipated was squelched under pasty white faces, looking worried and saddened.

At Atcham we came together from all the U.S. training commands, and some combat veterans on rotation from the Far East joined us, too. In one month's time we would have to put in twenty hours flying support out of England. First, we were assigned to our permanent Groups.

The alphabet arrangement did me a great service here, again. Ollerton, Oplinger and Paisley all got assigned to the 366th Fighter Group which was made up of the 389th, 390th and the 391st Fighter Squadrons. The 366th Group was formed in the States just the year before and was assigned in March, 1944 to the 9th Air Force at Thruxton, England to prepare for coverage of the D-day landings at Normandy. We were the newest additions to the 390th squadron.

A week later, a new batch of pilots came in from the States and my group picked up Miller, DeWyke, Picton, Johnson and the two Ross brothers, Sandy and D.J. We had all graduated from Luke and Miller had graduated from Oxnard with me. My friend Ted got assigned to the 48th Fighter Group.

For the first time at Atcham, we were issued a .45 caliber automatic pistol. We were also issued a bright yellow Mae West, surely not to use but just to make us feel better when we crossed the channel. The flight gear we were so proud of, was replaced with helmets and radio jacks which were peculiar to the European Theater of Operations. In addition, we got three pairs of combat gloves. The Air Corps insisted all three pairs were needed to withstand the cold if we bailed out. The idea was to layer them on our hands, first the chamois, then the wool and lastly the leather. Most of us would never fly with any of them, fearing we would lose the feel of the airplane.

Next, we were decked out in ill-fitting and outmoded civies in a photography lab where the Brits took our photo. The photograph went into a survival kit we were issued later which also contained sulfa drugs and high-energy food. If we went down in France the Maquis would use the photo to make up the necessary papers for us to move about on the German-occupied continent. The Maquis didn't carry camera equipment to make up the papers themselves; they could lose their lives if the Germans caught them with such contraband.

Within days the U.S. and our training command seemed so far away. Now the only thing we talked about was when we would get our chance to show what we could do in combat. This was a Friday night drag race waiting to start, the frenzied tension was at a peak. And as the weeks wore on, we started to venture out more into the civilian world of England.

The British were generally hospitable, in a reserved sort of way, to the American servicemen who roamed their countryside. There was one exception; the British men in uniform got visibly peeved when they caught any of us wandering around the pubs of England with local lasses on our arms. The English servicemen liked to complain, "The only thing wrong with the Americans is they are over-paid, over-fed, over-sexed, and over here." Admittedly, we got paid a whole lot more than our British counterparts, but I don't know how much anyone really believed about the rest.

We had our share of problems getting used to a new accent and the wealth of unfamiliar expressions. If a Brit wanted to pay you a visit, he'd say, "I'm going to knock you up sometime." That comment startled us the first time we heard it. Then, when a Brit answered the phone he'd say, "Are you there?" "What is the answer to that question?" we wondered. Actually, it wasn't a question and didn't call for an answer.

In addition, the British pilots were quick to teach us some of their terminology associated with flying. If we were flying at very low altitude we were *on the deck*. If we had on full power, we were going *balls out*. That was a real grabber for most Yanks. If you got killed, you *bought the farm*. And, if anything was easy, but not really, it was a *piece of cake*. We all got used to the expressions and soon we were using them as though we had invented them ourselves.

One thing we seriously doubted we would ever get used to was peas and potatoes, wrapped in greasy newspaper. The old days with fish and chips had to have been better, or at least easier to eat. But we all understood rationing by now. And, though England was even tighter than the U.S. as far as that went, we'd learned a little of how to get around the problem. The trick was to work your way into the back of the mess hall and make a swap with the supply sergeant. Maybe he'd give you some Spam for some cigarettes. With the Spam you could strike a deal to get yourself invited out, even if it was only to drink piss-warm beer. But with a little more effort, a can of Spam could get you invited to most English houses for a Sunday night social around the radio. The goal was to charm your hosts so thoroughly that the willing young birdie pleaded with her parents to escort you part-way back to the base on her bicycle, which was a perfect opportunity to stop at the pub for a nightcap and whatever else she would go for.

It was particularly enjoyable to sit around the officers' club at the Spitfire base at Northolt and listen to the pilots, both Brits and Yanks who had fought in combat, talk and argue about the capability of their different aircraft. Mostly they talked of Jugs and Spitfires. Everyone seemed to use the term Jug when they talked about the P-47. It was a term we first heard in transition, but it hadn't stuck with us. Now it would.

From what I heard, the R.A.F. as a whole didn't think the Jug could hold its own against the Jerry's Focke-Wulf 190. All the combat vets considered the 190 to be the best they had been up against. It was both speedy and maneuverable; and it packed a heavy wallop, carrying four 20-mm. cannons and two 13-mm. machine guns. The yellow-nosed 190s were said to be the ones we should be particularly wary of. They were piloted by Goering's boys, probably the best pilots in the whole German Air Force.

The Americans complained that the Spitfire was slower than the Jug, with lighter armament and essentially no armour. But the Brits argued the Spit could outmaneuver any of the combat aircraft in the theater on either side. Still the combat-wise Yanks could not understand the Brits' love for the Spitfire since its record couldn't match that of the Thunderbolt. The 56th Fighter Group of the 8th Air Force had over five hundred kills with the Thunderbolt. My buddies and I rarely missed a word of the arguments and we were convinced we would prove once and for all, when we got the chance, that the Jug was King.

It was our singing which brought the blue R.A.F. uniforms and the pink and green U. S. Army Air Force uniforms together. A favorite in England was *I've got Sixpence*. After a few drinks we joined in, catching only half the words and bumbling the rest:

> I've got sixpence
> Jolly, jolly sixpence.
> I've got sixpence to last me all my life.
> I've got twopence to spend,
> And twopence to lend,
> And two pence to send home to my wife--poor wife.
> No cares have I to grieve me,
> No pretty little girls to deceive me,
> I'm happy as a lark believe me,
> As we go rolling, rolling home.

Rolling home (rolling home).
Rolling home (rolling home),
By the light of the silvery mo-oooon.
Happy is the day when the airman gets his pay
As we go rolling, rolling home. . .

As the evenings wore, our arguing faded, and the warm beer kept
flowing. Then the mood was ripe for the Brits to teach us some other songs,
some of their more tasteless ones. "You blokes give us a tune and we'll sing
you a melody," they taunted us. They recognized immediately the tune of
the *Battle Hymn of the Republic*, and sang stoutly:

We fly our fucking Jugs at 10,000 fucking feet.
We fly our fucking Jugs through the rain and through the sleet.
And though we think we're flying south,
We're flying fucking north.
And we make our fucking landfall of the
Firth of fucking Forth.

Glory, glory what a helluva way to die,
Glory, glory what a helluva way to die.
Glory, glory what a helluva way to die,
And we make our fucking landfall on the
Firth of Fucking Forth.

We sang into the early hours of the morning with the lyrics deterio-
rating to the height of vulgarity. Nights like this always promised the
greatest of hangovers, a concern withheld for later. Still, the fun was over
and we stumbled to our Nissen huts through the murky night, made even
darker by the absence of all artificial lights.

Our orders came at last. We were to join the 366th Fighter Group
in St. Pierre duMont in France, which was under the IX Tactical Air
Command of the 9th Air Force. We were fortunate, however; the orders
gave us a few days leave before we were due on assignment. London was
our destination, which we decided without so much as a second thought.
But as we came into the city, we noticed that most of the girls were in
uniform and looked much too dour and single-minded. The city reflected
much of the wartime seriousness we'd come to know. And our trip through
Harrods showed what rationing had done to both the talked-about food and
gift stores. The purchase of everything required a coupon.

All the effects of the war didn't stop us from touring the town in a charcoal-powered London taxi and doing a little flying talk around the bar at the Grosvenor House. Our last night at the Grosvenor House bar, coupled with the rich food at the Mirabelle restaurant in Mayfair, were all the excesses we could fittingly tolerate. The Mirabelle was one of few restaurants where one could get a really fine meal in London. To our good fortune, many luxury foods in Britain had escaped the wrath of rationing. The meal we had there was as good and as expensive as everyone promised. Most of all we liked the waiter's attitude on our extravagance as he said to us, "What the hell, you are off to war and all that old rot."

The next day we took the train to Portsmouth where we boarded an LST crammed full of servicemen going to the continent. Through the clamor, Paul and I slept peacefully until we reached Omaha Beach. Op, however, spent the short crossing sitting on the pot with a heave bucket between his legs. He still had not recovered from our last night in London.

Our boots still sloshed with sea water as we came to the flight strip above the beach. There we learned the reason for our having not been ordered to fly into the field; our group had moved to Dreux where it would stay for a week then move on to Laon/Cuvron, France. The only reminder of the group's activity in St. Pierre duMont was a few trenches, the trampled ground and some wooden structures the men once occupied. A couple of speckled black and white cows grazed peacefully on the last few remaining tufts of green grass growing amongst the wreckage of a P-47. The cows wouldn't stay long because the area was rapidly being transformed into a marshalling yard for supplies moving to the front.

After a little discussion over a few beers in the local bistro, we decided our orders allowed us to catch up with the group in any manner that was *expeditious*. The wording on the orders was somewhat tricky and was surely open for interpretation, according to Op. He came into the cadet program out of Stanford University where he was studying to be a lawyer, and that was his best legal reading on the statement. So we mapped out our plan.

We had heard Paris had just been liberated, and our surrogate lawyer friend informed us that we could logically go through the city on the way to Laon. Without much discussion, that's what we decided to do. Paul, Op and I hitched a series of rides on the Red Ball Express, an army convoy system carrying supplies from the beach to different front-line activities, including Paris. When we got to Paris, there was scattered fighting still going on. A few Jerry tanks smoldered in the Place de la Concorde. Overall, the city appeared to be functioning, despite the confusion.

We learned there was a French school the army had taken over, close to the center of town, where we could get lodging and draw money against our orders. The advice from our *lawyer* was to get the eagle to shit as much as he would and spend all the money on the spirited Parisian night life. After all, we were getting closer and closer to the war, and all that old rot. About this time, D.J. Ross met up with us in Paris. D.J. accepted our *lawyer's* advice and did the town with us.

We settled into the Pigalle district of Paris, staying in the obscure Moncey-Hotel. Our first evening was spent in a nearby basement cafe called the Laise en Rose, which was jammed with young French men and women chattering away about the wartimes. On the way to the cafe, D.J. introduced us to the unique Paris toilets, ones he had read about in Ernest Hemingway's books. The pissotieres were stand-up urinals situated in the open air on the sidewalks for all to use and see. They looked like huge wooden barrels, with the side cut out and a hole in the bottom which went somewhere; we didn't care to know. Lacking the gall to try them out for their intended purpose, we all agreed they would be very useful when we drank too much. What did the women do, we wondered?

D.J. was the only one of us who could semi-communicate with the locals. His French couldn't get us anywhere, but he could do a reasonable job of speaking Spanish, since most everyone in Southern California was taught Spanish as a second language in high school. Now, it was coming in handy, since quite a few of the non-English speaking French spoke Spanish. Surely the details of our conversations got lost in the translations, but we picked up the gist of things.

Though we hadn't even so much as set foot on the front lines, the locals treated us as though we were *the* guys who liberated Paris. We didn't mind the locals thinking of us as their heroes, so we never told them otherwise. In the jubilant crowd, we met some members of the French resistance, called Maquisards. They were a defiant group who were damned proud of what they were doing. In listening to their stories, there was no doubt in my mind, they led extremely dangerous lives, more dangerous than I ever envisioned mine to become.

Their stories brought a chill to my bones. Blowing up bridges, sabotaging rail lines, and helping allied pilots escape, while all the time evading Gestapo plainclothesmen, spies and paid informers. Many bystanders told me it was the Maquisard's success which bred the German's hatred for them and which motivated a passionate stalking of the Maquisards, like rats as they crept through the nights on their missions. If any were caught, the Gestapo tortured them, then imprisoned them or more likely ordered them shot.

After sharing their stories with us, the Maquisards invited us to the place where they lived. They had taken over the luxurious Rothschild estate, not far from the Place de la Concorde. Earlier the German

Luftwaffe had confiscated the estate from the renowned Jewish banking family for the use of Hermann Goering and his staff. In Goering's rush to vacate the facility, he overlooked Rothschild's fabulous art collection, which was hidden in a secret room behind a bookcase. He also left the entire wine cellar, stocked with some of Rothschild's finest wines. That was a grievous oversight by the German Luftwaffe and a tremendous perquisite to those who followed.

While lunching almost royally at the estate on a black-market meal and a perfectly aged bottle of Chateauneuf-du-Pape, a middle-aged French gent named Jacques approached me, speaking what I considered lumbering but understandable English. Jacques was recovering from injuries he had received when his Maquis group got in a tiff with the German First Army in the south of France. After he recovered he planned to join the Free French Army of General Charles De Gaulle, who had just recently invited the Maquis to join him.

Jacques asked me where I was from. That wasn't always such an easy question to answer for Europeans since Portland, Oregon was so rarely known. So when anyone asked me that question I always said north of Hollywood since that was a reference point most understood. Jacques asked me how far from Hollywood and I told him some odd number of miles. That must be close to Portland, Oregon, he said. It turns out that he was a circuit wrestler during the Depression and had been everywhere in the U.S., billed as *Jacques, the terrible Frenchman.*

Jacques asked me if I knew Erickson's Saloon in Portland. He went on to say that it was noted for having the longest bar in town, one fifth of a kilometer long. No one needed to remind me of that because Erickson's was where my dad played poker in his logging days. After exchanging a few stories on Portland, Jacques and I became instant friends. He laughed at my French pronunciation of his name saying, "Just because I'm an athletic supporter, don't call me *Jock.*" Knowing we were on a tight budget, Jacques asked us to stay with his freedom fighters at the estate. We accepted graciously, but also kept a couple rooms at the Moncey-Hotel just in case we got a little action.

Through Jacques I met a girl named Annie who was a soldier of the Maquis. Annie had that very potent, feminine mystique which only French women seemed to possess. She was confident, strong, and deliciously alluring. My willpower faltered upon our first introduction, and I realized immediately I did not possess the strength to resist her charms. She was a mature twenty-seven years old and I was a young nineteen, but that mattered to neither of us. This was love. Pure, passionate love. A blazing attraction bound us. We writhed in its clutches, savoring every moment of our togetherness.

It didn't concern us that we could not speak each other's language with the eloquence we would have liked. Eventually, I'm sure she would have taught me her language, or I would have taught her mine. But, it wasn't meant to be this time.

We had to move on. Our group was just getting settled and would be looking for us soon. Besides, we had squeezed the eagle to the limit on our orders and were altogether out of money. D.J. stopped by Annie's apartment to pick me up on the morning we planned to leave. As I walked from Annie's now familiar apartment, I reflected on how much I had learned from her. I knew I would be back. As I left her arms she handed me her Maquis pin, the Cross of Lorraine. I was so touched, I gave her a pair of wings and promised to send another for her friend.

D.J. and I planned to meet Paul at the Moncey-Hotel. We thought Op would be there as well. As we walked up the narrow street leading to the hotel, Paul was coming from the other direction. He had made connections with a gorgeous blonde Polish girl he described earlier as capable of inflicting very deep and painful fingernail scratches in a guy's back. Paul didn't look good at all; in the early morning mist he looked as though he had been flattened by a flour truck which had lost its load. We guessed his appearance was the penalty for this being our last night of fun for awhile.

Together we walked into the hotel and studied the bulletin board. There were the fruits of our prearranged code system, telling who was in what room. Since none of the hotel clerks could speak English, we always left a hotel card with the information posted on the wall. Op was on the first floor. As we rolled him out of the sack, we reminded him to leave a little something for the girl. We must be off to Laon, despite the pleadings to the contrary from our lawyer.

33. D.J. Ross and Mel with Annie Simsen
at the *Laise en Rose*, Paris 1944.

CHAPTER 10

ON GOD'S SIDE

The field at Laon was just a few miles from Rheims, the capital of France's premier champagne country. As we passed through the quaint little village on the way to our field, we asked our driver to stop and let us buy a couple bottles of champagne at the equivalent of fifteen cents each. Op paid the merchant fifty cents a bottle and said lavishly, "Monsieur, your champagne is worth at least that much." The Frenchman smiled with an unknowing look, and responded graciously with some silky French utterance. We chuckled that the old man didn't understand a single word we said.

Arriving at the group in mid afternoon, we reported to the bustling operations tent. The supply officer looked over his shoulder and said to us, "Grab a tent at supply and pitch it anywhere you like in our area this side of the runway." Amidst the scurry, we missed the expected welcome.

The airdrome, we surmised, had once been taken over from the French by the Germans. Now the U.S. had taken control of the field and had squadrons stationed in tents at three different locations alongside the runway. Each squadron had a building or two they called their own; some were for storage and others were for mess halls. One of our buildings was being turned into an officers' club for use by the squadron.

Our choice of a site for our tent was an easy one -- a barren area laid just short of the strip, in line with the rest of the squadron tents. It was as good as any piece of real estate around. Paul, Op, Picton and I spent the remainder of the first evening assembling the mass of faded green canvas and characterless stakes that was to be our home for the duration. At dusk, the deep drone of the familiar P-47 engines quieted and we bedded down to an eerie calm, anxiously awaiting the next day.

At the crack of dawn the next morning, a brief convened in the operations hut. There, we met the old hands of the squadron. Major "Marty" Martin was the Commander; in Army terms he was the C.O., although some called him *the old man* since he was the boss and somewhere close to twenty-five years of age. He looked all business, though we decided it would take some time before we found out if the rumor was true that rank really didn't mean so much in combat.

Captain Lowell Smith was the squadron operations officer, or *ops officer*. A well-stained meerschaum pipe always hung from the captain's mouth and he had an odd habit of talking through it. His interest seemed genuine as he asked each of us about our home towns.

Captain Doc Clark was the flight surgeon. Since corpsmen generally gave recruits their shots and whatever else they needed for a cold or such,

I had not had that many contacts with army doctors. That is, except for the brief I'd received on the Clap and the flight physical, neither of which I remembered with great fondness. However, the Doc had every appearance of what I expected a doctor to be, and I suspected he was more than just another pecker-checker.

Captain Wilcox was the intelligence officer; efficient sounding, but pleasant. Business was never far from his mind, but we liked what we heard. "We'll get to know one another a lot better," he said; "I'll be the first one you talk to when you come back from a mission."

We also met the flight leaders, Bertza, Horgan, Burnes and White. That day we got a quick hello, but we hoped to talk to them some more over a round of drinks.

Three squadrons were in our group. All the men in our squadron appeared eager to introduce themselves, but it seemed the other two tended to stick to themselves. The commanders said hello, but none of their men.

Before the operations pitch began, we studied the situation chart, which was essentially a map of England and the Continent. The intel officer was carefully tacking a blue ribbon which denoted the FEBA or forward edge of the battle area, a line just seventy short miles away. The Allies were moving forward, but slowly, and the density of red splotches (indicating gun emplacements) which peppered the map told us our progress wasn't going to be much faster in the near future.

As the operations officer took his place behind the apple-box podium, we scrambled for a chair as most of the men had already taken their seats in the classroom like setting. "Ten-hut," the Officer of the Day called, and we rose to our feet, then sat once more.

Captain Smith announced that we had six allied armies facing seven German armies along a five-hundred-mile front between the North Sea and the Swiss border.˙ Our ground troops had covered a lot of territory in ten weeks since the landing at Normandy and they were dragging their butts. The supply lines were three hundred and fifty miles long, all the way back to the Normandy beaches. The Port of Antwerp could provide some relief, but it was not open. Only the Siegfried Line and the Ruhr and Rhine Rivers stood between us and the German heartland. The captain turned to us after the summary and said, "The group has lost about one hundred and fifty planes since June. A lot of pilots got back, but somewhere close to eighty didn't. We're glad to have you boys with us; we really need your help."

With a measured degree of humor, the Major added that Eisenhower had a wager with Montgomery that the war would be over by the end of '44 and we had plenty of work to do to make the general a winner.

The tactical mission brief for the afternoon flight mission was scheduled for 1100. We received direct orders to be there. This would be our first introduction to real combat, but we wouldn't be personally involved, not this time. Our only responsibility was to observe and learn.

As we walked into the operations hut, the mission brief was within moments of starting. The C.O. was arguing with the ops officer about the merits of the newly reported long-nosed FW-190. Horgan and Burnes were debating the best way to knock out a Tiger tank with either rockets or five-hundred pounders. Op said to me, "What the hell is a long-nosed FW-190?" I responded with a shrug, not wanting to miss a word of what was being said by the others.

No one seemed to talk about the merits of the P-47 in this squadron. They all knew their plane was the best. By the unspoken law of all fighter pilots, the plane they fly is the best made, no matter what it is or what it was built to do. Any pilot who was worth a damn would *make* his plane do whatever he needed it to do. The only argument was over the best way to do it, and that's what everyone talked about when they weren't flying.

According to the manuals, the P-47 Thunderbolt was built to fly above thirty thousand feet and its primary mission was to escort bombers. But this squadron knew the 47 also performed flawlessly at low altitude for ground support. And if the enemy dared swoop down for a little dogfight with them while they were busy doing their ground support mission, the Thunderbolt would respond in the best of tradition. All those P-47s on the runway took care of us, and we respected that fact.

The ops officer gave a little history about the Germans inventing the battle strategy of supporting ground troops with tactical air when they overran Europe. His unblinking eyes focused on us as he said, "We'll show them what it's all about." My squadron would prove the Thunderbolt was the best ground support aircraft of the war. Our enemy was tanks, bridges, trains, truck convoys, airfields and roadblocks of any kind. Anything on the ground that moved and anything in the air that interfered was at risk. On a moment's notice, our steel mesh fields rolled up like our tents and we could move right along with our ground troops, hopefully forward.

The next best thing to flying was talking about flying, and talk was all we were going to do until we got to know the operation a bit better. Day after day we attended the operations and mission briefs as nonparticipants, sitting silently in the back of the tent. A couple times we flew our planes around the area so we became familiar with the landmarks, many of which we knew only from geography books. We settled in as comfortably as one does.

Our first challenge was to make the most of our temporary home perched on the cold sodden earth. Between being dragged mercilessly through the mud from field to field following the ground troops, and the unforgiving stiffness of the canvas, the wear and tear showed on the tent. We didn't know what shape it was really in, until the first day it rained. The once invisible pinholes in the canvas turned into floodgates, and everything we owned was soaked with moisture and cold. Early the next morning we patched the holes as best we could, although we knew our soggy bedding and other belongings wouldn't dry for weeks.

In the early afternoons, we covered the surrounding area by foot and bicycle. Of course, we returned to the old man with the champagne. This time though, the champagne was fifty cents a bottle. It was still a bargain, and we told him so.

About a half mile away, we came across a bombed-out cottage which we scrounged for anything of use to either ourselves or our squadron-mates. We traded some tables we found for a couple of rubber entrance mats. Our most significant find was a pair of glass door panels which were in remarkably good shape. The panels added a little class to our home and allowed us to monitor the weather in relatively dry comfort.

Mostly we hung around the base, talking, listening and observing. We attended all the mission briefs, then talked to all the guys returning from their flights. Battered and tired, they would slouch around their drinks and pour out their tales. As they re-staged the attacks with twisting, pointing hands, life seemed to pour back into them. Altogether the stories they told were staggering to all of the newcomers, and the mangled planes on the runway reflected their truthfulness.

Keeping full squadron strength for missions was close to impossible and with the winter coming on, the ground crew had an even more difficult task ahead of them. The crew repaired and maintained all the planes outside, fighting against all the elements. They did only an occasional engine change in the relative protection of a tent. Because of the perpetual dampness, the cold was brutal and the crew's hands became stiffer and slower each day as the dead of winter grew nearer.

My squadron had a slight advantage over some in the area of maintenance. The group commander, Colonel Norman Holt, came from the 390th and kept his aircraft the *Magic Carpet* and its maintenance crew with our squadron. Our operations officer was free to schedule the *Magic Carpet* as a squadron asset. Other senior pilots in the squadron had specific planes assigned to them, also. The new pilots used these planes on assigned missions, with the threat of, "Scratch my plane and I'll have your ass." No one dared say what would happen if someone scratched the colonel's *Magic Carpet*.

At last our day came. On 13 October, the captain told us to get set for the next mission. Real combat was only two unrestful nights' sleep away.

Five o'clock the next morning came much too early, it seemed. Through the glass panels on our tent we could see that the clammy haze still hung low over the field. Dressing quickly in the darkness, we took little time to think. The strong smell of *Joe*, the strong black soot which cooked for hours on the potbelly stove, wafted from the half-filled briefing room. By now we had learned, mission pilots sat in the front row and the pilots who were not going to fly sat in the back of the tent. For the first time, we moved up in the pecking order. We took our places in the front row. With only a slight bit of apprehension, we were smug.

The briefing started promptly, with little commotion. The C.O. announced the squadron was going out with twelve aircraft; another aircraft would be covering in case there was an abort by one of the twelve. This backup aircraft would fly out for ten minutes; if there was no need for it by then, it would return.

The mission was a strike on a transportation system along the Rhine River, which would hopefully slow the movement of supplies to the front. Boiled down, we would be doing what the Army Air Force called rail cutting and road interdiction. Since the target was not time urgent, the strike would be worked into the planned schedule sometime within the next twenty-four hours. The brief, like all the others we had listened to, wound up with Wilcox giving his rundown on the location of AA guns in the target area. Wilcox riveted his eyes on all the new guys and reminded us again that these guns were a bigger threat to our Jugs than enemy fighters.

The mission was tentatively planned for 0500 the next morning. Paul, Op, and I would be flying second man in the elements until we showed our capability to take on an element lead, or until the squadron lost so many pilots they had to use us for the first position. Our flight leader for the morning flight was identified, and we walked out of the tent ten feet off the ground.

That night we wandered to the southwest edge of our area. This was our officer's club built by a couple of ingenious squadron flyers. As we entered the salvaged, miss-fit door I glanced at the sign over the makeshift wooden crate bar. It read, *No Guts, No Glory*, which was our squadron slogan.

Liquor always flowed freely at the bar. Flyers got two ounces of American whiskey for each sortie they flew. The flight surgeon kept the records and held everyone's allotment until they called for it. On rare occasions, the guys ferried scotch from England in the modified belly tank of a Jug. Since we weren't accustomed to Scotch, we bought French brandy and champagne in Rheims from our Frenchman friend and from almost any other street corner. Although brandy took some getting used to, that was what we usually drank.

For this special night we dusted off the old New Orleans recipe for Ramos Gin Fizz, and with a little urging of the supply guys, got a couple of packages of powdered lemonade, some canned cherries, and canned milk. We mixed all the ingredients together and sampled the product, just as we had seen only the most discriminating wine tasters do. The concoction got a little better as the evening passed. We roared as we listened to Paul telling tales about his Polish girlfriend in Paris. Girls, food, airplanes and weather, that's all anyone ever seemed to talk about. Singing was a great pastime too. We wound up the night singing *Rag Mop*, and with my thick shaggy mop of hair, now grown out from the crew cut, Op tagged me with the nickname *Mop*. It stuck, as did so many other nicknames cast on our buddies in the height of deliriousness.

Early the next morning we rolled out of our dank fart sacks, in what promised to be another brisk autumn day. Gazing out our makeshift window, I could tell even in the dark that snow was starting to fall. Without wasting a minute, Op stepped outside in his ratty woolen long johns, stuck a rag in a can of gas, and popped it into the potbelly stove setting in the middle of the tent. We had instant, though admittedly high-risk heat.

We dressed hastily in the cold and hustled to the mess tent, which generally was warmer than our own. It seemed the army never failed to serve SOS when our stomachs were queazy. (SOS was chipped beef and milk gravy on toast, more aptly called *slop on a shingle*). Despite our uneasiness we struggled to eat a bite or two, slouching over our trays, then we shoveled in the remainder of the disgusting mound. Things were uncomfortably quiet. Perhaps the reason had more to do with the last night's activity than the uncertainty of our first combat flight.

As we walked into the operations hut a single bulb lighted the room and the map of the battle area. "Ten-hut," the O.D. called and we stood at attention for a brief moment, then scrambled for our seats. The captain announced immediately, our mission had changed and was now time urgent. We were going out to an area just over the front lines across the Sure River, in support of the 1st Army. Attentively, we listened to the intel officer as he gave his front line status brief. We knew we needed to know the lay of the land if we went down.

The nervousness of the group mounted as we jotted our course figures on the backs of our hands with our black fountain pens. Then we carefully calibrated our watches. At precisely 0736 a.m., the apprehension paralyzed me, suspending my thoughts in animation. The jittery combat film I'd seen the previous day played slowly across the frontal lobe of my brain. Of more immediate concern, piercing knives sliced at my stomach in disgust of the huge mound of slop I had consumed earlier. I prayed my gurgling insides would not reveal the anxiety that gripped me.

"Good luck," the captain said as we filed out of the room. His voice reflected an attitude of business as usual, still unfamiliar to me. No one responded to the captain; they simply walked on, laughing and joking amongst themselves. "Kid's stuff, a piece of cake," they said. "Probably won't come across any bandits."

Moments later we all arrived at the aircraft with a devil-may-care easiness. The props of our Jugs were already turning and my time for brooding was over.

After our twelve-man flight lifted off the field, we never saw the ground again until we landed. The clouds shrouded the tree tops and all that lurked below, just as the captain feared. Our primary target would have to wait; it was far too close to our own ground troops to permit even slight miscalculations of its location. For now we headed to our alternate target, a dead-reckoned hit on the town of Aachen.

The enemy let us know they were beneath the thick cloud cover, sending up fiery balls of flak that exploded into large dingy, cotton-like, puffs. We knew then, we had crossed the FEBA into enemy territory. The sky blackened and the sound reminded me of the kettle drum of the Grant High marching band. Bum........bum. Bum......bum. Each boom shook the plane madly. The closer ones shook a little harder. However, other than this little bit of flak which didn't get dangerously close, the flight was uneventful, no more than a milk run. We dropped our five-hundred pound bombs through the clouds, softening Aachen for the 1st Division. Although we couldn't see if we hit our target, the town was so big it would have been difficult to miss.

On the 21st of October the 1st Division took the town of Aachen, the first German town to fall to American forces. On the heels of that victory, the front settled into stability with the coming of winter. Over the next few weeks we flew many ground support missions over the Hurtgen Forest and the Ardennes. The 366th was the first group to ever use the P. 47 as a dive bomber, and it was showing its worth every day. This was the Jug at its best.

The Hurtgen Forest was a plague for ground troops. No larger than ten miles by twenty miles, it was saturated with pill boxes on the fringe of the Siegfried Line. Our squadron was supporting the 1st Army in an attempt to penetrate and take the forest. Trees one hundred feet tall made visibility of targets a hopeless task. And while we fought over the Hurtgen Forest, the Germans regrouped. They had been pushed back by our forces in a series of engagements ever since the breakthrough at the Falaise gap. The Hurtgen Forest gave the Germans their first chance to regroup and fight back. They dug in hard and found order out of the chaos which the two previous months had known.

Paul, Op, Picton and I settled in with the squadron. First names or nicknames were all that were called for, except for the C.O. and the ops officer. Personalities and flying habits were something we grew to understand as generally one and the same. We got to know each of the guys, which helped us anticipate their moves in the sky. Sometimes we were surprised, but not often.

A head stuck in our tent, as Op sat and listened to my tales of hot rods and drag racing. "Mop, you're on in the morning and they want you up in the briefing hut *tout de suite*."

We were scheduled for an early morning flight the next day. The weather in the target area was low clouds at five thousand feet. Elements of the 1st Army were attempting to break through the Hurtgen Forest to the town of Schmidt. Our mission was to provide ground support and I was assigned the wing position of the element leader of Relic Blue Flight. Flak was reportedly light, weak and inaccurate, a piece of cake.

The flight took off on schedule. As we dipped down through the clouds, we broke into elements and started looking for our targets. Wilcox was wrong again; heavy flak sprouted all around us in shaggy blobs. Unmercifully, our planes jerked through the thick dark air, bolting and belching. Our eyes were glued to the ground.

Sitting at the east end of the forest was the key target area of Schmidt. As we crossed the bomb line, I caught a glimpse of a German tank preparing to back into a dirt revetment, and I called him out. Then my view was obscured by several bursts of ominous flak puffs. By now I had ten sorties under my belt and had taken my share of flak at both low and high altitude, but this flak was the hottest I had encountered to date. Pressing on, I wanted badly to make mincemeat out of this tank; my victory would be one small godsend to the 28th Division, which was acutely aware of the horrors of battling through the Hurtgen. My element leader scanned the ground, "Mop, I'm looking all over, and I don't see any damn tank down there, you take the lead." "Roger, we're going in," I responded.

I had what many considered as the essential physical asset for a pilot, that is keen eyesight. My 20-10 vision was a real plus for aerial combat, and it was a blessing for ground support work.

However, to date, I had no real experience with tanks. I knew German tanks tended to be heavier, better armed and protected with more armor than the allied tanks. They were also supposedly less maneuverable than allied tanks and would dig into a dirt revetment and act as a heavy piece of artillery firing their 88-mm., high-velocity cannon at road level. That's what this one appeared to be doing as I watched from the air.

My Jug was dropping in and out of low clouds at thirty-five hundred feet. Our mission brief had missed the weather by fifteen hundred feet. "Stay close and pick off any ack-ack sight you see flashing at us," I instructed my wingman. "Roger Wilco!" came the quick response. My total concentration was on the tank. To blast him, I had a full load of five-hundred pound bombs under my wings but no antitank rockets. The bombs were set with delayed fuzes, which would allow them to penetrate the earth before they exploded.

Making a short run parallel to the road, I gave my wingman the head's up, "This is it, stay close. Tallyho!" Racking a sharp wingover, I flipped the arming toggle switch for my bombs. "Steady now," I said to my Jug. Jerking though my mind was the tune, *I don't want to set the world on fire, I just want to start a flame in your heart.* As my mind snapped back to the task at hand, I noticed my heartbeat had doubled. This was it.

Incessant flak puffs shook my plane violently. My big old Jug reacted almost like it was spooked by the grimy puffs. Brilliant flashes soared into the sky from a gun emplacement on the side of a hill to the north. Still, I held my concentration on the tank. I wanted to lay all I was carrying right beside him. A direct hit could ricochet harmlessly off the heavy armor plate. Closer. . . closer. The tank filled more and more of my florescent gun sight. I wanted to go as close as I could and still pull out. As the center of the sight settled in alongside the tank, I yanked the release handle and the bombs dropped free from the plane.

Breaking hard to the left I pointed my nose into the gun emplacement on the hill with my guns blazing and gave him a short burst at three hundred yards. Seventy-two hundred rounds a minute of .50-caliber ammo spewed out at the Jerry hole-up. I was confident. The glowing burning tracers told me I was right on. Breaking hard, I roared into the clouds. My wingman stayed on me all the way. Rolling back out of the clouds for just a moment, I took a quick look downward. The tank was lifted onto its side, mangled beyond repair. Everything had worked just like the book said in Abilene. As my element leader took over the lead again, I mused, "That tank looked as good as any old Me-109."

Getting shot down often did irreparable damage to a pilot's spirit or courage, providing of course he lived to talk about it. More often than not these pilots lost the all-essential devil-may-care nerve, fearing the same could happen again and that maybe the second time their luck would have run out. Therefore most of the downed pilots who found their way back to the squadron were shipped back to the States for rest leave. Sometimes the men were dismissed, other times they were rotated. Since my arrival, Lt. Emil Bertza was one of the first to detach from the squadron under these circumstances.

Doc told me the details of Bertza getting shot down and being captured by the Germans. It was the 12th of August when he bailed out at two thousand feet after being struck by flak. He landed close to Domfront in Normandy in the midst of German gunfire, leaving him no viable alternative but to surrender. After being questioned at the German command post, he shared a bottle of wine and some friendly conversation with his captors, then was taken to the German Headquarters which was located at a farmhouse nearby. With some other prisoners, he was again moved to yet another farmhouse. As the men settled in, a couple of P-47s strafed the area, causing the Germans to scatter. The prisoners, including Bertza, escaped in the confusion and hid in a ditch beside a hedgerow. In an amazing turn of fate, six German officers joined the prisoners in the ditch, offering to surrender to the Americans if they agreed to take them across the American lines. To do this, the men first had to pass through a division of SS troops. The only way they could figure to get past the SS troops was to have the Americans act as prisoners to the Germans.

The Germans argued their way out of the SS Headquarters but were forced to hole up in an obliging Frenchman's barn to avoid some more gunfire. Bertza feared their plan was doomed when he saw a whole column of Germans approaching their hide-out. Mindful that he was surely defeated, Bertza approached the officers in a friendly manner, shaking their hands and offering cigarettes. The officers, who were Austrian, asked Bertza the location of the American lines. Bertza told the Austrians that they were surrounded by Americans, and there was no longer a German line in the area. He offered the men protection if they would surrender to him as prisoners. The Americans, he rationalized to the Austrians, would treat them much better than the French civilians. So Bertza's party grew and they moved towards the American lines. Only a few prisoners absconded along the way, having fled when it became clear there was not enough food to feed everyone. Bertza let them go without so much as an argument, since he was unarmed. Finally the saga was over, when Bertza came across the Free French 2nd Armored Division, who accepted the prisoners. Eighteen August, Bertza hitchhiked his way back to the squadron and was sent on leave shortly thereafter.

Mail call often brought a letter from my friend Mort, or less frequently from the other members of the old gang or my mother. Today brought a V-mail letter from Portland which I assumed came from Mom and a sweet-scented envelope with a Parisian post-mark. My heart skipped a beat; the envelope had to be from Annie. I'd written her a letter telling her about my first couple weeks with my squadron and also letting her know

I'd sent a pair of wings for her friend. I carefully opened the envelope and smiled as I read her letter:

Paris 25/10/44

"My Little Mop," she addressed the letter, obviously amused by my new nickname I had told her about.

"At last I receive good news from you. I was very impatient to get them and am happy to know that you are OK and that we'll soon meet again.

The photo of us with Donald taken at "Laise en Rose" is fine. Did you get it? It is here on a chest of drawers looking at me every evening when I come back home. XXX

Everybody at Rothschild's sends you their best wishes.

Inés will be very glad to receive that pin and she thanks you for it in advance. I think very often of you my little Mop.
So Long Your,
Annie"

I re-sealed the letter and placed it with my 201 file, where I kept all my important records. Every time I reached into the file, I would be reminded of Annie, dear sweet Annie.

Mom's letter was newsy as usual. She and Dad were managing fine.

September 28, 1944

Dear Mel,

I hope this letter gets to you before your birthday. It's hard for me to believe you will be 20 years old. Did you get the candy I sent? There aren't any nuts in it, hope you don't mind. I had the ration points and everything to get them, but your old boss at Teeny's grocery said there just weren't any to be had. Next time I'll see if Dorothy Gallager has some from her tree.

Dad and I are doing fine at work, we both got promotions of sorts. Still working a lot of hours. You should be proud of me becoming a lead welder. Your dad is now the swing shift foreman for the rigger crews. The money is better, we'll put everything we don't need into war bonds. Not much to buy anyway, sure could use a new refrigerator but that is going to have to wait.

Sorry I wrote so large. Will tell you more in my next letter -- running out of room.
Love,
Mom and Dad

I hoped Mom's package would come on a day when at least some of the guys were too busy to attend mail call. Maybe that way I could secretly squirrel away a couple pieces of candy, rather than having the whole box consumed in the typical three-minute frenzy. Unfortunately, both secrets and candy had a very short life expectancy in this environment.

At last, I was assigned a Jug of my own, and I needed to come up with a name to be painted on the side of the plane. Paul was assigned one at the same time and he named his *Lucky Marie*. We wanted to get the squadron art expert to do both of the planes together.

I knew the naming of an airplane was a ritual which must be done right and after some thought I chose the name *La Mort*, which to me had a double connotation. My good friend Mort, would be pleased when I told him of his new namesake; I appreciated his many letters over the short time I had been in Europe. The namesake was also symbolic of Annie's grieving for the Maquisards who had died in service of their country. *Mort* meant *dead* in French, a poignant reminder of those who departed before.

Paul put a full-bodied Betty Boop on his Jug, with two knockers the size of cantaloupes. On mine, the squadron artist drew the head of a blonde who reminded me only accidently of Polly Green, a casual romance never forgotten. He also repainted my plane designator, a big *M* on the back of the fuselage.

With the airplane came a crew. The chief's name, Staff Sergeant Michano, appeared just below mine on the plane's cockpit. Chief Michano was about fifteen years older than me. He had all the good nature of the corn-fed farm mechanic he was before Uncle Sam put him through aero-mechanic training. The chief told me he would push *La Mort* as hard as I wanted, and after a little discussion we agreed he should reset the gate to let more exhaust into the turbine. He estimated that a little more exhaust coupled with water injection would increase performance by an estimated twenty-five percent over the rated output. I'd keep quiet about the soup-up job since I didn't want the head maintenance officer to cause the chief a problem.

The chief liked the fact I was mechanically inclined, saying the last pilot he had didn't know much about that kind of thing and every little noise he heard threw him into a panic. Dad would be pleased to hear all that tinkering I did on my cars finally paid off. The chief and I understood each other and I was going to pay attention to what he had to say. It was obvious he would sweat every mission I flew.

Op, Paul and I stayed close together whenever we were doing anything on the ground or in the air. One day we took some time to go into Laon to return the requisitioned door we had in our tent. Seems the management thought we would establish a bad relationship with our French allies if we absconded with their fixtures. Like everyone else, we'd have to make do with the flap that came with the tent.

We stopped for a beer in one of the local cafes when Aageberg sat down and told me he would be flying with me on a flight in the morning. Though we knew each other reasonably well, we'd never flown together. Aageberg waved and said as he walked off, "I look forward to flying with you. I can use your help." As we returned to the field Op warned, "You be sure to watch Aageberg; I *have* flown with him."

At the morning brief the captain told us about the afternoon flight and the crews were posted for the flight. I was flying as element leader in Relic Red Flight. At last, I was an element leader. And it was that old Jerry tank which paved the way! Now my wingman would have to take care of me from behind while I did what I liked to do best, pressing the target. Second passes were my call. I would never leave a target area as long as I had any ordnance left on my undercarriage. Feeling smug with the new responsibility, I listened even closer to every detail of the mission brief.

We were going to the east bank of the Rhine. Our target was another train marshalling yard. For the mission the ground crew loaded us out with two five-hundred pound bombs and belly tanks. Immediately after the planes were refueled, we lifted off since we had to get back before dark. Night flight was treacherous without navigation aids or direction-finding capability. These aids were strictly forbidden on the Continent, lest we find the enemy on our doorstep.

When we got to the target area, the control told us to find targets of opportunity since the rail yard was socked in by weather. We separated into elements and soon we were on our own. The bridge at Cologne was my choice for a target. I told my wingman what we were up to and instructed him to stay loose and follow me in but to drop his own load wherever he wished on the bridge. We had to make the pass on the bridge from east to west to be sure to stay clear of the cathedral not far from the east end of the bridge. The word was, we were to avoid a drop on the cathedral at all cost. As we made our approach we passed over the city and the worst flak emplacements along the Rhine. The sky turned a greasy black and my wingman and I bobbed about in the sky like helium-filled balloons at the county fair.

The Blue Flight element made a run for the bridge and the leader took a hit that came close to flipping him over. I told my wingman to arm up and we started to make our run. If this was worth doing, we should go all the way down on the bridge before we released our loads. I told my Jug not to worry, we were going to make it, despite all the flak. Then as I crossed over the cathedral I saw a freight train steaming out of the station.

If I wasn't already committed to this run, I would have gone after him. He was safe, for today. Steady, steady. The intensity of the flak grew stronger, still. What was I doing here in all this muck? Holding to five hundred feet, I let the two five-hundred pounders go. As I broke off the target, I stomped on the rudders, one after the other and rolled the stick, forcing my Jug in a series of skids. Hopefully those maneuvers, as ungraceful as they were, would throw off the ground gunners. The strike looked good but we couldn't stick around to find out how good it was.

As we turned back to the field I heard the Relic Red Leader bellowing "MAYDAY! MAYDAY! MAYDAY!" over Aachen. He was in trouble and within minutes I was on his wing. Lieutenant Aageberg's voice was trembling with terror. He said he was losing fuel and I confirmed that his left wing was awash with some liquid he thought to be gasoline. In a total state of panic he readied to hit the silk. "Hang tough," I told him over the radio. Bailing out here didn't look like all that great an idea. Aageberg responded, "What?" He had never heard the expression. That inadvertent little delay got him to settle back for a moment, long enough for me to figure out that it wasn't gasoline all over the wing, but hydraulic fluid. He wasn't in any immediate danger.

We escorted him back to the field and he got his wheels down with a quick nose-up maneuver to give gravity a little assist. It was a good thing for Aageberg, New Yorkers don't talk like those of us from the West.

Aerial recon showed we left the bridge standing. Every time we ever used the bridge at Cologne as a target, the results were the same. The Germans knew how to build bridges and their bridges were the toughest targets we had.

There were days when Wilcox took advantage of the lousy winter weather to give us updates on the threat. No one flew on those days. We gathered around with our *Joe*, still cooking on the potbelly stove. The one to take the last cup made a new pot of side boil, which was just a pot of water with a handful of coffee grounds thrown in. The longer it cooked, the stronger and more bitter it got.

Still being reasonably new to the squadron, we were generally anxious to hear every brief we could, concentrating on every word. About the only thing we really knew about enemy aircraft until these briefs was what we learned in training on how to identify their silhouettes. Wilcox talked about the Me-262 pointing to a drawing of one hanging on the wall. This was the first jet to fly in combat and it was just starting to show itself on the front. IX Tac intelligence said one hundred new twin-engine 262 jets had just come into the inventory on the Western Front. They saw the first 262 only six months before. Supposedly this plane was a product of the finest aeronautical engineering Hitler had. It could carry three 30-mm. cannons and took a bomb load similar to the Jug, while cruising at five hundred and forty miles per hour. Also, it was capable of loading out with R4M rockets, twelve under each wing which could be launched simultaneously and could saturate an area the size of two baseball fields with metal frag. In terms of maneuverability it had the capability to fly on the deck, then bound almost straight up at you from underneath as you fly over. Wilcox told us, "When attacking the 262, go for the engine and wings. The body is not as vulnerable." Op gave me a little jab. He didn't have to say it, but I understood, "Wouldn't it be great to tangle with one of those bandits?"

Then Wilcox talked about the long-nosed FW-190 (inverted V12 cylinder) armed with four 20-mm. cannons and two 13-mm. machine guns. Everyone considered the FW-190 to be the best piston-driven aircraft in the Luftwaffe. The word was, "Don't expect this aircraft to act like the standard FW-190. It's faster and climbs with more agility. Watch you don't get sucked into the wrong position." In a way, Wilcox's remarks reminded me of those guys that used to tell everyone how to goon shift when they never had their asses in a real drag. By now, we had about twenty-five sorties of combat experience and felt like we were going to be old hands soon. Wilcox was a ground-pounder and we never let him forget it, in a friendly sort of way.

The brief was wrapped up with a warning, "The V-1 buzz bombs are out in larger numbers than last month. Don't shoot at them or you're liable to get caught in the blast from their warheads." *Doodlebugs*, as they were sometimes called, were fast becoming the German's preferred way to terrorize civilians in England and on the Continent.

Op, Paul and I seemed to be moving up the squadron ladder at the same pace. Largely, it was the luck of the call, being at the right place on the right mission. More important, we became close friends who would lay everything we had on the line for the others. We never mentioned the subtle competition between us, but it was there just the same.

We easily took on the relaxed ways of the old-timers, spending the evenings in the club introducing the new batches of pilots from the States to gin fizzes made from brandy. Having been on the continent just three months, we had great stories to pass onto the uninitiated. After all, they hadn't heard of the long-nosed FW-190, how to roll over a Tiger tank or the charms of Paul's Polish girlfriend. We could never hear too much about her.

Op and I were called to the briefing tent at 1100 hours on the 19th of November. I was to take the lead of the second element of Yellow Flight and Op was to lead the second element of Red Flight. We were going to fly top cover for the IX Bomber Command. They had eight A-26s making a low-level attack on a marshalling yard outside of Trier.

Three days before, the 1st Army made its drive north of the Hurtgen, towards the Rhine. The IX Bomber Command with its heavy bombers softened up the front for the drive. Over twenty-seven hundred aircraft dropped more than ten thousand tons of ordnance on the target area; still the First was hardly moving. Now it was the 9th's job to stop German supplies moving north to the plains behind Aachen.

Our job was to keep the bandits off the bombers. The plan was to make a run on the rail area north of town, drop our bombs, clear the area and circle back to cover the A-26s on their run.

Within hours we were in the sky. The crisp, clear air reminded us winter was nearing. Flying was such a delight on these cloudless days, I mused almost in a trance. As we lined to pummel the rail station with our loads, the familiar surge of sooty flak stirred the calm and jolted my Jug. I quickly studied the target, seeing that the front end of our flight had done a tremendous job of cutting the rail. My five-hundred pounders were going right behind them. As I looked back, I saw a train building up steam. Damn! I always hated to let those guys go. But we had an escort role to play, and a second pass through that flak would surely get someone killed.

We joined with the A-26s east of Trier. They were dropping to the deck so they could strafe on the way in. With their ten .50-caliber machine guns as protection, the A-26s used a technique which fighter bombers always used, approaching their target slightly spread in echelon. They would unload their ordnance, then veer off the target, breaking hard while staying low on the deck below the flak. These planes were not fighter bombers, but they were probably the most maneuverable light bombers in use.

As the A-26s dropped their bombs and broke from the target, all hell broke loose. They got caught fully exposed in a turn which was way too slow for such low altitude and there was no way to escape the flak alley once they fell into the trap. Before our eyes, the Jerries had a bloody turkey-- shoot. The first two bombers lost a wing and the second element leader lost an engine and his wingman was on fire. Yellow Flight was in even worse shape because they had taken so many hits before they got to the drop area. At the debrief, we reported that none of us saw any of our bombers come away from the target area. And there was nothing we could do to help.

Later, we were all subdued at the club. That deadly mission scenario would never be tried again. We felt so horrible, and so helpless -- as we watched. Our orders were to cover from above; under no circumstances were we to swoop down on the gun emplacements. There we were, flying around high in the sky, not being able to do anything about the devastation which assaulted our gaping eyes.

34. Be it ever so humble -- Laon, France.
Our first home on the Continent.

35. Lt. Russell "Op" Oplinger enjoys
the modern conveniences at Y-29.

36. The shower was as cold as it looks.

37. What a 500 pounder will do when it
falls off on landing. The pilot fortunately
escaped with only a few scratches.

38. Lt. D.J. Ross seeing his brother Sandy off on a mission.

39. A 40 mm strike on Lt. Sandy Ross' jug.
Despite the damage, she was still airworthy, barely.

Paris 25/10/44 -

My little hof,

At last I receive good news
from you. I was very impatient
to get them and am happy
to know that you are OK
and that we'll soon meet
again.

The photo of us with Donaldo
taken at "La vie en Rose" is fine.
Did you get it.

It is here on a chest of drawers looking at me every evening
when Il came back back
home xxx .

Everybody at Ratchild's sends
you their best wishes

Dnes will be very glad to
receive that pin. and the
thanks you for it in advance

40. News from Annie Simsen. What a lift!

41. News from Annie Simsen. What a lift! (cont)

42. Strafing an ammo train in Belgium.

43. An unexpected payload can sometimes raise havoc
with a low flying P-47 on a strafing run.

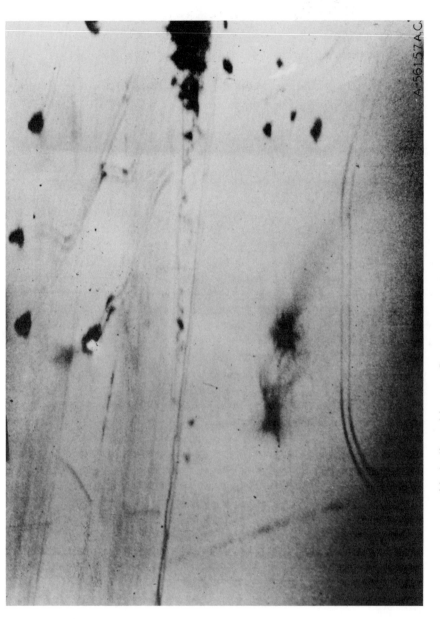

44. A direct hit on a German tank with an air-launched rocket.

45. What a rocket will do to a well-armored tank.

46. President Roosevelt and General of the Air Force "Hap" Arnold at a front line location. Generals Patton and Clark are in the background on the left.

A-26829 A.C.

47. Closing in on a FW-190.

48. Another bogey, out for good.

49. An early morning brief of the 390th Fighter Squadron.

50. The 366th Fighter Group Officers' Bar.

51. *La Mort*, a plane of my own.

CHAPTER 11

THE FUHRER'S FURY

On the 26th of November we moved our field to Asch, Belgium (Y-29), much closer to the line and much closer to the action. We were thirty miles from the Hurtgen Forest and forty-five miles from the Ardennes, just outside the town of Genk. From the time we would lean on the throttle until we crossed the German border was a brief five minutes. Before we left France, however, we loaded up on champagne which we bought from our friend at the new low, low price of five dollars a bottle.

Our field at Asch had a temporary air, sitting on a nondescript piece of unwooded land off to the side of a scrub pine forest. The landing strip was a transportable steel mat, plopped onto the barren earth and mashed down by the weight of the bulky P-47s. Our briefing room was now housed in a musty tent and took on a eerie look irrespective of the time of day. One single light glowed overhead casting dancing shadows in the cavernous darkness.

It wasn't long before we were back in the air and back in the thick of the war. The first mission out, I heard a frantic call over the radio from the last man off the target, as I broke away from the target. Tail-end Charlie screamed to his element leader, "Break hard, left. Bogey coming in on your left. Nine o'clock. High!" I passed into some low clouds and before I knew it, I was in the muck all on my own. Climbing above the overcast I took a look, then started an immediate let down. Our field was not far away. At eight thousand feet I broke out of the clouds, and as I emerged, an object caught my eye at eight o'clock. It was low, maybe two thousand feet below me, steady on course and black as night. With a brisk "put... put... put," the Jerry V-1 buzz bomb sped on its course to England or maybe Antwerp.

Wilcox's lecture wasn't much help with anything in the sky other than Jerry aircraft with pilots in them, but I recalled something one of my squadron mates had told me over a gin fizz. He talked about a gyro which guided the V-1s straight ahead until they ran out of fuel, "I bet if you garbled up the gyro somehow, maybe by tipping the damned thing over, it would fall to the ground." I shoved the throttle to the wall and went into a shallow dive, following close behind the V-1 for fifty miles, plotting its course on my knee-pad map. It was on a line to Brussels and in just a matter of time it would be there. If the Jerries had everything set just right, it would run out of fuel just as it got to the city. Now was the time to try what we had talked about as we sat under our squadron slogan, drinking gin fizzes.

Surveying the area, I noticed there was mostly farmland ahead of the V-1 path. The land was plowed, but the tiny houses were far apart from one another. It looked good enough to me, so I switched on the water injection and moved up on the V-1, carefully placing my wing under its wing tip. The Doodlebug was much steadier than my Jug, probably owing to the absence of a nervous pilot flying it. "Steady, now old Jug! This is for Mom's relatives down there." With a prodding right roll of my aileron, my Jug friend tipped the V-1's right wing to the sky. Within seconds, the V-1 lost its brains and tumbled downward. Rolling back, I took a short blast at the black body as it fell, hoping to get a little camera coverage for Wilcox. What a stupid move that was. My plane lurched upwards as the V-1 burst into the open field below, barely escaping the explosion which sent hordes of mud spurting into the air.

Our club at Y-29 was built from packing crates, painstakingly arranged by members of my squadron. Op, Paul, and I shared a tent again while Picton bedded down with two of the new pilots he had gotten to know at Laon. This time we took great care to get our location close to the club so it was downhill all the way home. As we initiated the club, I had a great story to tell about my one and only encounter with a buzz bomb. Op sneered, "Mop, where in the oath did it say you had to do that? You're a damned lunatic!" He only wished he had as good of story to tell.

Coming out of a late mess, we heard the unfamiliar drone of several low flying aircraft. Instantly, the chatter of guns strafing our airfield obscured the sounds of their engines. We bolted for cover just as the planes dropped a series of green and white flares. The whole area lit up as if it were daylight, and we saw the action in the sky clearly. A British Mosquito night fighter closed on the attacking JU-88. It was a dead hit! The Junker burst out of the sky with a trail of bluish-white flames mixed with black smoke. In the fire-lit sky we could see four stark white parachutes billowing to the ground. Sandy, Paul, and I ran for a jeep and rushed toward the area where we thought the parachutes landed.

First we found a parachute and then the plane. The wreckage had impacted into a bank just outside Genk. The idea of Jerries roaming around the area was worrisome. For some time we had been on alert just in case the counter-offensive overran the base. Our instructions were to keep a side arm with us always, something we were often lax about doing.

It was late when we got back to the base. There we learned two German airmen had been captured by the local Belgians. The night proved to be a restless one with several strafing attacks piercing the quiet. I sure wished the supply sergeant would get that Thompson he promised me; I'd sleep a lot better.

Having accumulated about forty sorties I had done my share of high gravity pull-outs, and was starting to get something which only could be described as a pain in the ass. Doc Clark's prognosis was not enormously surprising, "Mop, you have a case of the piles from too many high-G pullouts." He and I both knew it wasn't from sitting on too many concrete steps, like Virginia's granny used to say. But this problem was an easy one to solve, he assured me. In fact, right in the dispensary tent he concocted some fish oil salve to slather on my underside. A bit messy, but he said a Kotex would take care of that. All I needed to do was get one of the Red Cross girls from group headquarters to give me a few Kotexs and a sanitary belt for holding them in place.

While it wasn't easy to get up the courage to ask for what I needed, I thought it was the only way to get rid of the problem. So I swallowed my pride and approached the girls with my request. "Now there's one thing I'd like to ask you," I said with complete sincerity as I prepared to leave, "Could you please keep this just between you and me? The Kotexs, I mean. You know, the guys might not understand." With a satisfying smile, she gave me her assurance, "Of course, you can trust me."

For almost a week, I dressed in the outdoor shower, so my bunk mates didn't get any funny ideas. A couple nights later as I walked into the crowded club, Sandy Ross snickered, "Mop, you're looking a little flushed this evening. I hope you don't have your sanitary belt on too tight." Clark looked up with a chuckle, "I forgot to tell you those Red Cross girls can't be trusted, they talk a lot." "Maybe you should have called your plane *The Flying Rag*," D.J. cooed.

The brief for the mission on the 17th of December was not splattered with the usual ribald joking that was such good therapy for some pilots who tended to get a little tense and needed some distraction to keep them from thinking about what has happened or what might happen. Cutting the jokes was okay with me. While I enjoyed them, I didn't think I needed them. Combat flying really got my adrenaline pumping and I thrived on it, as much as one does. I liked to treat it like it was a piece of cake, but every once in a while, the seriousness came through. Maybe this time, more than the others.

Different from most mission briefings, this one started with Wilcox's intel pitch. "Yesterday I told you there was activity developing on the front in the Ardennes. Today we have a much clearer picture of what is happening. A major counter-offensive has developed."

We had not been able to get off the ground for three days. That was the longest period we had been pinned down by the weather. The light bombers had been making their drops through the cloud cover, but all the fighter bomber activity, which was down on the deck where you can see things, had been canceled. The Germans had planned their counter offensive attack well as they were totally protected beneath the clouds. The Jerries could predict the weather on the continent down to the last snowflake, much better than we could.

Wilcox continued, "On an eighty-five mile front from Monschau in the north to Echternach in the south, the Germans have been laying ordnance of all types since early yesterday. Two SS Panzer Divisions made a deep penetration in the line and a bulge is developing on the Ardennes front. General Gerow's V Corps, which as you all know we've been supporting since early November, is under severe attack."

Operations took over and explained our function: "This mission is extremely important to the 99th Division, which is sitting right in front of this counter-offensive. We will take three flights into the target area, then break up into individual flights. The flight leaders will brief their flights separately. One final point: I know you are all eager to get back out there, but we have chosen only element leaders to make the first run. If the weather holds out, the rest of you will get a chance this afternoon."

I was to fly the wing of the Blue Flight leader, Lt. Clair Cullinan. Kennedy and Picton made up the balance of the flight. Lt. Cecil Brotton was to take Red Flight and lead the squadron. Dutch, Sandy and Johnson filled out that flight. Marv Miller was in Yellow Flight. As we formed up over the field, we turned toward the bomb line in a southeasterly direction. The weather was cold and the ground was covered with a fresh snow, anywhere from six to twelve inches. Looking down at the ground, there was no traffic on any road. All was so peaceful.

Before we had time to think about what it might be like to make an attack on a major tank offensive, we were in the target area. Blue Flight covered the area to the west of the Losheim Gap. Cloud cover was from six thousand down to three thousand feet, with the threat that our sparse views of the ground could disappear any minute. The Germans once again had the weather on their side.

Coming into the target area, I saw in full view a tank formation entering the crossroad at Bullingen. As Blue Leader positioned himself to make a run and winged over, I caught a glimpse of a flight of Me-109s closing in fast. Excitedly, I called, "Cullinan, break left!" but Blue Leader was already on his dive-bombing run. I decided to take the risk of keeping my bombs on, just in case I might get back to my primary mission. That's not what the book says to do; you're supposed to jettison your belly tank and all ordnance before boring in on the enemy. But what the hell; I had to let this thing unfold some more before I decided what to do. Who could pass up an opportunity to get one or two of those tanks sometime later? The ground-pounders really needed the help. Besides, these were SS Tankers, known for the worst kind of treatment of their enemy.

I climbed into a tight turn, full throttle. Coaching myself, I thought aloud, "I'll need water injection with these two bombs. Watch the water carefully; you can't over-do it or you'll get the engine in trouble." On my right, I saw Kennedy take a hit from ground flak. That shot was surely a mobile AA gun traveling with the tanks. I passed Kennedy as his wheels started to come down. Oh damn, they got his hydraulic supply. The attacking 109 started a tight turn to the left, pulled a wingover and started down. His wingman peeled off to the right and followed. That was his first mistake, right there; his ass was mine! There wasn't a plane in the theater that could out-dive the Jug. I could taste the victory.

If the two of them had stayed at my altitude, I never could have turned with them because of the load I was carrying. Rolling with him, I rammed the throttle forward, keeping the water off. I might need to use the water again, I thought. As I pulled closer, he must have realized he had made a mistake and racked his plane in a tight climbing turn. Quickly I took a look for his wingman. I was traveling without a wingman myself and could have been worrying about my own mistake. There was his wingman plain as day. I'd set him up at the same time, I thought. Pulling a ninety-degree deflection shot on the lead plane, the job was almost done. He was dead center, looking so pretty on the glowing orange circle which hung in front of my face. This shot would take a full deflection of one circle. I had him, and I fired.

The blitz of .50-caliber ammo hammered at the metal and the sparkle of the incendiary projectiles danced on his engine cowl only moments before a blast of deadly flames engulfed the cockpit. The burning rubble of the 109 took a slow roll to the left, then plummeted to the ground in a violent explosion which reached back to the sky. His wingman was still up there. There he was, on my tail! He had worked his way behind me as I concentrated on getting his leader. Chopping my throttle all the way back and dropping the flaps, I stomped on the left rudder and went into a skid. As long as I was in uncoordinated flight, he would have trouble getting a lead on me, which he needed to take a shot. Pulling the Jug into a tight turn, the wingman over-shot me. Thank God!

In an instant, I was on the wingman's tail, flaps up, full throttle. With about one third circle of the sight for this angle, I gave him a short burst at thirty degrees and followed him around to a tail-end chase. Then, I put the dot right on him. He had made his last mistake. I hit him at two hundred yards with a fatal burst. The plexiglas canopy blasted up first and then out shot the pilot, high into the smoke from his plane. The skeet shooting at Luke really paid off.

Pulling into a steep climb, I tried to get some altitude quickly since I was still loaded with bombs. Blinking to clear my eyes, I concentrated on every breath. Slower, I coached myself, deeper. As I sucked in the oil-drenched air of the cockpit, I felt a sweaty dampness under my jacket. Gradually each one of my senses returned. But this was no time to get too comfortable. The enemy was all around, both under me and over me. Unfortunately, the weather was starting to close in. Maybe the risk of carrying these bombs around wouldn't pay off after all.

As the sky cleared for a moment, I noticed on my left a Jug with a Me-109 going round and round in a Lufbery. I made a pass through the circle and gave the bandit a short burst, beating a tattoo of machine gun fire on his body and tail. Evasively, he rolled over into a split-S out of range. I said to my Jug, "Not today, my friend, not with these five-hundred pounders." I could never pull out at this altitude, and I'm not sure he did. By now, the weather had blanketed the ground and it was time to head for home.

Meanwhile Dutch's flight had been jumped by sixteen long-nosed FW-190s. As he started his run on the target, one FW-190 used the same technique the Me-109s had used with us. Dutch sustained damage right at the start as he turned into a climb. He dropped his bombs and with a quick wingover was on the tail of a Jerry that was closing in on his element leader. A short well-placed burst blew the 190 into a thousand pieces of metal.

Then, two 109s made a head-on pass at him and one got a cannon shot into his fuselage. Dutch managed to get his eight .50s focused on the leader, then slid over and picked off his wingman, too. The tail burst off one 109 and the other was shooting fire. With smoke pouring out of Dutch's engine and flashes of fire breaking out of the cowl, he managed to damage even another 109 before he hobbled home. Dutch pulled what the Brits called the hat trick -- three on one sortie. He brought his ship, the *Flying Dutchman*, home safely with a big limp.

Sandy saw Cullinan knock out two FW-190s. Later he flashed by a 190 pilot dropping in a parachute. Either Miller or Picton got him, both of them having dropped a 190 at the same time. Sandy got two of them himself. He blew the cockpit section out of the second 190 as he skimmed the trees while Johnson passed him driving another one into the ground.

Altogether, it was a great day. As I approached the field, I called the control van and asked permission to do a couple of victory rolls over the field. The reply came back, "Damn it, not with those five-hundred pounders under your wings!" This was the only time I had ever brought ordnance back to the field. My armament sergeant would have a little less work to do, but with the ammo I used, he had enough to keep him busy. As I shut down *La Mort's* engine, the chief crawled on the wing. I was ecstatic, saying to him, "Get out the paint brush and put a couple of swastikas on her. And be sure to leave room for more!"

Walking towards the briefing tent my thoughts turned to Ray Kennedy. I remembered last seeing him with his wheels dropping after having taken some bad flak hits. Going down was nothing new to Kennedy; he was already a member of the Caterpillar Club, comprised of pilots who had bailed out and survived. Just three months ago, he bailed out at two thousand feet when his Jug caught on fire after taking some flak. The Germans fired at him all the way to the ground, where he discarded his chute in a hedgerow and proceeded north. For two days and nights, he successfully avoided the enemy and worked his way close to our lines. He had more than enough close calls and eventually was hit by a shell fragment when he got caught in the crossfire of an artillery barrage. Confined to a hedgerow through the night, the 83rd Infantry found him and put him in the hands of Doc Clark, who had him back on flying status in two months. Kennedy surely didn't need another dose of that and I was disturbed by the thought. As though my prayers were answered, as I walked into the briefing tent, I overheard a call coming into Marmite control that Kennedy was on his approach to our field. What a relief!

That night at the club the fizzes flowed freely around the potbelly stove. With Miller and Picton each having shot down a 190 in the same engagement and with Sandy and me bagging two each, the Luke class of 44-D had six out of the mission total of thirteen. This was the highest mission count to date for the 390th. As the first squadron to give support to the Battle of the Bulge, this was only a taste of the action which would come.

Our troops lost ground as the Battle of the Bulge pressed in our direction. Hitler's grandiose plan to retake Liege and forge on to the Port of Antwerp was not as wild an idea as some of his generals thought. The German troops were heading in that direction and moving fast.

After the 17 December engagement, the lead forward air controller for the 99th Division requested that our squadron send a tactical liaison pilot to work with them. I was selected for the duty and I reckoned after forty sorties, maybe it was time to take a little break. The job called for spending a week in the front lines with a tank outfit. Specifically, I would be directing fighter bombers to their targets by radio while operating in the relative safety of a Sherman tank. My new boss was an armor commander.

With an understanding of aircraft capabilities, a pilot was better equipped to help map out the attack corridor and set priorities for the targets. There was a lot of good solid logic to that thinking, but there was still something distasteful to me about taking cover in a tank. I couldn't talk to tanks like I did my faithful Jug; they surely didn't understand pilot talk. Worse yet, tanks weren't as safe as my plane. But I was due to be grounded for a while anyway, because I was getting ahead of my squadron-mates in sorties flown.

The 2nd and 99th Divisions had taken heavy losses and were merged into one division. General Gerow put the two divisions under the command of General Robertson. I joined the battered command and was assigned to an armored division. Passing through Malmedy my jeep driver was stopped by an M.P., then diverted to the area behind Elsenborn Ridge. As we pulled away the M.P. said to the driver that our boss just got his fifth star. Eisenhower deserved the promotion; few would dispute that.

Just one day before, I had identified Elsenborn Ridge for Wilcox as the area where one of the 109s I shot, had gone down. The command area where we were headed was on the edge of the Ridge. Perhaps it was a morbid thought, but I always wanted to see one of those Jerry planes close up, in a heap on the ground.

When we entered the command area, the duty officer told me to join the 2nd Armored Division to the South. On the drive down the jeep driver related a first-hand story of two Sherman tanks that had broken down near Rocherath. They dug into an enclosed area off the road and let five Tiger tanks pass, then knocked them out by hitting their soft armor in the back. The tail-end approach seemed to be as good for the tankers as it was for the fighter pilots. Maybe we did have something in common with them after all.

All said, duty with tankers was an interesting experience, though not one I wished to repeat. They had a language all their own. Also, they had one way of doing things. That way was their own, which was proscribed to the most trifling level of detail. Instead of the army-issue OD woolen jackets, I normally wore the winter sheepskin outfit used by bomber pilots. While it was warm, it sure stood out and the ground-pounders liked to remind me just how much it did. If the tenseness of the battle had not been hanging over these tankers, I am sure I would have taken an even more relentless ribbing. There was nothing they could say, however, which would convince me to trade our jobs.

Pilots of the 8th Air Force and the 9th always had an image of ground-pounders having a risky, dirty job. The ground-pounders thought of us as being a little soft, since we always returned from a mission to a warm bed and some friendly conversation. Many of them didn't even get to take their boots off at night.

To dispel some of the tension between the two groups, General Hoyt. S. Vandenberg, who commanded the 9th Air Force, passed the word down to his pilots that we were an outfit that was there for one reason, that was to support the ground forces. The word got around to the ground troops that they would be getting a little more respect, but by then our differences were really not so noticeable. Many pilots were now living in soggy mildewed tents right on the front-line battle area, close to where the troops were holed up.

The way the German drive was going, our temporary field at Asch was under the threat of being overrun any day. XXIX Tac moved from Maastricht to Saint-Trond to avert difficulties if a hasty withdrawal was necessary. IX Tac remained at Liege for now, but was on alert to move at a moment's notice.

Weather kept the fighter bombers on the ground for most of my time with the 2nd Armored Division. In addition, both IX and XXIX Tac were transferred on the 21st of December to temporarily support the British 2nd Tactical Air. This left me with little control action, so the tankers merely put me to work at their sides. I became one of them, whether I liked it or not. The second night in my new role, we bedded down in a basement of a shelled-out building. The tank commander told me to sleep on top of the stored flour in a sleeping bag, fully clothed and ready to go. We were the lucky ones; we were able to stop to let the supplies and ammo catch up. Artillery kept up their harassment throughout the night.

All night long, shells blasted over the front line. Although the tankers sharing the flour sacks could tell whether a shell was coming in or going out, I didn't know the difference, so I was the only one that got some sleep.

It soon became apparent to intel that a German drive was on to split American and British forces by plowing right through them and charging on to Antwerp. While the air action was minimal, the action on the ground was fierce. Most of our skirmishes were with infantry units and fortunately not with Panzer tank columns. Still, our own Sherman tanks moving full bore were enough to shake the kidneys out of an orangutan, and my kidneys and I were damned happy when my replacement showed up, and I went back to the squadron.

Three days later a driver from the 2nd Armored Support came to pick up another pilot for control duty. He told me the 2nd had a tremendously successful engagement with a Panzer division. A forward column of the 2nd Panzer was spotted by someone in a jeep who got the word to the task force commander, Lt. Colonel O'Farrell. Setting up their Shermans along the road in ambush position, they annihilated the German column without much trouble. The Panzers were carrying gas strapped to the sides of their tanks and a well-placed blast set off a show as spectacular as the Fourth of July fireworks.

The night I got back, Op told me about a mission he flew the day I departed. While making a run on a marshalling yard, his flight leader Bob Goff had taken a 20-mm. AA hit which took the top piston or two off his engine. With oil spewing over the cowl and canopy of Bob's plane, Op and a couple others tried to lead him back to the base. Bob's visibility was zero under the oiled canopy. His crippled Jug was losing altitude rapidly and with one Jug on each wing, Op and the others decided to guide him into a farm field so he could belly in, wheels up. Approaching a wind-breaking row of tall alders alongside a large field, they told Bob to lock his shoulder straps. Op eased Bob in, "Okay Bob, easy does it. Pick up the nose and we are going up over some trees and into an empty field......OH SHIT!" As they broke over the trees, there stood a two story brick farmhouse, as big as day. Bob slammed into the second story. And, when the dust settled Op and the others could see he didn't come out. Their hearts sank, and the field sadly reported that Bob Goff had bought the farm.

The next day Goff showed up back at the squadron, almost as good as new. He had shinnied out of the old Jug. It was a tight squeeze because the turbo-charger was shoved against him; but he made it with hardly a scrape. Then he walked down the staircase, apologized to the lady of the house for the damages and flagged a ride to the field. Goff was rotated back to the States and I didn't even have a chance to say good-bye.

On the 24th, the weather broke and the field came alive again. Everyone was restless and eager to get into the air. The 101st Airborne Division was in Bastogne surrounded by Germans. Patton's 4th Armored Division had been driving hard against the opposition since the 22nd and had only twenty more miles to Bastogne. That was not an unreasonable distance for Patton's outfit, which usually outran its own supply support, then had to slow up for them. But in front of Patton was the German crack 5th Parachute Division, equipped with a large complement of antitank guns.

Our Tac brief showed the 4th Armored Division broken into two columns, separated East to West by about four miles. We were to support the western column's effort to retake the town of Chaumont. A strong enemy contingent of infantry, tanks and antitank guns held the advance of our commands.

Wilcox warned us, "The German troops are moving with their own AA guns and there are lots of them. Remember, you can expect the largest concentration of Jerry fighters that we've ever seen on the continent. The allied tanks are carrying two yellow stripes on their tops to designate them.

But, be awful damned cautious, they sometimes forget to change from yesterday's designator."

We were loaded out with four five-inch rockets and one five-hundred pound bomb. I was flying the lead of the second element of Blue Flight, my favorite element lead. In a matter of minutes, we were off.

We took a little more time than usual to look over the ground activity from the air. We knew the flak would be stirred when we dropped down, but that would give us more to strafe on the way out. This time we had to be careful though, since we were as close as we had ever worked to our own troops. Circling close to the town, we waited to see if we would get an input from a forward air controller. No such luck; we would have to find our own targets.

As Blue Leader winged over to make a drop on what he had called out as a small concentration of supplies stored north of town, I spotted two vehicles ahead of a tank going into the north end of town moving parallel to the Sure River.

I pointed the targets out to my wingman, but he had trouble seeing them. I told him, "Lag a bit behind and watch my tracers." It would be best if I could get within gun range before launching my rockets, I thought. While doing a wingover, I took a quick look across my shoulder to see if there were any bogies in sight. Checking my ass was too important a task to leave to a wingman with whom I'd never flown. I needed to get up to speed to insure the right trajectory for the rockets. Pouring on the coal, I held my Jug steady on course.

As I started down, three more tanks appeared along the river coming out of a small wooded area about a half mile farther North. Nervously I hummed, *I'll be home for Christmas*. Tomorrow was Christmas Day and it looked like the 101st would have to spend it alone. At one thousand yards I let all the rockets go and hastily put my gun sight on the vehicles. The Jug spit out enough ammo to make hamburger out of the trucks. One of the trucks exploded into a massive fireball. My rockets undershot; I just didn't have enough speed. I needed more altitude for the dive.

Rapidly turning my attention to the tanks along the river, I pulled out of my dive at three hundred feet. There was not a puff of flak in the sky. That was no reason to drop my guard, however. Some of those bandits could get you before you saw them. I aimed to place the five-hundred pounder in the center of the tanks alongside the river. It now looked like there were more than three. As I did a quick break off the target and started into a climb, I glanced over my shoulder at my target. My luck was much better with the bomb than with the rockets. The delayed fuse allowed the bomb to embed itself in the soft earth under one of the tanks before going off. The mangled tanks toppled over the edge of the bank before anyone could tell them, *Kilroy was here.*

Christmas morning was quiet. Before the squadron woke, I slipped into the makeshift shower, which we had made from a wing tank placed on top of a wood stand high enough to give us pressure at the shower head. A potbellied stove heated the water through a jerry-built coil. The whole thingamajig worked about as good as it sounds. Mom would be proud of me, crouched in this tent in the subzero weather, getting all clean to celebrate her birthday. Today she would be forty-four and I had just turned twenty, two months before.

After my quick shower, I hurriedly trotted back to my tent to see if Paul and Op would like to get up and have a little SOS with me for breakfast. D.J. called to me, breaking my stride. A frosty fog spewed out with each word, "Mop you're on for the afternoon mission. The brief is in ten minutes. But don't go and get yourself killed, 'cause we have a dance in Hasselt tonight."

The brief started at 0100 hours with the captain giving his usual spiel: "The 101st repelled an attack on the northern perimeter of Bastogne. Over twenty tanks participated in the attack, so we know they're still in the area. We're going out with two flights. Yellow Flight will go on a recon north of Bastogne. Red Flight will go south of Bastogne to support the 4th Armored Division. Both Flights would get target instructions from the forward air controller in the area." We had orders to stay as a squadron until we got into the vicinity of Bastogne. The intent was to fly over Bastogne and let them know, even though it was Christmas Day, we were braced for action.

Wilcox came on next, "The captain has told you the situation on the north side of Bastogne. On the south side of town, the 4th Armored Division is now split into three columns, all heading toward Bastogne. The column to the far west is in the lead. You will be working close to our troops, so you *must* have positive target identification. AA in the area is reportedly light, and our vehicles are marked with a red fore and aft stripe. Merry Christmas and see you before dark!"

I was leading the Red Flight second element, which was the best position to be in for supporting a tank column. Once the first element spotted a target, the second element had plenty of time to set up to make the kill. The armament sergeant would load us out with two five-hundred pounders and a belly tank. That's almost max load for the old Jug. We were going to stay in the area for some time.

It had snowed that night, so we could see the tracks in the open fields. We'd track those Jerries just the way Koke and I used to track muskrats by the Willamette River. I snickered to myself; things had not changed so much, we were after the rats again. The tank tracks would show up like roads from above, we couldn't miss them. We split up. Heading south for about a minute, Yellow Leader made contact with a liaison flight officer on the ground. The *angel on the ground*, as the tankers called them, saw us overhead and requested help for his outfit. There were antitank guns holding up the right column of the 4th Armored Division at Remicham-pagne, about five miles from Bastogne. He offered assistance, saying "I'll put some smoke markers on the target area and call out the position from those markers." Within a few minutes smoke was drifting up from the ground, two red plumes and one yellow. The voice on the radio guided us from there, "The guns are dug in about one hundred yards from the yellow marker on a line that runs to the center of the baseline between the two red markers." We had to think a moment about that one. What did we have, some damned mathematician as a forward air controller?

The day was starting to wane; we had taken off from Asch later than we planned because two aircraft were forced to abort while still on the ground. Circling the field we waited for replacements before pressing on to the target area. Ground fog was starting to build, and it was getting hard to see. But we got the target identified after a little more talk among the flight leader, the angel and myself. Jointly we agreed we would unload the whole four thousand pounds, all at once. Dropping our belly tanks, we went into a series of wingovers toward the target. Thunderous flak started to pop; soon the sky filled with fluffy white puffs from Jerry's mobile 20-mms. Wouldn't intel ever get this right?

As we broke from the target, my Jug began to lose power. One of those puffs of white cotton must have clobbered me, but I hadn't felt it. "What's the problem old Jug, you in a little trouble?" I asked almost sulkily. No one else was in sight. Everyone had separated in the scattered fog and low clouds, so I started back to Asch alone. On the way home, my fuel gauge rocked too close to low and my engine sputtered disturbingly. Things felt a little better as I cruised at six thousand feet, where the clouds had cleared away in spots and the sun was out again. It would be a good night for a dance.

Dropping down into Liege, I saw four Me-109s at two thousand feet. Bad timing, I thought. I had to use my head on these bandits. Not only was I traveling short of power, I was probably carrying some of Jerry's iron in me. I tried to set up a pass out of the sun but it just didn't come together. There would be no time to devise a strategy if they saw me; I would lose the advantage.

The only way out of this mess was to take on all four of them at the same time. Rolling over I did a split-S to get max speed out of my ailing Jug, then a half roll, going straight for tail-end charlie who was lagging a little behind. It's just plain dumb to lag in that position. They saw me just as I got within range. I held my Jug at four hundred yards, then let the Jug eat on the laggard just a little. Closing in to the perfect range, I gave him another blast. The 109 wrenched to the left and the canopy exploded as the .50-caliber ammo sprayed his cockpit.

The balance of the flight scattered in every direction. That was the end of whatever the hell they were up to. Tail-end charlie rolled into a screaming dive to the ground and I gave him one last blast in the tail section for good measure. He went into the ground on the outskirts of Liege. But, I had been so intent on trying to get all four Jerries that I had violated the cardinal rule; cover your ass when you are alone.

"What the hell! Typhoons! Careful you bastards, watch what you're doing." Before I knew what happened, four British Typhoons blew out of the sun and blasted me hard, no doubt mistaking me for a 109 or more probably for a FW-190. No sooner did I feel the shock of bullets rip at my plane than the flight broke, surely having realized their mistake. "Just my luck, running into a bunch of bloody limeys who can't tell a Nazi from a Yank. Damn those half-blind s.o.b.s!" Lucky they didn't get more strikes on me; I wasn't yet sure if I would make it home.

Coming back into Asch, it was starting to get dark. My crippled bird sounded rough, too rough for that victory roll I always wanted to do. But there was little time to worry about that; first I had to get my Jug and me on the ground. Enemy fighters had a field day with crippled birds, but I wasn't all that sure my ill fate would be so glorious. Having sustained damage to the right aileron, my right wing was acting like it wanted to get on the ground ahead of the rest of the plane. My Jug was complaining bitterly at every instruction I gave it. Anticipating the worst, I snapped my shoulder harness in the locked position. It pulled snug against me; I knew the whole Jug could fall apart and the seat wouldn't release the grip I felt. Rocking downward toward the runway, I prayed for the best. Suddenly, *La Mort* lurched to the ground with her injured wing dangerously low. Before I could react, the right landing gear smashed into the runway. Only a Jug would hold up under such abuse.

As the chief checked out *La Mort*, he shook his head, "It's lucky you got on the ground on the first pass. You wouldn't have made it around the field for a second try." Only when *La Mort* came home a little too shot up, was it obvious that the chief considered the iron beast his plane too. *La Mort* was just as much his baby as it was mine, and he fretted every little scratch and lost a little sleep over every major calamity.

The guys thought it was nothing short of hilarious that the British tried to shoot me down. It was an accident, I'm sure, but it became just another great story to tell around a gin fizz this Christmas day.

On the way to the dance at Hasselt, we stopped at a coal mine that was on the way. Brulle had made arrangements for us to take showers in the miners' locker room. The Flemish which Brulle learned from his Belgian mom came in handy on such occasions. Because almost everyone was going out, there was no hot water in our shower and we had to get all the sweat off us somehow. Hardly a mission went by that I didn't sweat through a flight suit and this one today was a little worse than usual.

We drew a weapons carrier out of the motor pool and a sergeant to go with it. After the shower, Op, Paul, and I planned to stop at a cafe on the edge of Hasselt and pick up three girls we had met on previous trips. Their father owned the cafe, which was also a pretty good place for a black market meal. As we came out of the shower, I noticed my .45 Colt was missing from its holster. If it wasn't bad enough that someone stole my status symbol, they had to do it while I was jaybird naked. Though it was annoying to have lost it in such an undramatic way, the .45 to this point had served little purpose to me. Maybe now I could get that Thompson submachine gun I had requested. That wise-cracking Camp Pendleton marine sergeant told me I would have to do that anyway if I wanted to hit anything.

Our driver dropped us off at the cafe, then proceeded to the dance with a few other guys. In practically no time the three of us had consumed a greasy plate of eggs and bacon, which was far superior to our normal rations. Twenty dollars was what it cost, which seemed a hefty sum for friends of the family like us. We paid the price without voicing our complaint, then walked the Belgian restaurateur's daughters to the center of town.

The sergeant hovered over the weapons carrier he had parked in the town square. There was no reason for him to stand in the cold alone, so we told the sarge to take the rotor out of the distributor and go have some fun himself. We would meet him back in the square at midnight.

The local band did a fair job of playing some American songs we all knew, but we didn't do much dancing. Seems we talked about girls when we were at the field and talked about flying when we were with girls. If anyone wanted to have fun with a girl, he had to get away from this group. The guys were always clowning or harping on someone for doing something. I was the topic of conversation this night with Op grabbing the microphone and ranting about the great Battle of Britain which took place with me on the wrong side. The belief grew until it became a fact that the Brits had shot me down.

About 2300 hours the sarge came running frantically to us. Sheer panic squeezed his gut as he belched, "Someone stole our truck!" Only then did we wonder if maybe everyone who wanted free transportation carried their own rotor. Regardless, the dance was over for us and we briskly walked the girls home. When Op, Paul and I got to the cafe, we called the field and leaned on the duty officer to drive the fifteen miles into Hasselt and retrieve all the stragglers. He agreed to meet us at the square in an hour.

I slipped out of the cafe in the arms of my girl, Marie. Without a word, she led me to the combination barn and blacksmith shop where a half dozen cows warmed the cold air. It was cozy enough for what we came to call the *English lay*. We'd learned by now that the Belgians were outdone only by the Brits when it came to doing it standing up. Although the girls claimed they wouldn't get pregnant if they were standing, I suspect the vertical position had more to do with the constant threat of war in their backyards or maybe just plain convenience. Regardless, we could all be thankful no priggish flight surgeon or anyone else had invented panty hose yet. There was nothing in our way, not even the threat of clap.

Marie was almost four inches taller than me, and the whole act called for a little Yankee ingenuity. I found a large anvil on the ground in the barn and stood precariously on it, balancing my hands around her waist. As I drew her nearer, I felt the mountain of clothing which separated us, every ill-placed button and every thick layer of scratchy wool. Fumbling in the cold air, I at last found intense warmth, and my legs turned to drifting columns of sand, slowly collapsing onto the frozen earth. We parted, our hands reaching to each other, knowing we may or may not come together again.

Strutting into town with the guys, I related the story which now felt strange, almost like a fleeting dream. Thinking to myself, I characterized the incident as swift, transient and intense, like most our engagements. Still Op wanted to hear every detail and I divulged them willingly, albeit slightly overblown. Me, standing resolutely on the anvil. Marie begging passionately for pure, unadulterated animal sex and nuzzling her soft breasts against my chest. The trembling of her moist lips as they met mine and her roving tongue.   Yes, ah yes, that soft tongue, the genuine ecstasy which it commanded. Marie was the seductress we'd all talked about so many times in the bar. The one we always longed to meet and the one we always bragged we had met. The intent of the stories we all told was to instill envy into the groin of every man who overheard. Sure, we all discounted much of the talk, but there were few listeners who didn't have a nagging thought they were somehow missing out. Something someone else had, which they didn't. After I finished the story, Op said mischievously, "Are you going to have to carry an anvil with you all the time?"

It took a little discussion, but we all agreed we would pay for the truck to keep the sarge from losing his stripes. The group lawyer prepared all the necessary papers; it was all very ridiculous. We scoffed: any vehicle like that would have to be in the hands of another unit. No one calls *that* stealing. The guys who appropriated the truck would simply grab a paintbrush and change our unit code on the bumper to theirs. The truck was still in the hands of Uncle Sam. Didn't this pencil-pushing lawyer know that? Something told us we wouldn't hear the end of this for a long time.

Late Christmas Day, 1944, Op and I were out walking our strip, reminiscing over our past year in the service. As we started back to the club, a plane loomed in the night. It was a clear cold night and we thought by its outline that it must be one of our P-61 Black Widow night fighters on its way back from a mission. Those guys could have all that night flying stuff they wanted. It sure wasn't for me. Just then, the night split open as the plane strafed the trees standing beside our club and tents. "ACK! ACK! ACK!" our field responded with a clamor. Every gun on the field cut lose. Blinding tracers engulfed the aircraft. It was a Junkers-88 Lotsen bomber that the Germans used as a night fighter. He had just unloaded a payload of anti-personnel bombs, which fortunately landed short of the area where our tents were situated. Seconds later, the engine on the plane lit up and exploded. The bomber went into a low shallow dive, out of sight of the field and into the ground. We ran back to the club. Fortunately, everyone was okay. No one had even considered jumping into the slit trenches dug alongside the tent since they were all full of snow. What the hell were these Germans up to?

Between Christmas and the end of the year we did not miss a day at the front and I got in another eight sorties, bringing my total to fifty-one. Adding to the long list of tanks, trains, guns and vehicles that we blasted out of service, our squadron was doing a good job of proving how well the Jug could perform in the role of ground support.

Lt. Col. Clure Smith was the deputy commander of our group and considered by many including myself to be the best all around pilot we had. On occasion he would take over the lead position of our squadron. On the 11th of December he had taken the 390th to Euskirchen, twenty miles south of Cologne. Two of our classmates, Johnson and DeWyke, had the good fortune to go along with their Jugs crammed full of rockets and bombs. They caught a trainload of flatcars loaded with tanks and got all fifty-two of them. That was one quarter of the tank strength of a German armored division on its way to support the largest single battle of the war. Lt. James Campsi strafed the train on the way down and the results were captured on some film which had just come back. I spent one whole night of the holiday season reviewing this action and picking up tips on what a squadron could do to a trainload of the toughest freight there is.

The fighting in the Bulge was grueling and took its toll. Everyday, flak in the area was building and we were losing more and more pilots. In a four-day period the R.A.F. 2nd and the U.S. 9th Air Force flew 17,500 sorties. An untold number of pilots and planes were lost during the same four days, though we never thought it wise to ask how many.

The year wound up with the squadron having a New Year's party in the club. "I want to go home this year," was the battle cry heard over the clinking beer glasses, a cry which grew more intense as the evening wore on.

Captain Lowell Smith motioned me to the door of the club, and asked me to take a stroll down the steel mat runway to talk about the next morning's mission. I wasn't drinking that night because I knew I was on early call to get off the ground right after daybreak. Captain Smith told me Sandy Ross had been put in for the Distinguished Flying Cross for his flight on the 1st of December and I had been put in for the Silver Star for the 17th of December and another Silver Star for Christmas Day. The news couldn't have made me happier. As crazy as it sounds, these things are important to combat men, including myself. *Gallantry in action* somehow sounded good to us and it was sort of a status symbol to hang new fruit salad on our uniforms. Probably more important, it would make my folks real proud. It was a real button-buster for all of us.

The moon was out, shining bright, through and around the clouds. It was a good night for the wolves to bay, but most of that happened at the club. The lyrics flowed from the pine trees onto the strip. *The Battle Hymn of the Republic* took on new words:

She wears her pink pajamas,
In the summer when it's hot;
She wears a woolen nightie,
In the winter when it's not;

And sometimes in the springtime,
And sometimes in the fall;
She jumps between the sheets,
With nothing on at all!

Glory, glory for the springtime and the fall,
Glory, glory for the springtime and the fall;
When she jumps between the sheets,
With nothing on at all!

Though most of the guys liked it, that song was a little too prissy for my taste. My favorite was the one we sang next, which was a carry-over from our days in the back room at the *Westward Ho* in Phoenix:

Oh, there are no fighter pilots down in hell.
Oh, there are no fighter pilots down in hell.
The place is full of queers, navigators, bombardiers.
But there are no fighter pilots down in hell!

Oh, there are no fighter pilots in the states.
Oh, there are no fighter pilots in the states.
They are off to foreign shores, making mothers out of whores.
Oh there are no fighter pilots in the states!

Oh, there are no fighter pilots up in Group.
Oh, there are no fighter pilots up in Group.
The place is full of brass, sitting 'round on their fat ass.
Oh there are no fighter pilots up in Group!

When, a bomber jockey walks into a club.
When, a bomber jockey walks into a club.
He doesn't drink his share of suds, all he does is flub his dub,
But there are no fighter pilots down in hell!

Oh, it's naughty, naughty, naughty, but it's nice.
If you ever do it once you'll do it twice.
It'll wreck your reputation, but increase the population,
Oh, it's naughty, naughty, naughty, but it's nice!

Our songs were always followed by a few toasts. It was Op's turn to do the honor. Op looked around and saw a couple of P-51 pilots leaning on the bar. He lifted his glass, saying, "I'm an asshole, I'm an asshole, I'm an asshole, yes, I am; but I'd rather be an asshole than to fly a P-51."

A rangy 51 pilot had a quick come-back, "A toast to you, my friend! I hope they bury me upside down, so you can kiss my ass." Unfortunately I was going to leave before the fun started; I had to fly the next day.

As I left the club I saw a poker game breaking up. D.C. Johnson had apparently been winning and was complaining about everyone not rushing back to the table. He surely had no cause to scream, because he never lost. As a California boy, he probably learned the game before he learned to walk. At Luke, he used to take my money, and I had learned not to play with him. I was glad the game was over. In fact, I hoped D.C. would hit the sack since he was flying my wing in the morning.

Still a little tired, I staggered to the mess hall before sunrise. A choice of powdered eggs or corn mush was offered. That was an easy decision since the powdered eggs always tasted like stale chalk. Johnson was nowhere in sight, so I stopped by his tent to roll him out. We didn't have much time to spare; it was getting light. Stretching his flight suit over his ragged woolen pajamas, he told me he got a game going last night in his tent and bragged he had gotten a piece of hide off the butts of two P-51 pilots from across the field. I told D.C., if they were going to try to play the game we play over in the Bulge, they'll lose their whole ass.

Sharing our field was the 352nd Fighter Group from the 8th Air Force, a bunch of hot rock P-51 fighter pilots who spent most of their careers escorting bombers. They had an impressive kill record, which we all had to admire. The Group Commander was Colonel J. C. Meyer, leading ace of the 8th Air Force. They were here to provide assistance in the Battle of the Bulge.

Ground support was a new mission for the 8th Air Force. There wasn't anyone who wouldn't tell you it was the riskiest work a fighter pilot could do. Many an ace from the 8th and 9th bought the farm on strafing runs. Wilcox always reminded us that *strafe* in German meant *to punish with death*, and the punishment went both ways. Few would disagree, when we gave away our altitude, we gave away the most important advantage we had. Unfortunately, the 51 had a built-in disadvantage, since it had a liquid-cooled engine and could be brought down with small arms fire from the ground.

We knew the 47 would take whatever it was given. Jugs had brought back pilots when the guts of their engines were hanging out like the transmission on Dad's car after a bad goon shift. But, when you got into a dogfight, the 51 was hard to beat. Comparing the 51 to the 47 was like comparing a ballerina to a stagehand. Given a choice though, I'd stick with my tough old Jug. That agile thin-skinned plane with light armor and light armament was for those who flew a bit higher than us.

At the brief, Captain Smith gave the mission rundown. We were going on an armed recon mission in the area contained by the Battle of the Bulge. Two flights were going up and we were to stay together. Smith would lead the squadron and I took the element lead in his Red Flight. D.C. Johnson was my wingman and Lt. Jack Kennedy was Smith's wingman.

Yellow Flight was led by Lt. John Feeney. His wingman was Joe Lackey. Bob Brulle led the second element, with Currie Davis on his wing. We were loaded out with antitank rockets and five-hundred pound bombs. Weather was the usual cloud cover and there was no sign we would have any trouble in the target area. Wilcox ended with a typical upbeat comment, "Happy New Year."

Walking out to the plane, I was glad I hadn't spent the night drinking. Still with all the interruptions, I felt like I had put a full night in at Samuel's cabin drinking our favorite gut-rot. We were going out about fifteen minutes early and the crew chiefs had just finished warming up the planes. In our winter flight boots, we kicked up glittery puffs of snow with each step. I was thinking of what this year would bring. My thoughts fell to the guys who were walking at my side. All had taken on a certain seriousness and sense of purpose. I, like them, considered ourselves men, yet we were still boys at heart. That was easy to tell simply by watching what we did with our free time and listening to us talk. However when we stepped into the cockpit it was serious, life-or-death business.

Captain Smith was the oldest of the group, reserved in a manner typical of the pipe smoker he was. Word was out he was going to be made squadron commander and he would stay in the service after the war was over. He didn't mingle with the other men of the squadron and must have thought of himself as a disciplined regular. Some guys called him *Smitty*, although I always called him *Sir*. His talk the night before with me was to show me he was really one of us. I wasn't convinced I could count on him in a pinch. There was no reason for saying this; it was just a gut feeling.

The captain's wingman, Jack Kennedy, was a red-headed East-coast boy I liked from the first time we met. He was aggressive and I knew he would be reliable. You could forget about him when you swooped down on a target; he would cover your ass. We flew together on other missions and I knew what he could do.

My wingman and classmate Johnson was a flight officer. Johnson flew the way he played poker, aggressive with one goal in mind--to win. I jokingly said once that I hoped he wouldn't wander off my tail trying to fill out a flush. But I felt comfortable with him on my wing. He would stay with me all the way to the ground on a bombing run. Not everyone would.

John Feeney, leading Yellow Flight, was like the captain. He was reserved and I noticed he always wandered off when we were sitting around telling stories about our amorous affairs. He was an enigma to me and in a way I was glad I didn't have to rely on him, because I didn't know him well enough. We would probably take the two flights down on separate targets.

John's wingman, Joe Lackey, was a F/O and was one of the newer pilots in the squadron. Joe was a good drinking buddy, enjoying all our stories whether they were about flying or girls. Perhaps I'd get to know him better but for now I didn't have to rely on him.

Bob Brulle was leading the last element. He had all the characteristics of the memories I had of my rugged Belgian relatives in Canada. We had flown together before and while we were going up in different flights, it was good to know he was up there with me.

Currie Davis was one of the newer pilots, flying tail-end charlie, the riskiest position going out and coming back. Bogies always tried to pick off the tail-end position first, with everyone taking a lick on the way past. We all had to start there. The most obvious thing about Davis was his good looks. He was one of those guys the public relations people liked to catch crawling out of a cockpit for a recruiting or bond drive poster. Since he came into the squadron with Lackey, I was sure they felt good about being on a mission together, just the way I did when one of my classmates was with me.

Some of the guys seemed uptight before they went out on these missions. It appeared as though they would fall apart if anyone slapped them on the back in jest. The rest of us seemed to take it more in stride. We were the risk-takers of the group, the ones who thrived on our aggressiveness. Maybe we were just too stupid to sense the danger; maybe it was just the way we were.

I don't know how anyone felt about flying on my wing. In the short time I had been with the squadron, I had earned a reputation of being able to see tiny flecks in the sky or on the ground long before anyone else -- and more importantly long before the enemy saw me. But the truth of the matter was, a pilot had to be damned careful he didn't lose his ass when he flew the wing of someone like me. Perhaps I would press into an area blurred to the wingman's eyes, forcing him to face dangers he did not see. His alternative was to hold back, where he risks falling easy prey to bandits which were forever lurking in the clouds.

As I approached my plane, the symmetry of all the aircraft setting along the edge of the mesh runway reflected the confidence of our not seeing enemy aircraft in the area. But after the JU-88 episode the previous week, I wasn't sure our confidence was warranted. Sergeant Michano was rubbing down *La Mort's* wings with wax as I walked up. "Trying to cut down the friction, sir. You'll need every little bit of speed I can get out of this baby. By the way, she's in rare form; sounded like a dream when I ran her up earlier."

As I crawled into the cockpit, the three black swastikas painted below the canopy caught my eye. "I'd sure like an opportunity to add a few more," I said to the chief as he helped me strap into my parachute and then checked my safety harness. He fretted over me like a mother hen, sweating every mission and worrying every detail. I handed my winter boots to him, and he gave me the thumbs up as I gave him a wink. It was strictly *verboten* to fly in dress shoes, but they gave me a better feel and more control on the rudders.

La Mort responded to the early morning start with a rough cough. Within moments she was purring and my crew chief and armament sergeant guided me, one on each side. Smith and his wingman pulled out, and I followed close behind. The time was 0915 according to the clock on my dash; we were out fifteen minutes early. The officer on the runway gave me the wave on to the flight strip. "Keep them rolling," he motioned with his arms. It was a brutally cold day to have wave-off duty; the Jug threw such a hurricane. As I rolled down the runway, vapor sprayed from the prop and wings, and a wreath of misty light with a tinge of rainbow obscured Smith's plane.

"Good luck, sir," my crew chief yelled to the sky as he threw a high-ball. His voice vanished under the deafening thunder of our engines. Seconds later I rocketed into the air directly behind the first element. Taking off to the west we started our first turn around the field for the join up. As we climbed over the field, I could see the 352nd group crew chiefs at the west end of the field readying their P-51s. After our first three-sixty of the field, Yellow Flight started to join up with us. Once more around and we would veer off to the target.

As Captain Smith started his turn westward, his wingman called out, "Flak puffs to the East!" Wilcox had not told us about any expected problems in that area so I quickly focused on the swarm of activity. Visibility was virtually unlimited and I saw the raid blasting towards us. Excitedly I alerted Smith to the incoming German fighter sweep, "RELIC RED FLIGHT LEADER, THIS IS MOP! BANDITS, LOTS OF 'EM. TWO O'CLOCK, LOW! COMING IN ON THE DECK!" Captain Smith could not see them at first, "Mop you take the lead!" "Roger!" I responded instinctively, still surveying the situation. The enemy planes were at treetop level, anywhere from fifty to eighty of them. They had just hit the British 2nd Tactical Airfield at Y-32, and it was the Brits' AA guns that Jack Kennedy had seen.

The adrenaline surged through every blood vessel in my body, and my heart pounded wildly. This was my first time leading the squadron and I was facing a raid the size of which we'd never seen before. I could feel a surge of sweat saturate my flight suit as I jettisoned my bombs and racked my plane around for a head-on pass at the closest 190. He broke left, whipping away from our field. Thrusting the throttle full forward, my Jug seized the distance between us and I was smack on his tail. With a couple short bursts, *La Mort* consumed him. First the armor-piercing and incendiary projectiles shattered the oil and gas lines, then a huge fireball belched from his engine. He plowed into the forest from about two hundred feet with a terrific explosion. "Good show!" yelled Johnson.

Turning slightly, I pulled onto the tail of what was probably his wingman cruising at treetop level. We started a Lufbery and got through the first three hundred and sixty degrees. Through the tight turn, I tried desperately to keep a full circle of gun sight lead on him. Then my Jug hesitated in what felt like a high speed stall, reminding me I was still carrying a full load of rockets. He was still in my sight as I squeezed the trigger, spraying the wingman with a stream of machine-gun fire. Fifty--caliber slugs were striking him everywhere as the deafening sound of ripping metal pierced the air. Seconds later the plane crashed to the ground and a mushroom of black smoke billowed upwards. This should have given the 51s an opportunity to get off the field, I hoped, though little time had passed. The eight of us needed help soon; ten to one odds in Jerry's favor were simply too overwhelming.

As I climbed to gain a little altitude, I spotted a FW-190 on Johnson's tail. "Johnson. . .Break left!" Before the 190 could react, I got in a good deflection, striking him in the fuselage. In the ruckus Johnson shook him. Another FW-190 lurked on the deck, an easy target I thought, since his low altitude would pay off. Within seconds I got on his tail and let go of two rockets. Both were low. Correcting, I fired another two rockets higher and the bandit burst into a massive ball of orange and red flames. Glancing back at my wingman, I spotted an Me-109 on his tail. Pulling a hard turn to the right, I slid behind the 109 as he pressed on Johnson's tail. As he came into my sight, I blasted him hard. His fuselage ripped into a thousand pieces to the pounding of my guns and he crashed to the ground in a fiery heap. The sky blackened as I climbed steeply in a turn, giving *La Mort* full power and water injection. In the muck below was a 51 on the tail of an Me-109. The 487th had arrived! God kiss them all!

Rolling over and pointing the Jug straight down, I made a ninety--degree deflection shot, inflicting strikes along the full length of the Me-109 and shaking him off the tail of the 51. Then I broke off the attack to take on another 109 heading for our field. The 109 was at two hundred feet; I was above him about one hundred feet. Turning on the water injection and full throttle, I hoped the extra manifold pressure which the chief had added would pay off. I was dangerously low on ammunition and this was the last time I dared use water injection. One try was all I had. I was gaining on him fast and didn't want to over-shoot. Letting the deflection angle go close to zero, his wings more than filled the gun sight circle. He was closer than the three hundred yards at which the guns converge. At two hundred yards, I let the guns run out as he took a full blast. The eight .50-caliber guns, which shot over seven thousand rounds a minute, hacked at his wing and engine. A stream of oily smoke trailed him as he blasted towards the ground and disappeared in the muck.

I called *Marmite*, the field control van and told him I was coming straight in. Seconds later I dropped my wheels and flaps and landed short on the strip, heading right into the parking area. As I pulled into *La Mort's* stall, I chopped the throttle immediately and yelled to the chief, "Load her up, I'm going back out." I didn't need any fuel; I had plenty.

Without so much as a word, Sergeant Michano jumped on the wing, unsnapped my harness and hauled me out of the plane. The field was still under attack and they weren't about to reload. He flung me into a slit trench alongside the plane. My flying was over for the day.

At the mission debrief, the events of the day unfolded. Johnson bagged two 109s but fell prey to a Jerry he didn't see until it was too late. He bailed out and landed near a German aircraft which had bellied in. The pilot was dead in his cockpit, so Johnson took his papers and also his pistol as ante for his next poker game. The papers showed, one of us had gotten Lt. Colonel Guenther Specht, leader of JG-11, who just happened to be a German ace with an impressive thirty-two victories to his name. Johnson borrowed a bicycle and rode back to the field in style, sort of like filling out a flush.

Captain Smith got two FW-190s and pointed out we caught them the way they often caught us, concentrating single-mindedly on a strafing run and leaving their tails unprotected. He pointed out we dulled the blow to our field by making them turn and fight.

Bob Brulle gave his Belgian relatives a gift by putting at least one FW-190 in the trees and taking enough skin off another's hide to make him start smoking before Brulle lost sight of him. Out of ammunition, Brulle headed west to get away from the battle. He inadvertently passed over our field and our AA guns grazed him. As he returned to the field later, he saw a 51 chasing two 109s. Our AA guns crippled the 51 by mistake, which dropped his wheels and came in just as Brulle was landing.

Jack Kennedy, like most of us, got separated from the others in the flight. He got on the tail of a 109 and just as he was getting in a few strikes, he paid the price of not having a wingman. Two 109s closed on him from behind and in an instant he was on fire. He dove to the deck, but the 109s followed with a pulverizing flow of cannon and machine gunfire. Jack said he gave thought to bailing out, but the fire deterred him. Just then, two P-51s drove off the two 109s and he only hoped they got them good. Kennedy slipped the Jug a little and put out the fire. He roared into the field hot, without flaps. But safe.

Feeney, Lackey and Davis each got one bogey. Added to my four, that made twelve for the squadron, which was not a bad morning's work.

Major Marty Martin told us of the activity on the ground. The Ack-Ack on the field was busy doing its share of damage too. Everyone around took in the action like they were out watching the Sunday football game. Jerry's strafing the field drove in the gawkers only temporarily since this was one of the few times they got to watch such action. Usually they just heard about it afterwards. Altogether, the engagement lasted about forty-five minutes and amazingly, we suffered only minimal damage.

Marty wound up by giving us a rundown on what happened with the 487th. The squadron got off the ground shortly after we had engaged the incoming raid, probably about the time I shot down the second FW-190. Lt. Col. Meyer leading the flight bagged two 190s, one while he was still pulling up his landing gear. The second one he nabbed while chasing him across our airfield. Unfortunately, this chase almost cost Meyer his plane. Our field's AA guns fired at both the 190 and his 51. They made a direct hit on one of Meyer's wings with a 40-mm. cannon and raked the fuselage with .50-caliber ammo. Meyer cleared the area heading west, like Brulle.

The 487th impressively confirmed what the 51 could do in a dogfight, claiming twenty-three kills in the engagement with a loss of only three planes in the air. Marty said we would get a rundown in the morning on the total battle damage. For now, we had to get started on the brief for the afternoon mission. "Don't you know there's a war on," Marty quipped as he told us we were heading back out to the Bulge. Anxiously, we awaited news about the other 47 fields, where some of our classmates flew. Particularly, I wanted to find out if my friend Ted was okay.

The results trickled in, and the whole story unfolded. The attack on Y-29 was one of nine German Gruppen Luftwaffe strafing attacks which comprised Hitler's and Marshal Hermann Goering's *Great Blow*. This New Year's strike employed one thousand aircraft, practically the entire available strength of the Luftwaffe's fighter arm. Hitler was convinced the surprise attack would destroy the allied tactical air capability which was proving to be so lethal in the Ardennes. According to plan, JG-11, with about seventy Me-109s and FW-190s, was to hit Y-29 and Y-32 at 0920 hours on the first of January. The other eight Gruppens were synchronized to strike simultaneously throughout the northern sector.

Lt. Colonel Guenther Specht, leading JG-11, swept across the plains of Aachen and arrived at Y-32 on schedule knocking out ten spitfires on the ground before they could get off. Fortunately, we at Y-29 had a five-minute jump on them.

Throughout the northern sector, the RAF 2nd Air knocked down about one hundred German planes, mostly with AA guns. The 9th got about one hundred, with about sixty-five downed with AA guns. Added to the thirty-five we got at Asch, the allies stood their ground. The loss of

German fighters was heavy -- very heavy, estimated at about two hundred and fifty aircraft. Even more important, the Luftwaffe lost many of its key commanders.

The 390th was the only 9th Air Force squadron to engage the attack and made it possible for the 8th to get involved. My wingman flew the only P-47 lost in air combat that day and only one P-47 was damaged on the ground. We didn't lose one pilot, and I had led the show. What a day for all of us.

For this effort, Marty put me in for the second highest decoration our country awards, the Distinguished Service Cross for extraordinary heroism. I was pleased, but that's not what it was really all about. I was just doing what I volunteered to do, defending my country. However, from now on, I planned on calling the captain, *Smitty*.

Wilcox got the photo boys to get a shot of me crawling in and out of *La Mort*. As he put me in position for a shot in the cockpit, he stuck a cigar in my mouth saying, "That's better, you look too young." I kind of liked the new look, and the cigar didn't really taste all that bad. Not a bad habit to take up, I thought. As we finished, Wilcox said we were due for a special brief in the evening, which meant I had enough time to get the motor pool to drive me down to see Ted.

Ted's 48th Fighter Group at Saint-Trond was just twenty miles away. As we pulled into the field the guard gave us instructions to the officers' club. Surely that's where I could find him or at least word of him, since all good war stories eventually landed at the club. The 48th had a much better facility than we did at Asch, having taken over an airfield that had been left in pretty good shape by the Germans. The airfield came with a chateau which had at least some of the comforts of home. As I walked into the club, I was glad to see Ted standing at the bar with his blond hair acting as a beacon in the smoke-filled room. He spotted me immediately, "Mel, I understand you had a little action up there at Asch. What are you doing down here, trying to get away from the war zone?" Casually, I took a place at the bar, "Oh, I tangled with about seven of them and got four or five." Ted's look said, "You must be bullshitting me!"

The 48th had taken a terrible beating. They were caught on the ground and lost over twenty planes. That morning they woke to the sounds of all hell breaking lose. The clamor didn't set well with the morning effects of the squadron's contest the night before to see who could drink the most on New Year's Eve. Just as Ted opened the shutters of his windows, blinking at the bright morning sun, a FW-190 strafed the side of the building. Another 190 was on the tail of the first, looking like it would blast right into his window. Ted dove to the floor and stayed there hoping everything would go away, including his hangover. For hours we told our tales and before the afternoon was over Ted's buddies had bought me enough drinks to help me sleep soundly all the way back to Asch.

That evening, Marty started off the brief by telling us how lucky we were that we hadn't lost more planes, the way they were lined up on the field for an easy kill. We would change that; starting immediately we would position the aircraft throughout the field.

The next discussion point was one that almost got Brulle and Meyer killed: That was the inability of our ground gunners to make fast recognition of enemy aircraft that were going balls out on the deck. The solution to this was to put a ring of large foxholes around the field with phones connected to each of the AA batteries. Everyone thought this was a great idea, until we found out each emplacement was to have in it an enlisted man and a pilot. The second day of the plan, I drew foxhole duty. "What a great way to put your eyesight to the test," Op chuckled.

52. A P-47 makes a strafing run on a German airfield.
This was one of the most hazardous duties for fighter aircraft.

53. Striking a German flak tower. WW II version of the
"fight at the O.K. corral."

54. Full strength P-47 squadron -- a rare sight with so
many of the aircraft grounded for battle damage repair.

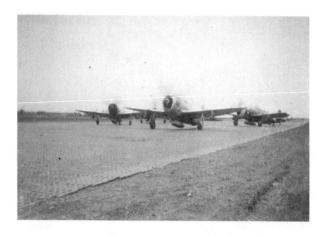

55. *La Mort* leads the squadron out of Y-29 in Asch, Belgium.

56. Adolf Hitler and Hermann Goering plan the January 1, 1945 "Great Blow" Luftwaffe attack on Allied Air Fields in Belgium, Holland and France. The 390th Fighter Squadron of P-47s at Asch, Belgium were the first U.S. aircraft to engage the attackers, contributing heavily to the largest single day loss the Luftwaffe encountered in the entire war.

57. Lieutenants Melvyn Paisley and Jack Kennedy take a look at one of the twelve aircraft the 390th Fighter Squadron shot down on New Year's day, 1945. The 390th was victorious in the scuffle, losing no pilots.

(GPR-366-1-9HPL)(16-FEB-45)(P-47 BURNS)

58. They don't always come back -- a P-47 burns after a fatal impact.

59. Standing room only at Asch, Belgium
for watching the frenzied dogfights
in the sky, January 1, 1945. The
The Luftwaffe lost a total of 253
aircraft in the attack which spanned
across the continent.

60. Counting the P-47s returning to the
field by Marmite control, Y-29, Asch, Belgium.

61. General Quesada decorates Lt. Paisley at Asch, Belgium.

CHAPTER 12

DOWN AND DIRTY

The raw earth of the freshly dug foxhole was dank despite the freezing cold. A chill penetrated my winter, leather bomber's jacket through its thick wool lining. It was probably the quiet which gave me even more time to think how cold I really was. By noon my limbs had stiffened painfully and I tapped at the shoulder of the sergeant, "I'm going down to the cafe at the crossroads and see if I can get a bite to eat. You can do the same when I get back."

As I entered the cafe, about ten locals sat around several small wooden tables drinking their beer and chatting quietly. Each looked up with a prolonged stare, then grew silent as they stared a little more. They must have been put aback by the outfit that I had on. It was not something we ever wore in town. Breaching the silence, I tried to convey to the proprietor that I wanted coffee and some food. Although a little Flemish would have helped the whole conversation, I felt pretty confident my food would be coming, particularly since the drink arrived almost immediately. Cabbage soup and yesterday's bread was perhaps all I would get, but at least it would be warm. I waited, sipping my coffee.

After a good deal of whispering and shuffling about, each one of the patrons filtered out of the bar, one by one, until I was alone. I waited some more, and my food did not come. I got up and walked to the kitchen, looking and calling. There was no one there, either; I was alone in the building. Returning to the front bar, I heard a voice on a hand-held speaker. Not all the words were understandable, but the message was clear, "Come out with your hands up, and do it fast!" Then there was a bit of what sounded like garbled German, crackling on the same speaker. With a thud in my heart I wondered, "Did the German's overrun the area? Was I about to be captured?" Peeking out the back and front window I saw the cafe was surrounded with British, not German troops. They had sinister--looking machine guns positioned fore and aft.

"These Brits must think I'm German," I thought to myself. The tank outfit I was with had informed their men that Commando Otto Skorzeny, under Hitler's personal command, organized a German panzer brigade which was outfitted in American uniforms, weapons, identification and jeeps and had dropped them behind the lines. Wilcox had warned us, if anyone ever questioned our nationality, we'd better be able to answer who won the world series, the last time they played, or some other very American question. There was little doubt in my mind, these guys were totally convinced they had a real live gestapo member in their grip right here on the edge of the town of Genk.

As I walked out the front door with my hands in the air I blurted out, "Mickey Mouse's girlfriend is Minnie Mouse." That didn't seem to help. The machine guns were still pointed my way. A British officer said brusquely, "All right Kraut, keep your hands up!" The guy on the machine gun looked too nervous for me to do anything besides breathe slowly. I requested permission to show them my identification, to no avail. At last a truck came barrelling down the road and I requested that my captors stop the truck, as it most assuredly was from my outfit. The driver would identify me, and resolve this whole mess.

As the truck slowed to a stop, I was relieved to see my squadron code on the bumper. Out stepped my armament sergeant, and I pleaded, "Sergeant, tell these people who I am." He replied curtly, "I don't know, who are you?" My knees sagged, and I gave him a glare that could kill. He came back, "Oh, I was only kidding. This is the hottest pilot in the 9th Air Force." I grumbled half under my breath, "I don't need all that extra stuff. Just vouch for me." But I knew that's the way the crews felt about all the pilots. The sergeant went on to tell them about the 1st of January, and soon we were all in the cafe having drinks on the owner. The proprietor couldn't get over the fact my mother was from Genk. I never could get him to understand it was *Ghent* not *Genk*.

The Allies stopped the drive in the Ardennes five and a half miles short of the Meuse River and the tide was starting to reverse. One of our last escort missions was to cover some A-20s dropping leaflets on all the towns between the bomb line and the Rhine River. All civilians were told to move east of the river, and the townsfolk were to leave no buildings occupied. There was no exception for hospitals, Red Cross facilities, churches, school houses or anything else of that nature.

The Germans had no compunction about using church belfries as observation posts, hiding behind young school children or amassing troops in hospital facilities. War was war. Everybody understood that. And we never expected it to be clean by any stretch of the imagination. Likewise from our perspective, when American lives were at stake, we simply couldn't count on the Germans honoring the internationally accepted precepts governing wartime activity.

Our orders were to hit anything that moved and blow up any buildings the Germans might have taken over. We would bomb the schools, the hospitals or anything which showed any sign of life. We hoped and prayed our demands to clear the area were followed by the civilians; every man, woman and child who once called the villages their home.

Atrocities were the by-product of failing to follow the gentlemanly rules of war. We knew both sides committed them, although the rumors of the German's viciousness were unsurpassed. By this time, we had all heard about the massacre at Malmedy. One hundred and twenty American G.I.s were captured by the 1st Panzer Division. Barbarically, they were herded into a field and gunned down with automatic weapons. The stories continued and we were all spoiling for a real cleanup when we got the Germans reversed.

On the 22nd of January, Marty went out on a recon mission with Sandy on his wing. Through some scattered clouds, he saw what looked like the traffic letting out of a New Year's football game. A B-26 had knocked out the Dasburg Bridge over the Our River and over fifteen hundred military vehicles were backed up for miles. Marty's flight got a radio fix on the exact location and for two days they had a turkey-shoot. The 366th accounted for over five hundred vehicles, including tanks and armored vehicles.

Of more magnitude, the Battle of the Bulge was over, at last. It was in no way an easy fight on the ground or in the air. We lost about the same number of American lives that both sides had lost in the Battle of Gettysburg, and sadly we lost Aageberg, Maurer, Feeney and Halterman from our squadron. Aageberg finally got his chance to bail out when he was hit with AA, but no one in the flight saw his chute blossom. Maurer was on the short end of a dogfight and Feeney got it coming off a target. Halterman went down in Brulle's Jug, *Virginia*. Brulle lost a friend and an airplane at the same time.

Now, the drive for the Rhine was on and we had yet to encounter some of the heaviest flak installations the Germans had. It wasn't going to be easy. Wilcox gave us the warning, "Get ready to pull the skin of your ass over your head and hope for the best!" The heaviest flak on all the continent was to the west of the Rhine, between the German border and the river, and we were going to start working that area every day.

On one mission, Op and I flew together. He took one flight and I took the other in a two-flight mission. We went after the supply shipments moving to Wesel from the south. In his brief, Wilcox said that flak was heavy in the target area; it was the heaviest yet reported.

The night before, we spent time in the club talking about girls and when we might get into Paris again. Op started working on me about writing his sister. He knew I didn't write any girls at home and he thought this would be something to keep me busy. Sort of a blind date on paper, Op called it.

As we flew to our target, Op talked to me about his kid sister and said he would have her send me a picture. I suspected this was part of his plan to get me to move to Illinois after the war because I was trying to get him thinking about Oregon. We had both given up on Paul because he had the sands of Arizona in his blood.

Close to the Rhine, the heavy, high-altitude flak turned the sky a murky black. We changed our directions continuously, trying to throw off the gunners. I saw the first string of barges just north of Dusseldorf and we decided to go after them simultaneously from the north and south. We had enough to do the job, since we were loaded with rockets and five-hundred pounders. Op was to bring his flight from the north and go after the barges on the east, while I was to come from the south and take those on the west. This strategy promised to give the AA guns the most trouble.

As we rolled over on the target and started down, I was convinced this would be a good flight. We would stay until we were completely out of everything we had to give the Germans. There was no substitute for flying with someone you spent so much time with, talking over every minute detail of how you do everything. We knew what each other would do, under most any circumstance.

D.J. had lost Bennett, his flight leader, in this area the day before. Though he bailed out and was seen landing in the water, we weren't sure what happened to him. The 40-mm. stuff which we were now up against had ripped his wing off with little difficulty.

We took a lot of strikes, but it was mostly light stuff. That's not to say the light stuff wasn't capable of doing a lot of damage. A 20-mm. hit could be fatal to the engine or controls if it hit just right. However, the 40-mm. just had to be close to blow the wing or engine clean off any plane, including a Jug. If the real heavies got close they could blow you right out of the sky, turning your plane into giant hunks of metal.

Skidding the plane was effective against any form of flak, unless the Germans were saturating the air with it, but the real trick was to hold steady long enough to make the bomb drop or rocket launch.

We coordinated three passes at the targets, the last was from east to west. Success was ours; one barge sank and another was on fire. Two others were damaged with strafing passes. We all made it back to the field, but as usual tail-end charlie took the most damage.

As the troops started the slow drive to the Rhine, we confiscated a handful of commercial vehicles that the Germans had stored in buildings along the way. The vehicles were makes from almost every country. With a little army olive-drab paint, we all had transportation for as long as we could keep it running. Our pride and joy was an Indian motorcycle that was sure to kill one of us, eventually.

Op and I were cruising the perimeter of the field late one afternoon on the bike, and through the falling snow everything looked dusky, without shadows. Then there was a deafening rough roar, which was unfamiliar. We looked overhead to see a B-17 Flying Fortress making an approach into the field. A heavy bomber like this, even if it was empty and even if the pilot gave it full flaps, couldn't get into our fighter strip. So, we reasoned it was merely dropping down for a position check.

Watching him descend further, we determined three of his engines were out of commission. One was mangled beyond recognition and the other two had their props feathered. It looked like he was going to set it down on the field, wheels up. As she plopped down, mud squirted in all directions through the holes in the steel mat. Then she skidded halfway down the runway on her belly, with sparks flying in all directions and the horrific sound of metal on metal piercing the air. We raced along the runway and came to the crippled plane about the same time as the emergency trucks.

The emergency crew washed the tail-gunner out of the turret with a hose and the half-conscious belly-gunner was dragged from the ball turret, where he had, through some miracle, escaped being crushed during the skid down the runway. Why hadn't he crawled into the aircraft ahead of time? About half the crew was dead, and the plane was far beyond repair. The bomber had been hit by flak over its target, and dropped behind. The Jerries stalked enemy aircraft just like wolves. Once they cut their prey from the pack, they descended upon it and tore it to shreds. The results were devastating, right here before my eyes. I stared in awe at the ruin. Now, I was even more sure that being a fighter pilot was the only way to fly.

As Op, Paul, Picton and I strolled into the operation tent in late January, we found two pieces of good news posted on the bulletin board. Major Martin had promoted the entire class of 44-D. He said we had done a good job for the 390th, and told us in the right way that we were now first lieutenants and our friends, Sandy and Johnson were now shavetails. Also, we had a leave to Paris coming. We would be flying our Jugs into Le Bourget for an engine inspection. Things just didn't get any better than that.

As I broke through the clouds over Paris and saw the sprawling city for the first time from the air, I marveled at the sight. My Jug careened effortlessly around the towering Butte-Montmartre over the northern rim of the city, and I located the field. After making a down-the-runway pass and a hot-rock 360-degree tight turn back into the field, I dropped my wheels and flaps, roaring onto the runway. Three to four days and the job would be done, according to the inspection crew.

Picton rushed to the Pigalle district. Op, Paul and I made fast tracks to the Place de la Concorde. Two blocks from the circle was our favorite watering hole at the Maquis residence. Jacques greeted us at the door and said he had some great war stories to tell. But not until he rolled out the wine. We spent the whole evening telling stories.

Op and Paul told their adventures on the trip to the Riviera. I was getting bored with the story by now, but Jacques and his friends seemed to appreciate it. Op had met a Countess at a dance in the Cannes Carlton Hotel and they became close friends. The affair progressed to what Op termed the royal lay, the details of which got more potent over time. We added a few more stories about the girls in Hasselt, and by then we were almost fresh out of girl talk.

Then, we got down to the more serious stories of what was happening on the front. Op and I jointly related the time we went after two trains pulling a string of box cars. We were on a four-plane flight; I was flying tail-end charlie and Op was flying the flight leader's wing. On the edge of the town of Porz, along the Rhine River, I spotted the train gathering steam. We had unloaded our bombs earlier on a marshalling yard and the flak was so heavy the flight leader at first decided not to make a strafing pass on the rail cars.

Despite the heavy flak, this train was far too inviting and we couldn't resist the temptation. Our strategy was to approach our target in echelon formation, first strafing the engine, then running the length of the train. With our concentration focused on the locomotive, we did not see the box cars open. They were loaded with 20 and 40-mm. automatic AA guns, pointed straight at us. We knew we had been suckered into coming down.

Dropping in from behind, I was out of their range when they started firing at the flight leader. As they swung around, following the flight leader, I got a good shot at them strafing the full length of the train. Since we all took some damage, the flight leader told us not to break up but keep on the deck and stay under their minimum elevation angle until we got out of range.

The story was good for a few more toasts. Then Jacques stood up and said proudly, "I will tell you what we have been doing. I think you know, the other men and I joined the French Army. My assignment was with the group attached to the American 6th Army. We drove the Germans all the way to the Rhine and our French unit took the town of Strasbourg were I was born. During the counter-offensive in the Ardennes, we refused to abandon the town, and we held it although our support from the Americans was diminished."

With more toasts, we went back to a serious discussion of girls. Jacques told me Annie was now working with the headquarters office of the

First French Army in Paris, since the Maquis women were barred from joining the army units.

Paul and I left Jacques, each parting in our own direction and agreed to meet at the Laise en Rose the following evening. If for some reason we did not show at the Laise en Rose, we would meet at the Moncey-Hotel the morning of the day we were to leave. I made a beeline for Annie. Paul went to create more stories about his Polish girlfriend, even if he had to pay the price of a few more nail scratches. Op couldn't tear himself away from the exquisite wine cellar at the former Rothschild estate.

Annie was waiting when I arrived, peeking from the lace curtains of her room. She was captivating and lovely, everything I remembered. We embraced and suddenly my mind, my body and my soul was at peace. Everything was going to be all right. Soon our embrace turned to passionate kisses and my world became a fantasy, a beautiful, beautiful fantasy without war or the threat of no tomorrow. I wanted the feeling to endure forever and we prolonged it as long as we could until at last we were writhing in a world so heavenly and so satisfying. Finally we worked our way to her bedroom into an ecstasy, the heights of which I had never reached before.

I awoke the next day from a peaceful sleep. Annie and I talked and shared our dreams of the future and the dangers in our present. Then we made love again and again and again. In all, we spent three glorious days and nights together, and the days mingled with the nights. She taught me so much about love and about life, living every day to the fullest. I hated to leave her but I did, knowing I would get back somehow, some time.

Rendezvousing at the Moncey, Op and I found Picton still in his room. We dragged him out of bed and shared a cup of coffee before hitching a ride back to the field. Op nudged Picton saying, "That girl sure hated to leave you. What did you do to her?" Picton told us of the adventures of the night: "I was just nodding off to sleep after what I thought was a terrific lay, when I heard her creep out of bed. Through the faint stream of light from the window, I saw her rifling through all my pockets and my wallet. Without a word, I reached for my .45 pistol and she heard the double click of the hammer being cocked. She leapt back into bed in a single bound, then kept the entertainment level high enough to make sure I didn't get another ounce of sleep the rest of the night."

We slowly let down onto the steel mat runway at Asch a few hours later and started to think again about the job at hand. We were now placed under XXIX Tac, which had been turned back to the 9th Air Force. Our job was to support the continuing effort to break through to the Rhine.

On my first mission after returning, I had just climbed to three thousand feet after making a dive-bombing run on a string of gun emplacements. My wingman, Lt. Gibson, delayed his run until he could take a look at the damage caused by my bombing. This was not the safest way to do things, but it was the way to get the best results on the ground. Gibson was at the bottom of his dive, starting to pull up when he saw a Me-262 lurking overhead. Gibson poured the coal to his Jug in a sharp climb but could not get the airspeed he needed. Racking a wingover, I pointed *La Mort* directly at the intruder, and gave it full throttle with water injection. My nose pointed straight down, the direction the Jug knew best. *La Mort* ripped past Gibson like he was standing still. The 262 pilot was surely one of Jerry's best since the Germans gave these jets only to the most dedicated, combat-hardened Luftwaffe pilots. Looking him over, I hissed, "A wrong move here could cost you your ass."

The 262 still hadn't seen me as I closed. The unchanging tell-tale blur from his engines told me he was not accelerating, not yet. As his wings filled my gun sight, I was in perfect range to let the eight .50s work on him. Dead-hit strikes gashed his wings and fuselage, and on the right engine the incendiary projectiles worked like a damn. Pitch black smoke billowed out of the engine as the plane tumbled to the ground somewhere on the edge of Gladbeck. The troops would be there soon and they just might get a piece of him for a souvenir.

On the way into Asch, I called field control telling them I planned to ring out a handful of victory rolls over the field. For the first time, my plane wasn't too shot up or battered to do so. *La Mort* rotated smoothly over the runway, like a well-oiled drill. It felt so good. As I crawled out of the plane the crew chief gave me his congratulations. "Thanks," I beamed, "but the bad news is, the engine probably needs a change-out. I think I ran the water tank dry chasing that Me-262. By the way -- you can paint another swastika on the side."

That night I talked to the Doc and told him I had a ticking in my head which just wouldn't go away. I thought it might be affecting my hearing. Checking my story out, the Doc found that he could hear the tic himself. That was a real puzzler to him. Another one of those *G.O.K.* cases, known in the army medical profession as, "God only knows." His response was typical of the advice he usually gave in that situation, "Just wait awhile and see if it maybe goes away."

Doc checked back with me in a week or so, and things hadn't improved any. "Doc, it's getting where I can't hear myself fart," I complained. He didn't know what to do, and after thinking a moment and rummaging through a cabinet drawer, he reached out his hand, "Here, take these pills." I questioned Doc about the pills, wondering what they were supposed to do. He grinned, saying, "They won't help your hearing, but they'll make you fart louder." Op was with me and laughed, "Don't worry. Things aren't so bad after all. When you fart, you don't need to hear it to know you did." I never brought up the problem again to Doc.

Mail call brought a letter, the scent on which reminded me of three wonderful days in Paris. I didn't have to look to tell it was from Annie.

Paris 25/2/45

My Mop,

Only yesterday you left and I would like you to be back with me. I think the idea is silly, but I have enclosed a lock of my hair as you wished. I will not tell you where it came from. Keep it wherever you pelots [sic] keep those sorts of things. In your airplane perhaps? XXX Must I tell you to remember to keep your mind on what you are doing.

Onis said she was sorry to miss seeing you when you were here, but I told her we never left my apartment for the three days. She seemed to understand.

The way the battle is going we should be together soon. The thoughts of the wonderful time we had with each other will have to last us until we meet again. XXX

Love,
Annie

Thoughts of Annie distracted me, and I wished the war was over, leaving us free to love one another. I kept her black curly lock of hair in my wallet as a frequent reminder of our war-torn affair.

On the 6th of March, about that time of day we liked to start thinking of maybe a game of poker, a drink or a trip to Hasselt, Smitty popped into the club and said we had a late mission call for volunteers. Picton and I were there alone and we offered to go, saying we would find a couple more guys right away. As always, we looked first for our classmates. Sandy was in his dress uniform, waiting for a ride to Hasselt, but he was always the first one to put his hand in the air and say "Count me in." The girl in town could wait; Sandy probably thought this might be as good as sex anyhow.

Smitty was in the briefing tent when we walked in. He was laying out some blue and red lines on a map of the northern sector of the Rhine. The blue allied troop line was moving to the red German line, close to the Rhine River. The 9th Army was moving to get a foothold on a piece of real estate on the Rhine big enough to set up a bridgehead. General Simpson, head of the 9th, called for help out of XXIX Tac to soften a resistance he could not budge. It was important he move on schedule to support Montgomery's crossing of the Rhine at Wesel. The XVI Corps was to cross just south of Wesel at Rheinberg and hold off any advance from the south flank from the Ruhr. Our job was to go to the target area and work with an air controller for a column of the 2nd Armored Division which was under the command of Major James Hollingsworth. We could only use guns since we would be right on top of our own troops. To this day we had no knowledge of ever making the mistake of accidentally strafing or bombing our own troops, but we were always in fear of doing so.

Two flights were going out. Smitty led Red, with Sandy on his wing. Scholz had the second Red Element, with Picton on his wing. I had the second Blue Element with Sills on my wing. Leading my flight was Brotton, who had Davis on his wing. Op and Paul were on leave to the Riviera on the south coast of France or they would have worked themselves in on this mission, too.

There was a slight delay on our takeoff because a 47 had just landed with a five-hundred pound bomb which broke loose and rolled down the runway. It exploded on the side of the runway, sending hordes of dirt into the air. Unfortunately, the 47 didn't get away unscathed; the bomb blew off large hunks off both wings and the back two-thirds of the plane. It was a miracle the pilot was not hurt seriously. About fifteen minutes later, the runway was cleared and we took off.

By the time we approached the target area, it was already getting dark. Although our visibility was limited, we decided to stay in the area as long as we were doing some good. The flak in the area was as thick as we had experienced. The black cotton balls were churning all around, forcing us to veer continuously to throw off the gunners. We made our first pass working over the troops and light gun emplacements. The controller, hidden somewhere in a tank below, directed me into some buildings where enemy troops were holed up and where there was an antitank gun positioned alongside. On the second pass, Sills and I were abreast of one another. We started at four hundred yards from the building and stayed on our guns until we popped over the structure at fifty feet. With only two targets to focus on, the Germans let us have everything they had and the ground came alive in the ebbing light with golden flashes of all sizes and potency.

Minutes later darkness crept in and it was almost too dark for flying at this low altitude. We couldn't fly any higher; with the light background of the sky we'd leave a profile for the mobile ground guns. So, Smitty called us for a rendezvous and we turned back to the field. Ground control said we had finished the job and they were moving onward again. Right about then, Sandy must have been thinking how he could get a little press on his dress uniform which surely got a little crumpled in all the action. It wasn't too late to meet his girl.

For the first time, smudge pots were strategically placed along the field at Y-29, allowing us to navigate safely into the field. Sandy stepped out of his Jug as disheveled as I had envisioned him to be. Thinking of what Sandy had in store, I enviously wondered if this really was as good as sex.

Sandy and Picton were in the target area a week later, on a forward liaison job. They related a story of finding some dead bodies strewn throughout a field, as domestic pigs, turned wild, cleaned the bones. Though we could only imagine the shocking details, the thought alone bludgeoned our imaginations. War was terrifying as could be. We tried not to dwell on the horrors, but they served to heighten our drives.

Our next mission was an unusual one. No one in the squadron had ever dropped a jellied gasoline napalm bomb, not even in training. Smitty called on the armament officer to give us a run-down on how the ordnance worked. "These things don't drop like bombs," he said, "they will tumble as soon as you release them. In order to get them on the target, you must lay them right down on the deck. And if you get them on the target, they will stick like snot on your finger. Oh, and there's one more thing I have to tell you, if one of your canisters gets hit by flak you may have a fire on your hands. Or worse yet, the canister may explode. Bail out quickly if you must." This sounded to me like someone's great invention gone amiss. The armaments officer continued, reserving judgment on the obvious dangers of using the napalm, "You will have a seventy gallon canister under each wing and we are putting a two hundred and sixty pound frag on the belly. The napalm has impact fuzes and the frags are delayed so you can go as low as you want." After the armaments guy spoke, Wilcox took the podium and gave us the *good* news, "You will be going in on the marshalling yard at Dusseldorf. The flak is reported to be light." This had to be the biggest load of crap yet. Who ever heard of a marshalling yard in the Ruhr area with light flak? Had the Germans gone east to give the Russians a little action? I doubted that.

Coming into the target area, we had only eight aircraft out of the original squadron of eleven. Three aborted about ten minutes after departing from the field. This was the kind of mission, which tended to make some engines sound a little rough and maybe not fit for combat. The marshalling yard and a nearby parking area were loaded with motor transports and railroad cars. If we needed to go down on the deck to dump this stuff, we agreed we should let the whole load go on the first pass. We took the eight Jugs in, four abreast just far enough between the two flights to let the frags go off. The first flight dropped to the deck, jettisoning their tanks amid the flak. I led the second flight and as we came in on the deck we saw the flames from the burning freight cars rising from the yard. The first flight had hit their mark. Staying low and going through the flames was a piece of cake if we got rid of our tanks first, and with all the black smoke curling into the sky, the flak gunners would have difficulty staying on their targets. We dropped to the deck and dumped our loads on the near side of the yard, breaking left hard, through the flames and away from the flak. The entire yard of over one hundred cars became a massive inferno, belching orange-red flames and mountains of smoke. The buildings alongside the yard succumbed quickly to the flames. It was a horrible, frightening sight. This was the one and only napalm drop that we ever made and while it was effective, I had no desire to ever, ever use it on any area which was potentially populated. It just seemed too one-sided.

An all-pilots meeting was called on another one of those dreary days which seemed more suited for holing up in my warm sack. I dressed quickly and walked hazy-eyed out of the tent, doubting it would ever quit snowing in Belgium. No wonder my grandfather made light of those rough winters in Canada, if he grew up in a godforsaken place like this.

Marty was just starting the brief when Op and I sauntered in, at last. He looked up through the steam of everyone's coffee with a good-natured smile on his face, "Mop, you guys have to get to bed a little earlier if I'm going to make you two flight leaders." That was the way Op and I found out we had at last made it. Suddenly, this seemed just the kind of day we should rise up and kick the asses of a few Jerries.

Marty began, "Now that our couple of stars are here, we can get on with the brief." Op and I jabbed each other as we smiled to ourselves. "Montgomery has crossed the Rhine and General Simpson followed him to the south, thanks to the job you guys did a couple of weeks ago. I still keep getting congratulations on that one from Headquarters. I told them, you men are the ones who deserve all the credit, but still they've asked me to join them at TAC Headquarters. Smitty will be taking over for me, starting tomorrow."

Marty continued, "Now we need to open some resistance that has developed on the other side of Wesel. You will be going out with six, two hundred and sixty pound fragmentation bombs, the best things we have for disabling troops. Remember, get them on the target. They aren't five-hundred pounders -- you can't be sloppy. They will be armed to go off on impact with no delay." Wilcox added, " The flak in the target area is heavy. And on low approaches, watch for the flak towers. You can't do a thing to them unless you put those .50s you guys are so proud of, right up their nose.

You're just wasting your time bouncing ammo off the concrete, so if you can't get right on top, stay away from them."

I grumbled to myself, "What's this stuff, 'flak in the target area is heavy.' Wilcox should just post a sign to that effect. After all, that's what he means even when he says otherwise."

Wilcox continued, "We have a little extra work for you guys. A 35-mm. colored motion picture camera is in the wing well of one of your planes. A second camera which looks over the cockpit and forward, has been placed in the tail of another plane. This is the P.R. boys' way of getting some coverage for their movie *Fighter Squadron*. The Navy did a bang-up job on theirs, *Fighting Lady,* and we're going to do even better. Right men?"

We crossed the Rhine at fairly high altitude and then broke into three flights. Targets were called out by two different ground controllers. I took the one to the north. A roadblock backed up by a large concentration of troops was holding up the advance of a column, east of Wesel. Flying over the target at three thousand feet, I could see the activity clearly. My element went down first to go after the troop concentration; I told them to come from the east, strafing their way in, then dropping their frags on the roadblock. They went in too high, trying no doubt to avoid the string of flak towers to the east which loomed into the sky looking like giant concrete grain elevators with wide perchs on top. Hidden in each of the openings were lethal, high-velocity 20-mm. guns, like those we saw so often at the Siegfried Line.

The frags dropped by the first flight did not hit close enough to the target, so I told them to hold cover for my wingman and myself. We would make our pass from east of the city, down on the deck. On the way into the target we encountered several flak towers which appeared surprisingly debilitated. Wilcox would have been proud of us; we put some .50-calibers right in their noses. But it was just plain stupid not to have known our firing position would give the flak tower the same perfect shot at us. Savagely, the flak bit into my plane. The air became a dingy, threatening black as the plane wrestled in the muck. My hands trembled as I at last passed into a patch of calm air and took a deep breath. Fortunately, *La Mort* was tough enough to take the abuse it sometimes got.

I steered clear of the flak towers after that, going out of my way to avoid them. But in the whole ruckus my wingman lost me. Dipping close to the main road, I saw the roadblock, then dipped lower to fifty feet. Laboriously I hummed one of Sinatra's songs, *Don't throw bouquets at me*, and let the whole load of frags go. Instantly, my Jug lurched straight up in the air. Hunks of my frags mangled *La Mort's* already beaten body and wing sections. Hydraulic fluid trickled over both wings and I thought maybe I had punctured a wing tank.

My element watched from above and said we destroyed the road-block; there was nothing left of it. I hugged the deck as I crossed the Rhine. At last, we were over friendly territory. If *La Mort* wasn't going to make it home, that was important. I'd heard too many reports of the atrocities committed by the Nazis. Enemy pilots who bailed out on German soil stood a good chance of getting themselves killed or thrown in wretched prisons.

I nursed *La Mort* back to Asch and got the wheels down with some coaxing. We got the job done, but I learned a hard lesson about dropping frags so low with an instantaneous fuze. I also learned to have a little more respect for flak towers. It was a good thing those cameras were in someone else's plane. No matter about the cameras though, tomorrow was always another day. Our orders had already been prepared for the next mission.

The 9th Army, and specifically the 2nd Armored Division, was on the front end of a drive to the Elbe River. Moving fast, they were starting to get out of our range for support. We all knew we would be moving our field soon. Maybe we had even waited too long.

Mail call brought a letter from Mort, who was still the most consistent writer from the old gang. He kept me informed on the activities in the Pacific, where he was an executive officer in Roy's Raiders, having received a field commission in the infantry. Even though the censors cut out some of what he said, I could figure out what was happening by putting what he said in context of what I read in the Stars and Stripes. He could never say in his letter where he was, but the word *Cebu* slipped through this time and I knew he was involved in retaking the Philippines.

> March 5, 1945
> (Can't say where I am)

Hello Ol' buddy,

For some reason or other, Mel, your letter from Belgium really hit the spot, maybe because it was from a pal who means so much to me. From your last letter, it sounds like you have your hands full (with everything but girls!). At any rate, I'm throwing an armload of thanks out your way fella, from the front lines of Cebu and you know I mean it. You know how much the ground troops rely on the support from you pilots.

The action we had last week took us to -------------- and then to ---------------. We had a close call and I was able to ---------. The Command-er put me in for the Silver Star and I know my mom will boast about that to all her friends for years.

Heard from Red, and it looks like he will never get out of the States. He is stuck in the training command teaching dodos to be gunners.

Well that's all I have for the time being. Take care.

Your pal,
Jack

P.S. Charleen is either divorced or on the way. I will have to look her up when it is all over.

I suspected Mort was busy fighting in recent weeks because he usually had more to say in his letters about the girls in the islands. I missed hearing about the girls, since I didn't have much time to take the proper interest myself.

Smitty called Dutch and me in the next day and said we had been put on detached duty for six days to go to Bradley's headquarters in Luxembourg. It was customary to bring in combatants from the field to some unrelated function where the attending higher command officers gave out decorations. We made the trip in a jeep, which took most of the day. Passing through Bastogne, we stopped for lunch with an army unit. Though the damage to the city looked quite extensive, the civilians had returned. Life went on, despite the war. The torrent in my mind focused on the scores of cities we had used as targets.

Dutch and I were invited to an officer's reception for drinks and dinner at the hotel in which we were staying. After a lot of soap and hot water, I gazed into the mirror thinking I looked pretty damned sharp that evening, for having just come off the battlefield. Mostly I was proud of the special jacket I had made by a tailor in Hasselt. It was an Eisenhower jacket made famous by Eisenhower himself. The green gabardine jacket was lined with red velvet down to the tip of the sleeves. A little red poked out the end of the sleeves, letting everyone know my new status as a fighter ace.

Officially the War Department didn't recognize the term *ace*. Some said the officials were more interested in teamwork than individual performance. Still, everyone else, the pilots and the general public alike afforded a special status to all combat flyers who had attained five or more air combat victories, and the Army Air Force went along with it, letting us wear our status on the inside of our jackets.

We aarrived at the cocktail party before anyone else and greeted the officers as they walked through the door. There was General Vandenberg, head of the 9th Air Force; General Spaatz, head of the 8th Air Force; Army generals Bradley and Patton; and five star Generals Arnold and Eisenhower. Boy, oh boy, oh boy, we couldn't wait to tell the guys about this! Marveling at the Generals' awesome displays of fruit salad, we were humbled as never before.

At a special ceremony, Dutch and I each received the Distinguished Service Cross from General Henry *Hap* Arnold. Dutch got his for the 17th of December, and mine was for the 1st of January. The whole affair seemed a bit stuffy then, but the more we thought about it, the more we became the proudest damn twenty-year-olds there ever were. Still, there was no call to boast too much; we both knew the war wasn't over.

Returning from Luxembourg, I found orders on the bulletin board which sent me to the Riviera for a week of combat leave. With one hundred and twenty sorties under my belt, the Army thought it was time. Op and Paul gave me a couple of addresses, including the Countess'. I was now not so envious of them having gone there without me.

The extravagant Carlton Hotel in Cannes was the billet arranged for the 9th Air Force officers. I think the Army Air Force wanted to group us together so we didn't mingle so much with the Brits and the French. The higher ups said that's one of the reasons we were never put on combat leave in Paris or London. After all, this was a rest and not a place for just fun and games.

Regardless of where we went, it was almost impossible to forget the war. We always found enough good arguments with other fighter pilots from the 9th to keep the conversations lively and focused on the task at hand. We got into a great debate one night over some cognac. I was now to the point that I thought fine French cognac was a good drink.

We argued the merits of a Spitfire, a P-51 and the Jug. In short order, I beat my opponents down to admitting the Jug did not have a rival in ground support. My argument for the best dogfighter was a bit more obtuse, making the choice between the 51 or the Spit. Since neither of my opponents had ever taken a shot at a German, I felt a bit of an advantage. I bored in with the argument of armor and armament and they bored in on maneuverability. But as always, we never resolved the issue and if there was a winner, it was the cognac.

Quite by accident, I met the manager of Major Glenn Miller's band, who told me the tragic story about his boss. Miller was gone, lost over the English Channel back in December. His small plane went down, no one knew where or why for sure. No one ever ruled out enemy fire, though Glenn's manager was reluctant to pursue other possibilities in our conversation. He did say, however, that Glenn was on his way to Paris to do a show at the personal order of Eisenhower, who asked that the major take his outfit there.

He also told me of Glenn's apprehensions of that final plane ride across the Channel, a comment overheard. It seems when Glenn climbed into the single engine Norseman for his journey across the Channel, he asked, "Where are the parachutes?" His fellow passenger, who died as well, laughed off the comment, "What's wrong, Glenn, do you expect to live forever?" A chilling reflection, which obviously troubled the manager.

Just thinking about the many times I had enjoyed his music made his death difficult to comprehend. How I loved his music, and the little bit of home it brought to all of us. Death. How calloused we'd grown to its mention. Still, the realities hurt.

The second day on the beach, a couple Red Cross nurses rescued my ailing spirits and we made a week of it. My thought of helping Op with the Countess was short-lived because when I went to visit her, I discovered there was also a handsome Count. They turned out to be a chipper couple, and we had a good time doing the town together.

Saturday night was the dinner dance at the Carlton. I took one of the nurses and invited the Count and the Countess and the couple who lived next door to go with us. The chefs proved the French are truly the world's greatest cooks. They somehow turned G.I. field rations into a gourmet feast, the likes of which I hadn't tasted since London. As we danced into the night, it was as though the war didn't exist.

The Count's friend at dinner asked me if I had ever been hypnotized. I told him about a time at the theater in Portland, one Saturday matinee. The hypnotist had put me across two chairs with my neck on one and my heels on the other, then had three people stand on me. The question was now being asked to determine if I was one of those people who could be hypnotized easily. It all seemed harmless enough, so I let the Count's friend try to see what he could do. One minute I was looking at the pocket watch he held in front of him and the next thing I knew I was sitting at the table with everyone burbling about what I had done.

Whooping and hollering I had led a Conga line throughout the hotel. The crowd's choice, they said. If instead they had told me I stood on my head and sang Dixie I wouldn't have believed it either. The evening came to a close with the Countess and my nurse friend giggling and tittering together, away from the crowd. Only when I walked the nurse back to her hotel at four in the morning did I learn what they were laughing about. She said while I was under the trance the hypnotist proclaimed at one o'clock I would get an erection and it would not go down for four hours. She grinned and said, "You see he wasn't so good--it didn't work."

Word came over the radio the next day, President Roosevelt had died. The local military contingent conducted a formal ceremony on the beach and I was saddened. He was the only President I had ever really

known. Our country elected him when I was only six years old and his four
terms had carried him to this day. My father talked of him as the savior of
the working man.

After the ceremony, we returned to our field at Asch, which was
getting out of range of the front line troops more and more each day.
Major Hollingsworth, whom we had helped at the Rhine, had led the first
American column to reach the Elbe River just south of Magdeburg. Now
we were out of their range as were most American fighter units. Therefore,
it came as no surprise when the C.O. told us to land at our new field at
Munster after our mission the next day. Munster would put us back in the
action.

My first mission after our return was a fighter sweep to the west of
the Elbe. It was rare when we did fighter sweeps since we were generally
booked, doing ground support work to the south. When we did sweeps
however, we almost always used the entire squadron. But this day, there
were scattered clouds to three thousand feet from the deck and higher
clouds at fifteen thousand feet and Marty decided we should only take out
two flights and look around. That left us with twelve Jugs on the ground,
in case the weather improved. Our two flights broke up when the lead flight
got a call to cover the XIII Corps. The squadron leader left me to continue
the sweep.

As I burst off with my flight, I was thinking about my gear, hoping
someone would pack it up for me. It wasn't a big job; everything fit in my
B-4 bag and my sack. Scanning the sky, which was lulling gray, I spotted
two Me-109s milling around just under the upper cloud cover. Immediately
I alerted the flight and we started a slow climb. I wasn't about to let happen
to my flight what had happened to the squadron a few weeks earlier. They
had followed some 109s through a cloud cover and found a whole group of
long-nosed FW-190s sitting on top. They were lucky to get out, losing only
one plane. We would just let these bogeys go for now, but if we didn't see
something soon, we had no choice but to break through the clouds and see
what's up there. We couldn't let things pass that easily.

Within a short time, I made out a FW-190 sitting on top of the lower
cloud cover. I told the second element to stay above and give us cover. My
wingman, Lt. Davis, and I blasted toward the FW-190. This bandit was ours.
He saw us coming, but with our altitude edge he was in trouble. Darting
into the hole made by a break in the clouds, he looked like a rabbit chased
by a couple of foxes. It was clear below and we trailed him down. I would
get right on him before I fired. He started a turn to the right and my
wingman got a nice bite of him, then he swung back in front of me. Two on

one was such a delight! Damn, Davis was good. He had shown me what he could do on the 1st of January, too.

I was closing faster than I wanted to, and chopped all the way back on the power. As he filled the sight, with his wing tips just touching the edge of the circle, I let *La Mort* chew away at him. We were at one hundred feet and he was heading into a large field. "*Ha, Ha, Ha! Little brown jug, Don't I love thee,*" I sang out. That was one of Miller's best. As I passed him, I took a cut at taking off the top of his tail with my prop and got a nice chew off him just as he popped open his canopy.

Pulling up, I did a wingover and came back at him on the ground. We caught him scurrying across the field as we brutally strafed his plane. Lifting above the clouds, we settled back for an easy cruise for Munster. Davis and I would not have to buy a drink tonight, but we hoped there was a club at Munster for somebody else to buy the drinks. We'd hate to get beat out of the glory of this one. Regardless, we were going to be the first pilots to ring out a victory roll over our new field.

62. Get them into the air!

63. On the roll to the Rhine River. Tactical Air knocked out a major percentage of the enemies' armor.

64. A V-1 robot bomb -- 2000 pounds of death and
destruction, headed for the port of Antwerp, Belgium.

65. The way to attack an Me-262 is from behind. Hit them where they're soft, if you can catch them.

66. Getting the word from Generals Spaatz and Doolittle.

67. Captain "Dutch" Scholz receives the Distinguished Service Cross from General of the Air Force "Hap" Arnold. General Spaatz is to the right as Lt. Melvyn R. Paisley stands off camera waiting to receive the same decoration. Luxembourg, April 1945.

68. The French offer more than just a handshake with your decoration.

CHAPTER 13

FAREWELL FOR NOW

On the 20th of April, the group commander came to me saying, "Mop, with all the sorties you've flown, they will be rotating you to the South Pacific one of these days. How about the two of us taking a flight together so we can celebrate your becoming a captain? I know we can stir up a little action." Op and I beamed; we were the only two captains out of our class. At this rate we were on our way to becoming awfully young generals if the war in the Pacific and our luck held out.

As we taxied onto the runway, I thought the four-man flight looked like it might be a little small for this kind of activity but I knew the war in Europe was winding down. As we formed up after takeoff, it made me feel good to have Paul, my sand-hog friend from Arizona, on my wing. Like no one else, Paul would never let me down to save his ass. Hopefully we could stir a little action so *La Mort* and *Lucky Marie* could end their careers in Europe with a blazing victory.

We took off toward Potsdam and the Chief said we should head straight for one of the big Luftwaffe bases since there had not been many German aircraft reported flying in the theater. As we approached the field at Potsdam, I spotted a lone FW-190 circling at three thousand feet. "Bandit ten o'clock, low," I called. The Chief held back, "Go get him, Mop! But stay off the deck. Don't let him suck you into that flak on the field." Paul and I closed in on the bandit, barreling full throttle. I had him in range, but I was moving too fast and was going to over-shoot him. Still, I got a good blast at him, ripping off some of his hide; he looked like he was in trouble. Then I passed him up.

Paul used his head and held back, watching as I broke hard left and for the first time ever, let one of these guys get smack on my tail. This was the perfect way to get yourself killed. . . and it was just plain dumb! "Get him!" I screamed to Paul as I jerked *La Mort* hard to the right. "I'm coming! Look out! He's on you again!" Fortunately the bandit faltered, and didn't get a good shot off at me. "Paul, this time. Get him for God's sake."

A stream of bullets burst from *Lucky Marie* and I hoped Paul got him good. A quick glance behind me said he hadn't. I racked another tight turn and the bandit followed with Paul closing in on his tail. The Chief watched from above as I radioed Paul, "We're not going to get this problem taken care of, the way we're going. I'm going to roll over slow and pull out on the other side. You get ready to blast him when we start the roll. He'll surely follow me through." Halfway through the roll all hell broke lose. *La Mort* lurched, slamming me violently against my shoulder straps. The armor plate behind me rattled fiercely and I took some rounds in the fuselage. For a second, I wrestled feverishly with *La Mort's* controls, horrified by the thought of having to bail out over a Nazi airfield.

Damn it! I thought to myself. Paul must have blasted me with his .50-caliber gunfire. Jerry's .52-caliber explosive machine gun shells couldn't penetrate our armor like this hit. Right about then, the Chief slashed through the formation and bagged the 190. Just that easy. "You okay?" Paul asked sheepishly after things calmed down." "Yeah, just give me a couple seconds." Paul and I would talk about this when we got home.

On the way back to Munster I spotted a field loaded with Jerry aircraft. The Chief took us on a series of strafing runs across the field, until we were out of ammo. We couldn't get any of the planes to explode or burn, but we were pretty sure none would ever fly again. It was a great way to wind up what turned out to be my last and 172nd combat sortie. Paul and I had long debates over whether it was the 190 or him that mangled *La Mort* on this sortie.

Mail call brought me a letter from Op's sister, Ro. Op's effort to get me interested in his sister was paying off with very welcome letters and care packages:

Decatur, Illinois
May 1, 1945

Dear Mel,

I want to tell you how wonderful I think it is, that you are a captain, and only 20, too. Congratulations, from all my heart.

As you know, I am home from school. After being locked up all year long, I just don't know what to do with my freedom. No bells to wake me at seven, no exams to cram for, and no one to tell me to be in at 9:45 p.m.. Did I ever tell you we can't go out after 9:45 without a chaperone? You can imagine how much fun we have with a gray-haired woman tagging along everywhere we go. I shouldn't be so harsh, she's a nice lady, knows how to play a good game of chess, too.

Say Mel, if there is anything you want, just tell me and I'll see what I can do. Since I am home, I have access to a lot more shops.

I'll bet with the war going the way it is, you boys are seeing a lot of Europe, even if it is mostly from the air. When you return there some day, just think, you'll know where all the best places are.

My trunk from college just got here so I have to unpack, but remember if there is anything you want, just ask. I have sent a box of cookies for you and Russell. I hope they aren't all broken by the time they get to you.

Love,
Ro

"Russell," I thought. I always snickered when Ro called Op by his real name. It sounded so formal, so out of character from the guy I knew. Maybe the more cultured life is the life to which he would return someday. A life so different than the one we shared.

I told Op of the letter I had received when we settled in for the night, and I got a halfhearted moan in return. I pushed harder, wanting to talk, "Op, I've been thinking. . . what are you going to do after the war?"

"Oh, I don't know," he replied, "prop my feet on a comfortable davenport and enjoy a bottle of Canadian Club. Just me, in the peace and quiet. Drifting into oblivion. Dad wants me to help him at his ophthalmology clinic. I'd have to go to school forever, get a degree. Sounds exciting huh, a real dud. How about you?"

"I suppose I'll just mess around for awhile. Work over my hot-rod a million times. Mort wants me to start a garage with him. But I guess what I'd really like to do is find a girl; you know, make a little whoopie in the back of my rod on some secluded country road."

Op rolled away from me in his sack, "You're all talk, Mop. Don't expect any more action at home than what we've gotten in this rat-trap. Diddly-squat, that's what we'll both get. Same as here. That's right. Who wants to go out with some smelly guy who might get himself killed the next day."

Op was obviously disgusted with life today, which concerned me. He had been drinking again, which caused him to be frighteningly introspective and more negative than usual.

A couple weeks later we got some good news. Wilcox had heard from the field hospital which had our squadron-mates Bennett and Maurer in their care. Bennett had a broken leg he got from hitting the vertical stabilizer when he bailed out over the Rhine. Maurer was not as fortunate; he was badly burned and would be recuperating for some time. Wilcox had also received a letter from Feeney and passed it around:

May 6, 1945

"Dear George:

I understand that you boys back at the squadron thought that I'd had it, so I thought I'd better drop you a line and let you know that I made it OK. I also want to find out what happened after they nailed me.

I'll give you a short story about my adventure first of all. As you know I got hit by flak. They hit me in the gas tank and tore the left side out of the cockpit. Naturally the damned thing had to catch on fire, which made it rather uncomfortable in there. I didn't have much control and was losing altitude. I tried to get out and couldn't make it, so I sat back down and managed to roll it over and fall out. Outside of being burned a little around the eyes I was OK. I was pretty low when I got out but the "Goons" managed to get a few pot shots at me while I was floating down. I made a nice easy landing in about two feet of snow. Some flak gunner yelled at me and told me to come over there and all the time his friends were popping away at me. I decided to make a run for it. but after I'd gone a couple hundred yards and had a wagon load of ammunition shot at me I thought it best to give up, so I stopped and held my hands up. They kept right on shooting so I took off again. I ran about 3/4 of a mile across open country with the bullets skipping along beside me in the snow and whizzing by my head. I was really a frightened little boy. I finally made it to a patch of woods where they caught up with me. They pushed me around a little and cursed me out, but I was treated better than I expected. It was the SS boys who gave me this reception. I figured I got through pretty lucky. After that I went to Koln and Frankfurt, then to Nurnberg where we really starved. Then we marched down here to Moosberg. We lived pretty good on the march. We were liberated on the 29[th of] April and are still waiting here to be evacuated.' Jones, Lund, Ackerly, Luthy, and Taylor are here also. . . .

Your friend
John Feeney
P.S. Did I get credit for that 109? Give me all the poop. . ."

We were pleased to hear of our squadron-mates who made it back; there were twenty-two who never did. But the damage we had done helped pave the way to victory. I was particularly proud of the squadron's record of 158 tanks, 1100 motor transports, 800 railroad cars and 120 locomotives. The enemy aircraft were just the cream of our kills; we were truly a ground support outfit.

The war in Europe was declared officially over on the 7th of May. So ended another chapter of a war which appeared to have no bounds. We celebrated V-E Day by going into Munster to one of the few cafes that was operated for our use. In our drinking party was a fresh batch of pilots who had not seen so much as a single day of combat. The old-timers told them all the tales of combat they would probably never see. Our talking only made it worse for those who had worked so hard to get to where they were. Smitty said maybe we could get this bunch up and at least show them what the land around here looks like from above. So, the next week I took a flight of twelve up and let them try to feel a part of the action.

We were flying at five thousand feet and I spotted a British Mosquito flying on the deck. He looked somewhat like a Me-262 with his two engines and cigar-shaped fuselage. I told the flight to stay close together and we would make a pass at him. It would make for good practice, although I had strict instructions to keep these new kids up off the deck.

We made a pass at the Mosquito at thirty degrees. In the middle of the pass, I saw a series of high tension wires coming up fast. Over the radio, I called out, "Utility wires dead ahead! Stay alert 'cause we're going under them. Keep good and low. Fifty feet max altitude!" Two in the flight got goosy, maybe even piss-in-their-pants scared and they didn't stay quite low enough. With a horrendous crack their tails smacked the wires, but they recovered just in the nick of time with not too much damage. The radio exploded with the two of them chattering in a frenzy. They were rattled all right, and their concentration disintegrated, but they were okay. With luck, I got them back to the field. "For cripes sake, I thought that kind all bought the farm in training," I sniffed to Op. They could thank their lucky stars they would never see combat.

The Chief called me to group headquarters under the pretense of giving me hell for what I did. First I got a short reprimand with a tempered degree of sternness. Then with a twinkle in his eye he said to me, "Mop, you won't be happy 'til you get back into combat. I'm going to see what I can do about getting you transferred to the South Pacific. Maybe you can see how you like shooting at the Japs."

The next week the rotation plan came out and combat personnel received orders to go home based on a point system. Allowing for our length of time overseas, decorations, family situation and whatever else thrown in, I was number one to go home for rotation out of my class.

As I was getting ready to leave I stopped to see my crew and the chief told me to take my nameplate off my Jug; it was an access plate right below the cockpit that had my name and all the crew members names on it. I gave *La Mort* my last walk-around inspection. When I turned around, Op, Paul and the Ross brothers were standing there. We talked about the future in the States. It was so heartbreaking to leave the men who had grown up with me. We were friends joined by fate and bound by a spirit created only in times of extreme hardship. There was nothing that could ever break those bonds.

As I crawled into the C-47 for transport to England, Op gave me a jab, "Do you think you have room in there for your anvil?" The plane held on the end of the runway for some time and then the pilot's voice crackled over the radio, "Captain Paisley, if you look out the window, you will see your squadron fly escort as we leave the area." Once we were airborne, the Jugs flew by, one at time and I could see all the familiar names of the planes of my classmates. The last one fading out of sight was *Lucky Marie*. I'm sure Paul was right; she wouldn't have hurt her old friend *La Mort*.

Two weeks later I arrived in Portland. Seeing the Greek dampened the sad memories of leaving the men in Munster. Don Hoff, who was the captain of the football team at Grant when we played Waite, was just home from the SeaBees and we started celebrating the end of the war in Europe. He had been in the Pacific and was waiting for that activity to wind up so he could really celebrate. The next week, President Truman ordered the Atomic bomb dropped first on Hiroshima and then on Nagasaki. The war in the Pacific was over.

Hoff and I were on Broadway Street in downtown Portland when the announcement of V-J came. Hordes of people jammed the streets, yelling, crying and hugging one another. Both Don and I were in uniform and everyone acted as though we alone had won the war. It was a wild joyous time, a celebration of life free from the bonds of war, at last. This was the moment of euphoria every American had prayed would someday come. Don lifted a pretty girl and a sailor bit her right on the behind, as she screamed in delight. Anything was acceptable. And now we could start over where we left off.

69. The last drag across the field in *La Mort*.

70. Lt. Paul Ollerton's *Lucky Marie*.

71. Lieutenants Paul Ollerton and D.J. Ross,
and Captain Russell "Op" Oplinger see Mel
off to the states, with his swaggerstick
and a fifty-mission crush in the hat.

NICE-MARSEILLE EDITION

V-E Day | **THE STARS AND STRIPES** | **D+336**

Daily Newspaper of U.S. Armed Forces — in the European Theater of Operations

Vol. 1—No. 57 Wednesday, May 9, 1945 ONE FRANC

Allies Proclaim:

IT'S OVER

Surrender Is Signed At Rheims

By CHARLES F. KILEY
Stars and Stripes Staff Writer

RHEIMS, May 8 — The Third Reich surrendered unconditionally to the Allies here at Gen. Dwight D. Eisenhower's forward headquarters at 2:41 AM Monday.

The surrender terms, calling for cessations of hostilities on all fronts at one minute past midnight (Double British Summer Time) Wednesday, May 9, were signed on behalf of the German government by Col. Gen. Gustaf Jodl, Wehrmacht chief and Chief of Staff to Fuehrer Karl Doenitz.

Under Jodl's signature were those of Lt. Gen. Walter Bedell Smith, Chief of Staff to the Supreme Allied Commander; Gen. Ivan Susloparoff, head of the Russian mission to France who was authorized by Moscow to sign on behalf of Soviet forces, and Gen. Suvez of France.

The surrender was signed in five minutes in the SHAEF war room here, 95 miles east of Compiegne forest where Germany surrendered in the last war on Nov. 11, 1918, and the scene of the capitulation of France to the Third Reich in this war June 21, 1940.

Flew from Germany

The terms were signed in less than ten hours after the arrival of Jodl by plane from Germany, and at — ""— negotiations first begun on Saturday of Gen. Adm. Hans Georg von Friedeburg, commander in chief of German navy, who on Thursday headed the Nazi delegation which surrendered German forces in Denmark, Holland and Northwestern Germany to the 21st Army Gp.

Gen. Eisenhower did not take
(Continued on Page 8)

Announce the Victory

GEN. EISENHOWER **PRESIDENT TRUMAN**
"The crusade . . . has reached its glorious conclusion."

3rd Told Big News After Taking Prague

On the day of official announcement of the European war's end Third U.S. Army troops drove into Prague, and Marshal Joseph Stalin announced the fall of Breslau, Germany's ninth city, after an 80-day siege.

The Czech radio announced yesterday that the Czechoslovak commander of Prague defenses had welcomed the commander of the First Div. to Prague. The Germans, who surrendered effective the afternoon of May 9—today.

A Soviet correspondent reported that the German commander raised the surrender flag at Breslau at 1800 hours Monday. German defense efforts ended in almost complete destruction of the city.

Doughs Watch 'Final' Battle

ON THE ELBE RIVER, May 8—One of the last battles of the European war was fought on the east bank of the Elbe today—between the Russians and the Germans.

Everybody knew the end of hostilities was only a few hours away.

For the last week the German 12th Army was pushed back on the Elbe, and began surrendering to U.S. troops. The Germans built bridges while Americans as spectators to U.S. troops. The Germans built bridges while Americans watched and accepted their surrender.

SWEDES BREAK WITH GERMANY

Sweden yesterday severed diplomatic relations with Germany on the ground that there is no central government to be recognized. The Swedish radio said all German buildings in Sweden had been turned over.

Peace came to Europe at one minute past midnight this morning (Nice-Marseille time) when the cease-fire order to which Germany had agreed went into effect.

Formal announcement of Germany's unconditional surrender came nine hours earlier in radio proclamations by President Truman and Prime Minister Churchill.

As they spoke the last "all-clear" sirens sounded in London and Paris, and the streets in both cities were the scenes of frenzied celebrations. America took the announcement calmly and quietly, having staged its celebration Monday when the German announcement of the surrender was flashed.

All hostilities had not ceased yet, however. Some German pockets still were resisting the Russians in Czechoslovakia and on islands in the Baltic Sea. Moreover, up to a late hour last night Moscow had not proclaimed victory.

The surrender agreement, it was disclosed, was signed at 0241 hours Monday in Gen. Eisenhower's headquarters at Rheims, France. To the last the Germans attempted to split the Western Allies and Soviet Russia, offering surrender at first only to the Western Allies. This was rejected flatly by Gen. Eisenhower.

Defeat of Germany—concluded in the bomb-burned and
(Continued on Page 8)

Allied Soldiers Praised In Ike's Victory Order

The text of Gen. Eisenhower's victory order of the day follows:—
Men and women of the Allied Expeditionary Force:

The crusade on which we embarked in the early summer of 1944 has reached its glorious conclusion. It is my especial privilege, in the name of all nations represented in this theater of war, to commend each of you for valiant performance of duty. Though these words are feeble they come from the bottom of a heart overflowing with pride in your loyal service and admiration for you as warriors.

". . . Astonished the World . . ."

Our accomplishments at sea, in the air, on the ground and in the field of supply have astonished the world. Even before the final week of the conflict you had put 5,000,000 of the enemy permanently out of the war. You have taken in stride military tasks so difficult as to be classed as impossible. You have continued until our front was firmly joined up with the great Red Army coming from the east, and other Allied forces coming from the south.

Full victory in Europe has been
(Continued on Page 8)

72. The Stars and Stripes tells the world, "It's over!"

CHAPTER 14

DOLLARS AND NO SENSE

Eleanor Roosevelt recommended that returning servicemen be quarantined in Panama so they could be re-educated on how to behave in a civilized manner. Furthermore she recommended that the men be required to wear conspicuous arm-bands to warn decent girls of their status as potential rapists. That's what the grapevine said at least.

We scoffed at the underlying accusations of Mrs. Roosevelt, but we still took full benefit of the last vestiges of women who felt it was their patriotic duty to entertain servicemen. We toasted the girl's mothers for not locking them up, and we toasted their fathers for not finishing us off with their sawed-off shotguns. Patriotism was never so sweet.

Mom and Dad took contrasting approaches to my obvious preoccupation with women. Mom assumed, and rightfully so, that many of the women who courted the returning servicemen were seeking their future husbands. An admirable goal; one which she fully supported. For these women, Mom harbored a deep-seated protectionist tendency, and she offered to cook dinner for whomever I wished to bring home. Mom struck up a quick relationship with one young lady and offered to cook a special pot roast for the occasion of her meeting my Dad. The offer was made in kindness but the real reason I accepted it was my yearning for more privacy and comfort than I had in the back end of my hopped-up Ford.

Mom prepared my date a fine dinner, then we chatted and listened to the radio. It was Dad who first yawned, suggesting to Mom that they should retire to their bedroom.

My friend and I were left alone at last on the davenport. We talked softly, then I got up to close the venetian blinds, one by one, snapping the blades shut on each window. I slid back onto the davenport, close to my engaging friend and just as I slipped my arm around her shoulders, Mom reappeared like the wind in her quilted bathrobe. "Oh, don't mind me," she said in an unusually high pitched voice, "I just came out to get a glass of water." "Sure Mom," I replied in a slightly annoyed tone.

I listened as Mom turned on the kitchen tap, then turned it off. When she walked through the door with her glass, she glanced at the blinds. "Melvyn, you mustn't close the blinds," she scolded uneasily, as she sat her glass on the library table, "What will the neighbors think?" Within seconds she had the blinds open again displaying a full view of the neighbor's windows. Then she retreated to the bedroom without her glass.

Dad appeared a couple minutes later. "Forgot my cigar," he mumbled. He looked disapprovingly at the open blinds and closed them without any comment. "Sweet dreams," were his final words as he left the room for good. I couldn't help notice the great big grin on his face.

In general, Mom and Dad accepted the incessant partying, though I suspect Mom had more than a little coaxing from Dad. Day after day, night after night, I disappeared from the house to meet my friends. Then I would reappear joyously inebriated and smelling of perfume. Our tickets for free entry to the taverns and clubhouses were the uniforms we still wore and our tickets for free drinks were the stories we told. We returned heros, but now our job was done.

I received orders to muster out of the Army Air Force at Santa Ana Army Air Base, a couple day's drive from Portland. On the way to my last duty station, I stopped at Muroc Air Force Base, which had a flight test program that sounded somewhat appealing. I'd heard many fighter pilots were staying in the service so they could continue flying, and military test pilots were the elite of the flying community. I had to start thinking about a future and flying was all I knew.

For almost a week I knocked around the desert with a lot of guys just like myself, trying to decide what to do next while a few of the Air Force's test pilots mingled among us on a recruiting mission of sorts.

We gathered at a crude desert bar, an outpost just as inelegant and looking just as temporary as the officer's clubs our squadron had built from whatever materials they could scare up at the time. Pancho's Fly Inn was almost an institution in the flying business and it had all the comforts of a war-torn home. It was owned by a raw, crusty woman who called herself Pancho Barnes, an older woman whose rising age was exacerbated by the tight clothes she wore. She was an accomplished flyer herself, a dare-devil according to most of the men who knew her well, and maybe she could have done more of the things she liked to do if she had been born a man. But I suppose it was her shocking, unassuming ways which attracted the pilots, the wanna-be pilots and the women who loved silver wings.

Seems I spent most of the week there, drinking and talking up my flying days. Pancho overheard my tales of Luxembourg, and a big grin covered her leathery face. "I'll be go to hell," she said. "I'm an old associate of that old bastard George [Patton]. And Tooey [Spaatz], too. Sure would give anything I had to see them again, put 'em up at my ranch. They've been through hell and back over the past couple years. Maybe I could take them for a ride in my new airplane, that is if they still have the balls to do it." Pancho was a woman who squeezed every dram of fun she could out of life. There wasn't much she missed.

Just being around flyers again convinced me I should do everything possible to become a test pilot. There was a real thrill associated with flying our country's newest and best, and I wanted to be a part of what the Air Force was doing. I signed up to take my flight physical which was the first step in the process; mine was past due anyway.

The physical was as rigid as the first I ever took, with the flight surgeon poking at my body and sticking something into just about every orifice with the tenderness of a clumsy bull. The corpsmen did their usual tests, the results of which they would reveal at their own convenience. The pass rate, of course was rumored to be as dismal as before.

The Doc who gave me the bad news on the results. He told me my hearing was no longer good enough to meet the flight physical requirements for a pilot. Those pills I got in Belgium never did work, so that was the end of my thinking about flying for the military. It was a great week anyway and I was off to Santa Ana.

At Santa Ana, I was herded through all the paperwork required to process out of the service. The whole procedure took about a week, a surprisingly lengthy time, but that suited me fine because that gave me the time to look over California in a way I hadn't before. This was hot-rod heaven. The best irons in the country were here and in my meanderings around the hot-rod hangouts, I struck up a friendship with Vic Edelbrock, a young guy who was developing racing equipment. For two wool blankets, which the Army supply sergeant was more than happy to push off on someone as a going-away present, I talked Vic out of a set of racing heads and a manifold. This was the start of my next rod.

Vic reintroduced me to the beach fronts I had seen before, without benefit of a car. What an eye-opener! There was so much more to see and do. If I didn't have so many roots in Portland, including a newly discovered girl, this would have been a fine place to settle in.

Still decked out in my uniform, ribbons and all, I stopped at the Balboa Beach Club for a quick drink with Vic. It seemed an unpretentious place but I was set back more than a few steps when the bartender asked to see my identification. Could it be that this civilian was telling me I needed I.D. to buy a drink when I had put my life on the line every day while he poured drinks on the beach making himself rich? Vic's scowl discouraged me from knocking the guy on his ass, but if words could have, maybe I did anyway. Admittedly I was a little hard on the guy, which was maybe a reflection of our having stopped at a couple other drinking holes before the Beach Club. But if one cared to get right down to the facts, the bartender was right; I wasn't yet of legal age.

All my military records cleared, except for the issue still pending of my owing the U.S. government for some part of a truck *stolen* in Belgium. The Army Air Force put me on terminal leave and my discharge was to be effective on the day of my twenty-first birthday. On this day I was handed my *ruptured duck*, that small bronze lapel pin, signifying my new status as a vet.

I returned to the Santa Ana barracks for the last time. The buildings were as crowded and felt as unfamiliar as the first night I spent in the Army at Fresno. I sat alone with my thoughts as I carefully removed the ribbons from my dress shirt and placed them one by one in a small cardboard box. The Distinguished Service Cross, two Silver Stars, the Distinguished Flying Cross, the Air Medal with fifteen Oak Leaf Clusters, the Belgium Fourragere -- twenty-one decorations altogether. Three years ago I could never have foretold this.

My friends and I were heros in the eyes of so many who had counted on us -- foolhardy in the eyes of others. Risking everything we had, every day every mission. Risking our lives for others, sometimes out of duty and sometimes just hoping they would someday return the favor. I could not have done things any differently and likewise I am convinced that was true of the others with whom I served.

But now our goal had been accomplished and three vivid years of my life were just a memory. Gone were my wingmen who I had relied upon and gone was the pace of life to which I had grown accustomed. Now what?

I returned home wearing my uniform, not out of duty, but out of convenience. But the uniform somehow didn't feel the same now, and I decided to try on some of my old civies Mom had dragged from the closet. A moth had eaten through the jacket of the zoot suit, and Mom saw no way to alter it. The pants were hopelessly out of style, particularly in view of the government's past restrictions on the amount of fabric which could be used in clothing. My cords still reeked of grease and they somehow didn't fit the same as I remembered. The scuffed up English brogues seemed too juvenile, though they were still serviceable. My sweaters were also a possibility, but even they were too baggy. I needed to buy new clothes.

Jobs were nowhere to be found. I had no training to speak of, and I had no former job to which I could return by law. I wandered aimlessly, waiting for my friends to return from the war.

By summer's end, the gang had returned to Portland, all except one, that is. Jack Kendall was lost in action while flying patrol in a PB-Y for the Navy. I felt sad when I visited his folks. Two silken stars hung in their window; one was gold and the other was blue. Junior made it home safely, thank God. In Jack's old room, his mom preserved the memories of the days we had spent together. He was the best airplane model builder I knew and all his models still hung from the ceiling of the room where his mother and I sat and reminisced. It was not an easy thing to do for his mom or me.

I could not help but wonder if my coming made her feel cheated out of something she shouldn't have lost. She must have felt cheated, because in a way she was. As I left Jack's house I saw his Soap Box Derby trophy gleaming on the mantle. The sight of it reminded me I would never have had that experience if it weren't for Jack. I smiled, seeing myself as a young child, racing down the hill to the sounds of a cheering mass of people. Totally exhilarated, totally free. Free from the clutches of the Depression for just a fleeting moment. Through this victory I learned to set my goals high, higher than the men I'd come to know who spent their whole lives working in the fields and who squandered their dreams on booze. Reaching out required dedication and hard work, but the reward was there. I knew that to be true. Jack was the one who did this for me and now he was gone.

Mrs. Kendall would live with the memories of Jack and me coming in off our bikes and running to the refrigerator for a treat, a privilege I did not have at home. As I walked to my car I said to myself, "Jack you should not have always let me have the lucky bite, you needed a little luck, too."

The members of the old gang quickly set aside the three past years, almost like they hadn't happened and we picked up where we had left off, as carefree high school kids. That is, all except Koke. He seemed to have lost much of the spirit he once had and decided the city was no longer for him. He told me serving all that time on a submarine had given him too much time to think and he was ready to try to do what his father did all his life, which was being a farmer, far from masses in the peaceful countryside.

One morning, I got a surprise call from a girl named Bea Burdick who read an article about me in the *Portland Oregonian*. With a familiar giggle, she said she called just to say hello. Bea went to school with me at Gregory Heights and then moved to California where she went to high school and later became a dancer at Earl Carrolls, the top night spot in Hollywood. After tiring of the California pace, she moved back to Portland where she lived at the time of her call. I agreed to meet with her and when I saw her, I could hardly believe what a knock-out she was. We started seeing each other regularly, then a little more. I quickly forgot about the other girl I had just met, and Bea became a real buddy.

Mort was still on terminal leave like me which left us with plenty of money for necessities. That meant everything we had in the bank could be spent on our rods. Mort was back with Charleen and started to work on his '36 Ford. Having been inspired by a few of the irons he saw in California, he dropped the body about six inches, put a set of skirts over the back wheels, added Hollywood disks, replaced the standard door latches with push-button releases and recessed the license plate. Mort was happy to forget about the war. After his stint as a platoon leader with Roy's Raiders, he got a battlefield commission and came as close as he wanted to losing his ass. Though he won the Silver Star, he never wanted to talk much about it. During the war, we had stayed in touch with each other by mail better than any of the rest of the gang.

Red decided it was time for him to start thinking of continuing his education. He still wanted to be a veterinarian and he knew it would take a long time. We talked him into staying around, about six months for what we called *fun and games*. Before we knew it, he was off to college.

Lew lived at home and was doing what we were doing. He still didn't have a car so he helped us have a good time in ours. Meanwhile, he started driving midget racers at the Portland Speedway which was the newest thing in car racing. Midget racers had all the appearance of an Indianapolis racer looked at backwards through a spy glass. They were small, and were powered by a hopped-up 60-horsepower V-8 which came out of the smaller of the two Fords which were produced, starting in '37. The gang and I spent a lot of our time at the track cheering him on.

The Greek, different from the rest of us, had not set aside three years. He didn't share the adventure which consumed our conversations. All along, he worked as a trucker, driving the big rigs around the state. It looked like he might even get married. We did a lot together, although his job seemed to settle him down a bit more than the rest of us were ready to accept.

All of us, except for the Greek, joined the 52-20 club. The government decided veterans should have unemployment just like civilians, so we got twenty dollars a week for fifty-two weeks. Each week we'd stand in a block-long line at the VA building, most of us still wearing our threadbare uniforms. Since we didn't get our checks on the same day, there was always one of us who was good for financing a little get-together. After all, beer was only ten cents a glass.

Before I left for the service, I had stored a '29 Ford roadster body under the porch of a friend's house, with the idea of coming home and building the world's greatest hot rod. Throughout the duration of the War, I thought of it continually and drove Op crazy talking about it. To him a car was transportation, something his dad would give him so he could get to the places he needed to go. To me a car was an extension of myself, and that mothballed rod stuck in my mind even when I cruised out to a mission in my Jug.

But, now after what I had seen in California, I really knew what I wanted. I took a '46 Mercury V-8 engine, and did everything to wrench as much speed out of it as possible; I stroked and bored the engine and relieved and ported the block. On top went all the Edelbrock equipment and two Stromberg 97 downdrafts. And after adding a set of headers and twin Smitty mufflers, she purred like a ferocious kitten. Her engine was sheer perfection. Then I lowered the body, put on a drop-center front end, put motorcycle tires on the front; and I added the final touches -- a new lacquer paint job, an all leather interior and a new California Carson top, side curtains and all. She was a flawless creation with style and performance; and she was hankering to drag every scorcher in town.

A group of us formed the Oregon Roadster Racing Association with Red, the Greek, Mort, Lew, Emmy Payne, myself and five other hot-rodders as charter members. Three years had made a difference in automobiles and we wanted to bring hot rods to the tracks since the cops were making a dogged effort now to keep us from racing on the streets. Also the crowds and purses were becoming very attractive for organized racing.

Bea was real understanding, which she had to be if she wanted to run around with anyone in our gang. She, like the Greek, hadn't set aside three years, and it must have bothered her to see us acting like we were still in high school. Still, she hung in there. I think the uniform and wings got her hooked that first day and after that she just plain cared. She really showed herself one night after a wedding we attended. Mort and I were part of the wedding party, dressed in tuxes. After the ceremony we gathered at a local club where some other friends met us. Hoff was with his girl, Target, and a former football friend, Deeks and his girl were there, too. For hours we danced up a storm making a terrible ruckus. Hoff and Deeks, at 280-pounds each could really make the floor bounce to *Chattanooga Choo-choo*.

In a raucous tribute to all of us being together again we sang loudly:

Pardon me boy,
Is that the Chattanooga Choo-choo
Track twenty-nine
For you can give me a shine.

We partied into the night singing and dancing to all our favorites. Then, just as we were leaving, Mort leaned over and whispered in my ear, "Let's meet at my place afterwards." The guy sitting at the next table, noting no doubt, our carnations and princely get-ups, said in a sing-songy voice, "You two going together?" Tucked between Hoff and Deeks, I didn't hesitate to respond, "Stick it up your ass, asshole!" The first guy with the real big mouth stood up and never seemed to quit standing. He must have had his own line position on some football team. As he rose to full stance I thought, why not, and I gave him my best Sunday punch. He lurched back, grabbing the front of my ruffled shirt. Still gripping a clump of my shirt in his fist, he thrust his hands back and ripped the venetian blinds off the window as he crashed to the floor. Bea stood and hovered over him for a few seconds, then kicked him in the balls with her satin shoe. At that moment, she cinched her relationship with me and we scrambled out of the club with the guy looking like he would puke on the floor. Bea turned to look at him once more as we stepped out the door and she grinned, "With those two *achers*, he can go into the real estate business." She had learned a lot since leaving Gregory Heights and I knew she'd make a good wingman.

A girl like this, I just had to get up in an airplane. I hadn't been in a plane since returning from England and I was just itching to go. There was no problem getting a commercial license; I just showed my flight log and filled out the forms. The small airport in Troutdale had Ryan PT-22s for rent. The PT-22 was the two-seat open cockpit primary trainer which some schools had used when I was flying the Stearman PT-17 at Mira Loma. I strapped Bea in the backseat and started down the runway. The minute we were airborne, the memories came back of what it was like to be up amongst the wispy clouds, soaring through the air. I could see Bea in the backseat through the rearview mirror; she was laughing and loving every moment. This was the first time she had ever been up in a plane and I knew exactly what she felt.

Since it was Sunday afternoon, I thought some of the gang would be at Jim Dandy's. As we came in sight of the drive-in I made a low pass just to get everyone's attention, then went north a short distance and dropped to the deck in a Japanese farm field which the U.S. Government had closed for the duration of the war. Then I blasted toward the drive-in at full power, slipping under the telephone wires of the two poles across the street. As though that wasn't enough, I did a wingover above the Grotto built into a hill, alongside the drive-in. Had it not been Sunday, at the exact time of afternoon mass, I would have been all right. Most folks were still reasonably tolerant of war-time pilots. But, when I got back to the field, the manager said he had a complaint and would have to report it to the higher-ups. Within a week, a warning came to me in the mail. I vowed to be a little more cautious, or at least more discreet for awhile. I doubted the authorities would let my pilot's license fill on the back like my first driver's license.

Once I felt pretty comfortable again in the pilot's seat, I convinced my dad to go flying with me. He had never been in a plane and I wanted to see if it did for him what it did for me. I crumpled him in the backseat of the Ryan and with caution thrown to the wind, hot dogged it down the taxi strip.

Unfortunately, I wasn't looking where I was going and crashed into a Piper Cub setting in a 45-degree take-off position. I ate part of his wing, and after that Dad never even considered going up again. For awhile, I set the flying aside and got back to my rod. But there was something missing in my life; something I was still looking for.

Mort and I had always talked about starting a garage and Dad found a good deal for us. Like many small businesses, this garage was shut down when the owner joined the Navy after the Japanese attacked Pearl Harbor. The man was killed overseas and his wife had no interest in restoring the business. The whole idea sounded tempting, but we just couldn't bring ourselves to do it.

Racing was what interested us most and at every opportunity we raced our rods at the local tracks. We were going to make a big thing out of it. Then, disaster struck one day, when Lew, Mort and I went to a local horse track to race our rods. Lew plowed through the inside rail and smashed his car into a smaller-than-life grotesque mass of metal. When he came to, Lew found the top rail in the front seat with him. Only then, did we admit we weren't eighteen anymore. We had our fling but now the war was over and so were our days of our throwing panties at cheerleaders in the football games and acting crazy. It was time to seriously think of where we were going.

The Greek was going with a girl named Harriette who I always thought was first-class. He talked like he might settle down and started asking me when I would do the same. That wasn't for me though, not yet at least. I started to realize hot rodding wasn't something I could do forever, and something within me was saying "Do more." But like most of those vague messages which tend to hit you suddenly but seem to come from nowhere, this one came without a solution. Still, getting serious about marriage didn't fit in.

Ted and I got together one evening and he told me he planned to go to school and study to be a C.P.A., like his dad. Being a C.P.A didn't seem like such a good deal to me, until Ted told me some of the less obvious benefits. It was true Ted's father was the head of the local Internal Revenue office and they never had to worry about things during the Depression and that alone was enough to convince me. One never knew when another Depression might strike. Mom still refused to spend her money, like she thought another one was lurking around the corner.

I talked the idea up a little with the gang and before I knew it, Mort, Lew and I joined Ted at the Northwest Business College on the G.I. Bill. Our 52-20 payments were over and this was a good source of income for us all. We still thought of rods, though now they became primarily a source of transportation which was a status symbol only on the weekends. I was driving the same rod but Mort moved up to a '41 Buick convertible. We had been in the school about nine months when Ted started talking to me about taking the C.P.A. exam. Even though we were working hard at it every day, I didn't think we could pass the test without a whole lot more study. Still, Ted laid out a cram course for us and soon Ted and I sat for the exam. Ted passed all four elements and I passed three. The rules said I had two months to retake the fourth element.

Ted took a job as an accounting apprentice which he would do for two years before becoming a qualified C.P.A. Twenty-five dollars a week was his salary. Although I kept telling myself I was still serious about becoming a C.P.A., somehow the whole thing just didn't look all that attractive; maybe I should be thinking about something that moved a little faster.

Lew and Mort were passing time and maybe getting a little smarter along the way, although they weren't really heading anywhere in particular. Ted knew what he wanted and he was on his way. But I was still searching. It wasn't like I was alone; there were schools throughout the country catering to G.I.'s searching for that something. And some G.I.'s found it sooner than others.

Flying was still exciting to me and that's why I jumped at the opportunity to become a pilot for United Airlines. I was sure I was in. The examining official for United said not to worry about the physical, but the week before I left for their training school they gave me a preliminary check and my ears did me in, again. If I would do any more flying it would have to be for pleasure.

My brother got settled in a little more quickly than me. Shortly after he got back from Germany, he and Dad bought a neighborhood tavern together. Mac, a friend of mine, had another tavern on the edge of town where we all hung out on Saturday afternoons. Both taverns seemed to be making money and I wondered if maybe I shouldn't be thinking about owning a tavern, too.

Mac and I sat down one day and talked seriously about the tavern business. There was more to the business than met the eye, he said. Beer was in short supply and when you bought a tavern it should have a good beer allotment. You also needed to have some guarantee for getting the allotment increased if you built up the business. It was possible to make a lot of money on the punch boards and the jukebox too, he said, but you needed to have a place where the business could grow. Mac offered to help me here since his dad was a truck driver for a large brewery and knew all the good locations and soon we had found one. It wasn't the nice neighborhood kind, but it had good potential. It was right down on skid row, two blocks off the waterfront, close to Erickson's, my dad's and Jacques' former hangout.

Money was my next problem. The only way I could swing the deal was with a loan from Dad and Gord. I was completely tapped out, having spent all I had saved on cars and girls. As I knew they would, Dad and Gord came through and Dad even worked my problem of getting a tavern license. For eight thousand dollars I got the lease on the building, the previous owner's license, which he transferred to me, and the previous owner's beer allotment. At twenty-three I was the youngest tavern owner ever licensed in the State of Oregon.

The Greek's father had a grocery store a block from my tavern and the two of us got to know each other a lot better. He started to press me to go out with a girl who worked in his accountant's office. Bea and I had started to drift apart by this time since I was not thinking in terms of wedding bells. Maybe I could have used a new relationship but I was too busy for that sort of thing. Besides I was sure this girl would not have anything to do with anyone who owned a skidrow tavern.

The waterfront district seemed to be starving for a young bartender who was also a good listening partner. The other taverns in the district were owned by the same people since Prohibition and the owner-managers were had since tired of what they were doing. Managing their taverns was a job for them, that's all.

Unlike my disillusioned bar-owning neighbors in skid row, I attacked the business, opening at seven in the morning and closing at one in the morning. It was work all the time, but in six months I paid off my brother and Dad, and paid the balance I owed the owner. The money gushed in far exceeding my wildest dreams. Mac's dad kept me supplied with beer and even offered to sell me some special punch boards. I started learning fast.

Bea and I drifted even further apart, then it was all over. I didn't have time for women anymore. This period of my life reminded me of my days as a cadet. I had something I was trying to do and I gave it my undiluted concentration. Everything else was set aside, even recurring thoughts of Annie.

I had a real empathy for *down-and-outers* and they all liked me for it. My regulars were a real batch of Damon Runyon characters, some of which I even put to work. There was One-eyed Vic who became my swamper and kept the place clean. Waxey Gordon had a gimpy arm and tended bar on occasions when he had a dry spell, though that wasn't very often. Loud mouth Johnson became my best customer. He made most of his money in the fields in the summer and I always thought his money in the winter came from a family that paid him to stay away. Knot-head Whitey, No-legs

Whitey and Hickory were all my customers without legs. They made more money in a day hustling the crowds in town than most working stiffs.

And then there was Arnie Johnson, as tough a guy as I ever knew. He was an ex-cowhand, ex-longshoreman, ex-goon in the San Francisco riots of '34, ex-painter and ex-everything else, including ex-con. Rumor said he had gotten into a barroom fight in Seattle and threw a guy onto a water hydrant and killed him. For months after I started the bar, I thought if only I could get Arnie on the straight and narrow, he would make a great combination bouncer and bartender. And after a couple of false starts, he turned into a jewel. He showed me the ropes of doing business with the working class. That included some of those folks who didn't work regularly but still seemed to have enough money to buy a drink.

Arnie used to sing a little song written by a roving balladeer named Guthrie, which I always thought reflected his feelings on life,

> I've sung this song, but I'll sing it again,
> Of the people I've met, and the places I've seen,
> Of some of the troubles that bothered my mind,
> And a lot of good people that I've left behind.
> So it's,
> So long, it's been good to know yuh,
> So long it's been good to know yuh,
> So long it's been good to know yuh,
> What a long time since I've been home,
> And I got to be drifting along.

The rest of the clientele was a colorful smorgasbord of humanity. There were some Finnish fishermen from Astoria, a city at the mouth of the Columbia River. These men would leave their families in Portland and come home occasionally with the paycheck, sort of like my dad did. I had loggers, too. The logger business, I built up from almost nothing, though. The fact I had lived in a logging camp gave me an edge over other operators in the district. I would always give the loggers a grubstake when they went broke, then I'd drive them back to the woods. Come the next payday they'd be back yelling *Timber* which meant they were buying for everyone in the house.

My rangy mop of hair hadn't changed much, but the customers decided *Curly* was a more suitable nickname. So the name of my place became Curly's Roseway Tavern. Every hangers-on in the district knew to be at Curly's on the lumberjacks' payday where they'd get free drinks until the place closed.

As time passed, I also developed a good following of merchant marine hands who came in whenever the ships were in port. When Lew and Mort both gave up on accounting, they worked for me off and on. I credit them with building up the merchant marine trade. The sailors liked to talk to young people who knew something about the ways of the sea.

This mixture of patrons was as raucous a crowd as one could manage. Arnie almost always was the one who kept the crowd under a modicum of control but sometimes the crowd went wild anyway. There was always someone who felt they had to challenge the tough-talking beefy-looking bouncer. And what I didn't need was to lose my license for having the cops called too often. The cops didn't understand the working stiffs who frequented my bar; they called them bums, beggars and undesirables. So I spent a lot of time just settling disputes myself.

Working stiffs no matter what size, always seemed to be in able physical shape. They could hold their own with or without the booze. I found that out one evening when a fisherman got soused and started stirring up a little trouble. Trying a little reasoning first, I told him if he didn't straighten up he would have to leave. He acted like he didn't even hear me, and kept it right up. Normally I would have turned the situation over to Arnie, but I figured this old guy was pushing fifty or sixty years and I didn't need any help.

Wheeling around the end of the bar, I spun the fisherman around on the bar stool and grabbed him by the back of the neck and the seat of his pants. Then I hauled him right out toward the double swinging doors. On the final heave through the doors he grabbed each door case with surprisingly quick hands and it was like I had run up against a brick wall. I quickly regrouped and forced a smile," Okay, if you are going to stay, be good." Arnie gave me a big-brother lecture, cautioning, "Don't step around the bar after those guys. I'll do that; those fishermen all carry a shiv."

On another occasion, I again didn't heed Arnie's advice and made it all the way through the doors with a peppery seaman. Right then, the seaman took a swing at me. He was shorter than me and had plenty to drink so his not-so-hard a swing laid *him* to the ground, not me. I left him for out. Luckily, Arnie had followed me out the door and saw the guy push himself off the ground, looking to get even. As I turned around, Arnie kicked him between the eyes and he was down for good. Another lecture was appropriate, "Don't turn your back on those kind of guys until you are sure they are through."

The rough stuff was not the norm for the Roseway crowd. Most of my following were guys just trying to shake the strains of life off their backs with a little drinking and talking. From their viewpoint a visit to the tavern was what they knew as fellowship. It was medicine for the mind.

A few of my friends used to like to come and slum a little at my tavern. For that reason I never wanted for company. One or two would bring a girlfriend on a Saturday night to show them what skid row looked like. Hoff was driving a truck in the city, and he came down to see me on his run every day. And, on his way to visit his dad the Greek always dropped in to find out if I was ever going to be able to go fishing or hunting with him.

Finally, I got to the point where I thought I should start spending some of what I was making. Mac and I bought a houseboat on Tomahawk Island in the Columbia River. The houseboat came with a high-powered speedboat. In good weather, and sometimes in bad weather too, I motored down the Columbia. Skirting the city of Van Port, I turned into the Willamette and after a short haul parked on the waterfront and walked two blocks to the tavern. The whole trip took less than thirty minutes with the throttle to the wall.

Then I got to the point where I only really had to work half the day. My relaxed work schedule allowed me to spend more time just sort of tooling around, and enjoying my house with both a refrigerator and my first television. Next came a new Cadillac convertible and a Navion airplane which I kept right across from the houseboat at the field in Vancouver, Washington.

I found the Cad in a lot next to Vic Edelbrock's place in north Hollywood. It was still hard to find good cars and this one caught my eye. The singer Billy Eckstine owned the Cad, which had a genuine imitation leopard-skin boot that covered the top when it was down. She was a beauty, just like new and just what I needed to cruise Broadway.

On the way back to Portland, I passed a dance hall alongside the main highway into Sacramento. A guy who had just come out of the dance was thumbing a ride. He looked like my old friend R.B. might have looked all dressed in my zoot suit, complete with the pork hat. I picked him up, as it was my habit never to pass a hitchhiker. Anyone else would have done the same since most everyone hitchhiked at some time during the Depression and we all remembered how much we appreciated the lift.

I could just tell when this guy stepped through the door and sat down on the fine red leather seats, he felt like he had *arrived*. By the time we pulled into Sacramento, the radio was blaring "*Hey! Ba-Ba-Re-Bop, Oooh Bop!*" My fellow passenger had worked up the volume to a level that got folks looking our way. And, of course the top was down, what would anyone be doing in a convertible with the top buttoned up on a sunshiny day? A Packard convertible pulled alongside us. One quick glance reminded me that the bulky Packard had not caught up with the modern streamlined look of other cars. My friend glanced over at the Packard, as its occupants gaped at him with his over-brimmed hat and white shiny-tooth smile. He said to the Packard driver in a haughty tone, "Man you ain't riding. You ah walkin'." I couldn't have said it that good.

Skidrow taverns usually needed a good watchdog. So I got a gangly one-hundred-and-sixty-pound Great Dane who spent a good part of his life in and around my tavern. He often slept there at night with his huge snout pointed at the brass spittoon by the door. All my regular patrons knew him well, bringing him bones and a caring pat. The Greek hung the name of *Ace* on the friendly creature and that's what everyone called him. Arnie took great delight in donning a chauffeur hat while he cruised in my Cadillac. I took just as much delight sitting in the backseat with some good-looking gal while Ace stretched out on the leopard-skin boot. If it was attention we were after, we got it.

Off and on, I kept in touch with both Op and Paul. After the war, Paul went to Arizona State at Tempe and joined the Air National Guard. Op worked with his dad who was an optometrist in Decatur. Op's dad called me one day, although I hardly knew him. Op's sister put him up to it, she told me later since she knew me well enough from the letters we exchanged during the war. Their dad told me he thought Op was drinking too much, and if I could get Op to come out and work for me, he would give me the money for his salary. He said the doc blamed Op's drinking on the trauma of the War. Op drank to forget. He drank to cope.

I never hinted to Op's dad about his drinking in Europe. Op always had a habit of drinking more than most, though he never confided in us, why he did. I suspect he had no answer to give and we never pried. Everyone had their own way of coping and we could not judge what was right for someone else.

I told Mr. Oplinger I was on my way to Decatur to get Op and that I really did need his help in my bar. *I* would pay him. There was no way I could deceive Op by having his dad secretly pay his salary; you just don't treat friends that way. I didn't need another bartender, but that didn't make any difference. If Op needed help, I would do what I could.

The next day I flew my Navion back to Illinois and picked up Op. Before I knew it, he was behind the bar looking like he belonged there. A guy like Op was a great addition to the tavern and all the clientele liked him. He had finished his studies at Stanford and everyone, including me, liked having an educated guy around.

There were people on skid row who had wound up there for every reason under the sun. Most of them would say it was because of a woman. Some just never had a chance in life. And strangely enough, some were well-educated but just didn't want to do what they were educated to do. Those were the folks who liked talking to Op the most.

Arnie took me aside one day and warned I would get myself in trouble with the liquor inspector sometime. If they found Op drinking too much behind the bar, my license would be suspended. Getting closed down for a month would raise havoc with this type of business because people where hard to bring back into the fold, once they got out of the habit. It was painful but I had to do what I should have done sooner. Op helped by telling me he thought it was time for him to go home. I hated to see him go, as much as he hated to admit he was an alcoholic who needed serious help.

About that time, my old sand-hog friends from Arizona, Paul and Parry flew in for a visit in a couple of P-51s. Parry was in the Arizona Guard with Paul. I owed them a visit, so Op and I decided to go to Phoenix on the way back to Decatur. The Navion was a great plane for this kind of trip. It had room for four, and when you slid the canopy back you could get behind the backseat and store at least four suitcases. The same company that built Navion also built the P-51 and the AT-6. All those planes had the same wing designs which made them the great airplanes they were.

Arnie agreed to manage the bar while I made the trip. Lew and Mort were both pinch-hitting for me, helping Arnie. It was Arnie who came up with the idea that maybe I should take Waxey along so we had a valet. Arnie had more class than I gave him credit for. But Waxey had never been in an airplane and he wasn't enthusiastic about the idea. He knew I had gotten in a little trouble a while back for flying my Navion under the bridge which spanned the Columbia from Portland to Vancouver, Washington. I promised Waxey a small bonus for going because I didn't want to make the trip home alone.

Waxey was a great conversationalist having spent a good part of his life in New York City working for a family which had the run of the docks. He never talked about how he lost his arm or why he left New York and I never wanted to ask. Arnie was convinced he had something to do with the commies on the waterfront, but it didn't make any difference; he was always right by me.

We flew to Phoenix on a weekend and Paul put us up in a shack he was renting on the edge of town. It was not much of an improvement over the musty tents we shared in Belgium, except the unceasing open air ventilation was warm, instead of cold. We couldn't complain though, because we were really there to drink Tequila and at last, taste all the Mexican food Paul used to brag about making.

Paul took us to his favorite hang-out which was a four wall adobe squat building with a dirt floor. It was not far from the crossroads they called Scottsdale. The Camelback Inn was fairly close and frankly, that was more like what I had in mind. As it turned out Paul's favorite bar had a lot more character and we couldn't have had any more fun. In the center of the dirt floor was a large washtub which was full of ice and beer. The routine was to walk over and throw a quarter in the tomato can then take out a bottle of beer. It was that simple. As I looked around I saw that the only light in the place came through four square holes in the walls and from a part of the roof which was missing. Mismatched chairs and tables were scattered on the uneven floor and a fellow sat on the floor in the corner playing the guitar and singing familiar tunes in Spanish.

A whole cast of characters walked in the doorless opening and as they grabbed a beer you would hear the clink of the coin. More often than not, they walked right out the same opening they came in and took a spot leaning against the shady side of the building. Two women sat at a table in the corner, chatting one-on-one and surveying the customers as they walked by. For a one-night stand, they looked worth pursuing, I couldn't help notice their Mexican-style blouses purposely pulled low over their king-sized headlights. However, we were too busy talking about the Great War to take the proper interest.

Later that evening we returned to Paul's place and in short order had talked out the war and airplanes and were sitting around the house by ourselves. Only then did we realize, we had passed up a golden opportunity in the dusty bar. We knew how to entertain ourselves, however. We consumed a whole iron kettle full of refried beans and tortillas, laughing and telling raunchy jokes. Then Paul introduced us to the formality of placing a little touch of lemon juice on the back of the hand alongside a little pile of salt. The routine was to count, "One, two, three; lemon, salt and tequila, down the hatch." Within hours the house was sopped clean of every drop of tequila.

The tequila was a rare delight; at the bottom of each bottle was a pickled worm. It was some kind of Mexican ritual, Paul said, and I think we all ate at least one worm with all the proper sound effects. Late into the night we passed out on the back porch in the dry summer air.

The brilliant morning sun came painfully early and I wondered if the chickens running around the yard had slipped up in the night and shit on my face. My mouth tasted like a Russian wrestler's jockstrap and the stench pursued us all.

Fortunately, there's nothing like a reformed boozer to put a group of sickly drunks back on the straight and narrow, and Waxey played the role well. He packed the bags in the car and got us to the field in time for our scheduled early departure. We planned to fly into Decatur in one day's time and did not want to get in too late. With a fond adios we were off, with Op and me in the front and Waxey in the back.

The climb to our cruise altitude took some time. My Navion, like most private aircraft was designed to operate as cheaply as possible and it just didn't have the power of military planes. Patience is what one has to have to fly one. Just as we trimmed up the plane and leveled off with our course set for Kansas City, Op shifted in his seat grasping at his gut, "I've got a problem." His Midwest digestive system was not handling the mixture of the night before. It was probably all those peppers Paul was so proud of. "Please Mel," he begged, "you must land as quickly as possible. I need a men's room, now."

"It took too long to get up here," I complained. Instead I offered to slow down a little so we could slide open the canopy. That way Op could crawl into the luggage compartment and use the sack in which Paul had packed our lunch. Op wasn't happy at all with the suggestion and I heard some harsh, colorful language spew from his mouth, language I hadn't heard from him since we were in Europe together. But I had honed up on the use of such vulgarity while working in the tavern business and I wasn't about to give in to his threats and abusive references to my upbringing. Finally the urge got the better of Op, and gave me the edge in the argument.

Just as Op crawled over the seat, it happened. The time I helped Grandpa move the outdoor privy was roses compared to this. The foul odor made my eyes water and a film formed on my teeth. I wanted to bale out! Op changed clothes before he came forward but didn't say a word. In his hand was the lunch sack with his shorts sticking out the top. He opened the canopy and gave them the heave-ho, and the air cleared.

We got into Kansas City in the dark and had some trouble finding the refueling station. The tower put a spotlight on us and led us to the passenger unloading area in front of the spectators' window. Op and Waxey hopped out of the plane to go in the building. I planned to take the plane for a refuel. As I let my passengers out of the plane, I could see Op's shorts wrapped around the antenna which ran from the tail to the back of the canopy. Here was the Saturday laundry for all the airport gawkers to see in the spotlight, except it wasn't clean.

We decided to proceed to Decatur although we would get in much later than we had planned. The tower said there was weather in the Springfield/Decatur area but we thought it couldn't be any worse than what we had flown in before. Besides, we now had several flight control aids we didn't have then, including a direction finder.

As we set course out of Kansas City we picked up the beam to Chicago. After we had been on course about an hour Op put on the headset and started listening to the beacon identification code, then studied the flight map. When he was sure, he said, "Mop, you never were too good at code. It looks to me like you are on the beam to St. Louis." A little researching on my part proved him right. I told Op we would just turn north, take a fix with the direction finder then work our way back onto the Chicago beam. It didn't take long before we were hopelessly lost. We had overshot Decatur and were getting low on gas.

The field at Decatur was closed and so was the alternate at Springfield. The trouble was, we didn't have enough gas to make it into Chicago. So we decided to try to make a letdown into Springfield anyway, hoping to find that the heat of the city had lifted the overcast a crucial few hundred feet which would allow us to locate the runway. Op was still thinking reasonably clear and he said if we had a chute, the best thing to do would be to bail out. Up to this point, Waxey was taking all the conversation in stride. Now he panicked. Op tried to calm him down a bit, saying he made some sort of overstatement but it didn't help much.

This part of Illinois is as flat as a plate and under these conditions it was the best place to be. I thought a shallow letdown would allow us to see the ground in time to work our way into the town and find the field. One major problem loomed over us. The red warning light was telling me, we were about out of fuel. According to well-established procedures a slow spiral letdown was the customary thing to do now; we weren't the first to be caught in this situation.

As we broke through the clouds, we could see cars on the highway. At one hundred feet, patches of fog masked the view to the ground in most places. Op surmised we were right on the edge of the city. Then he got us located. We were in Springfield, he exclaimed. "Turn right, and you should see the field." That's what I wanted to hear, and just then a flash of a rotating beacon caught my left eye. There was the runway on my left about a mile ahead. The engine started coughing and then windmilled. I pointed the nose right at the runway, dropping the wheels and barrelling in. I knew I was coming in too hot and too high but I had to get us on the ground. As we slammed onto the runway, we sprung the nose gear. Everything else held together like a tough old Jug would. Looking up at the sign on the tower, I saw we made it into Decatur, not Springfield.

Waxey might have had a great story to tell all his cronies back at the Roseway, but he had no intention of getting back in the airplane. I put him on the bus and then told him I would meet him a week later in Portland. It would take me awhile to get the plane repaired.

The Greek worried about my ears ever since he found out about my problem. He told me he read a story in *Ripley's Believe it or Not* about a guy who had an audible tick in his ear, which sounded just like my problem.

That supposedly was the only known case. He kept after me to go to the Veterans Administration and try to get something done about it. This couldn't be a run-of-the-mill problem, he said, if only one other guy had it. I thought maybe he was right.

The VA hospital staff was hopelessly perplexed by the problem. One doctor said he had read about a case of a vet who had hiccups which wouldn't stop. They cured the hiccups by injecting novocaine into the nerve in his neck. The doctor said the analogy was admittedly remote to my case but he still thought this procedure might have application. So he planned an injection in my inner ear, hoping it might yield the same results. The head audiologist asked what if the hearing disappeared with the tick when the novocaine wore off. That was enough to scare me right out of the hospital. I wouldn't have anything to do with being a guinea pig.

The Greek didn't give up. He was now driving truck for *The Journal* and knew a reporter who said he would publish a story on my ticking head. The story made the front pages and the Veterans Administration had me on a small pension in short order. The press, lots of times got results when no one else could. However, publicity, bad or good, always brings out the crackpots. A couple of self-professed prophets wrote saying the immoral deeds I committed during the war provoked the devil to invade my body and I had to rid myself of him before the tick would go away. The good news was, if they were right at least I would know when he left. Meanwhile, the devil still lurked within me, raising havoc.

The Greek kept putting pressure on me to spend more time fishing. We tried once to fish the Smith River not far from Portland. The trip wound up with our getting thrown out of the lobby of the only hotel in the area. The manager didn't like it when we bedded down in the lobby. He didn't care if the weather was miserable and we couldn't stay awake at the wheel of our car. We knew the trip was really over when we found out that the road leading to the best part of the river had washed out in the rain.

The Greek wanted to try again. This time we were prepared to walk to the river if necessary. We planned to drive to the Vincent Creek guard station, about thirty-two miles from Gardiner, Oregon. The guard station wasn't far from the river, but at Sulfur Springs which was almost sixteen miles short of the guard station, we found ourselves stuck in almost a foot of thick mud. We decided if we didn't want to lose the truck we borrowed for the trip, we'd better walk from there. The walk was as beautiful as it was wearing. The trees hung with water and the smell of the damp forest was all around. We were alone in the world, it seemed; I had never experienced such peace. Continuing, we moved along at a pace we hoped would get us to the guard station by nightfall and to a cabin a friend of the Greek's dad owned. We came to the cabin in time to sit and watch the spring steelhead salmon bound over the falls on the way to their spawning grounds. There were hundreds of fish, all twenty to thirty pounds in size. We stayed for a week shooting enough grouse and catching enough fish to feed ourselves. The Greek was right, we had to do more of this. It was good for the soul.

On the way back to town we thought we should stop at the Mt. Vernon hot springs since a rancher told us it was a good place to get a steam bath. My Finnish fishermen friends from the tavern were the first to introduce me to the delights of steam baths and I wanted to introduce the Greek to the ritual. We came with clean clothes, soap, and towels. From the front, the springs didn't look all that impressive, an old hotel-like structure, probably built around the turn of the century, faded into the surroundings. In the parking lot were a couple of Cadillacs and a Lincoln with California and Nevada license plates. The springs must have special healing powers to attract all this out-of-town trade, we thought.

A pleasantly agreeable girl, probably about our age, met us at the door dressed like she was ready to do a nightclub act; complete with the frilly, half see-through dress and all. She looked at us, seeing we looked like we had just wallowed with the pigs and said, "Can I do something for you boys?" I responded truthfully, "We would like to take a steam bath." She lifted one eyebrow and crumpled her lips, "Take a what?" After a private conversation with another girl tucked behind the door, the first girl said, "There's a steam bath somewhere on the edge of the property and when you get through come back for a drink. By the way," she added with a threatening sneer, "would you mind parking that truck of yours around back."

After our steam bath, the Greek insisted we take one last look at the place and I didn't have a good argument against it. But I had a tough time luring the Greek away from a dark, long-legged Grecian-looking gal who claimed to be from the old country, but who talked with a distinctive syrupy southern twang. She told us the whole house was operated by girls from Nevada who were working their way through college. It didn't take us long to figure out this was not our time to be overly supportive of higher education. We kept on driving.

It was too early for breakfast eateries when we came upon the first small town, but we hoped to find something to eat anyway. The only restaurant was closed and we were getting mighty hungry. Our only hope for a meal was to stop at a farmhouse and see if we could buy one from the lady of the house. The place we stopped was a fairly large working farm and the hands were just coming in from having put in a couple hours work before breakfast. The farmer's wife told us to sit down and grab a bite before the crew got in. She put on a feed which took me back to the farm days in Canada. It started with pork chops and hot cakes, bacon, chicken livers, and oatmeal. The breakfast feast concluded with what we mistook for gravy, which was really plain cream almost too thick to pour. To go with the cream was almost anything anyone could want including my old favorite, stewed prunes. The missus wouldn't take anything for the meal but the Greek slipped a couple dollars under the plate just to make it easier for the next guys who asked the same favor.

Arnie kept things in good order at the bar and Mac came up with an interesting idea worth some consideration. He told me he thought my business was good enough we could cut the size of the glasses about two ounces. I thought the diminished size would be too noticeable. Arnie had already come up with a solution for that problem. He talked to the glass distributor who said we could taper down the size of our glasses about one-half ounce at a time. The change would never bother anyone, he said, and in short order the increased profits we made would cover the cost of all the extra glasses we had to buy. That's exactly what happened and my profits shot up twenty percent. This whole idea was really Arnie's and for that, I gave him a raise and sent him on a vacation. Ace and I ran the tavern while Arnie was away. Mort was now working full time for me as well.

Ace used to go across the street and beg for bones from the wholesale meat market, the bigger the better. He liked to drag the bones to the front door of the tavern and eat them there. One day a merchant marine sailor, with a little too much to drink or maybe even too much to smoke, staggered through the front doors and kicked at Ace's big old knuckle bone. With a growl, Ace held his position and the floater took a swing at him with his clenched fist. In an instant Ace pulled the man to the sidewalk and dragged him through the swinging doors, then all the way to the back of the bar. It was a good thing the guy had on a sturdy leather jacket.

Ace's adversary was no skidrow deadbeat, and before I knew it, I was being sued. With a quick settlement, Ace was restricted to the back room. But when Arnie returned, he didn't take too kindly to Ace's new restriction. I never realized Arnie and Ace were such pals. Unknown to me, Arnie got one of his merchant marine friends to lure the guy responsible for this trouble back into the tavern, then Arnie found a good reason to rough him up. We lost that customer for good, and Ace worked his way out of the back room and was put on probation.

Many of the guys who worked the fields in the Valley were what some folks called winos. I usually let them hang around, even though they weren't cash customers. They didn't drink beer and I didn't sell wine, since wine was only sold in the state liquor stores and in licensed food stores. One day two of these guys stood at the end of the bar. They were counting their money and had decided they had enough to buy two bottles of Muscatel. The guy who was the most sober went to the store to get the bottles. As he came back through the doors with both bottles, his partner rushed to meet him. Just then, the wino carrying the bottles dropped one and it broke on the concrete at the front door. He looked at his friend and said, "Oops, I dropped yours." This crowd was always good for one-liners.

Mom called one day and told me our old friend Dorothy from the logging camp days and my brother and his family were coming to the house for Easter dinner. I would never refuse an offer like that. Mom enjoyed cooking big dinners for the holidays and she was good at it. Unfortunately, Dad always took the opportunity to offer lots of advice on how I should run my life. I knew he would give me another one of his lectures on me spending too much money. The last time I had told him that money was only paper, he almost got angry.

As we sat around the table in our Sunday best, we must have looked like a classic Norman Rockwell painting. Our manners were formal and almost stilted, mostly for the benefit of our honored guest. Without thinking much about it, I reached across the table to pick up a bowl of mashed potatoes and accidently spilled the gravy boat. As if Mom wasn't already horrified enough I blurted out, "Oh Fuck!" Dad didn't bat an eye as he said, "Now, there is a word you don't hear too often." His remark spared me for the moment. But I knew then, I had been around those guys on skid row too long and I was starting to talk like them.

My Easter dinner at home made me start to think about an idea Lew brought up. We were both getting restless. All the gang was filtering off trying to make a career out of whatever. Even Mort tired of bartending and settled down. He bought a conventional '46 Buick convertible and went to work for U.S. Steel as a salesman in their chain link fence division. Red was still working hard to become a veterinarian, Koke was becoming a successful farmer and the Greek would be a truck driver forever.

Lew wasn't sure what he wanted to do yet. He did know he wasn't ready to settle down and neither was I. And, although I was now making barrels of money, the business wasn't all that satisfying. Worse yet, I knew my dwindling interest would soon start to show in the receipts. Lew's idea sounded attractive.

"Sailing," Lew said, "that's the thing to do. We could dock our boat at the mouth of the Columbia and make short trips to Hawaii and down the coast." Then that talk grew into, why not sail around the world? Lew argued this was the only way we could see all the fascinating things and places all over the world. "Just think about it," he said, "nice warm breezes, a bee-utiful girl in every port." Soon the idea flourished, and we became convinced that sailing around the world offered the thrill and excitement we craved.

71. Mel's hopped-up '46 Mercury A-V8.

72. A little more class, Jack Morton's
'41 chopped Buick.

73. The one Jack "Lew" Lewis always wanted.

74. The Roseway Tavern dividend.

77. The Navion in Decatur, Illinois recuperating
from its hard landing.

78. John "the Greek" Peacheos and Harriette meet
Don Parry and Paul Ollerton, who arrived
in Portland, Oregon in their P-51 to share
a beer at the Roseway Tavern.

CHAPTER 15

THE FINAL BLOW

"Frankly, you wouldn't know a sailboat from a washtub," Dad snapped as I told him my plan to buy a fast sailboat and sail around the world." Yes, he was right, I had never been sailing in anything but a washtub, the one in which I sailed the Columbia as a kid. Dad never hesitated to revive past indiscretions to make his points.

Still it was time for me to do something different with my life. I had learned a lot about people while operating my bar. Somehow the fundamental human tendencies, both good and bad, come to the forefront when people drink too much booze. The same thing happens in combat, when a man is forced to make a decision between his own safety and the life of another.

The insight was valuable but I'd learned enough. "Now what?" I had said to myself. And the answer that came to me was about as boring as finding a couple dead cockroaches in my bar glasses.

Dad should have known I was going to set my plan in motion anyway with Arnie and Lew as my shipmates. First, we needed to find a ship so Lew and I started looking for one while Arnie kept the bar operating. We helped Arnie when we weren't working on the sailing trip and we divided the other responsibilities. Arnie had the job of getting all the fishing and hunting gear in order. My job was to see we had proper navigation and radio equipment. Lew was responsible for everything else except the food for what promised to be a four-year voyage. And since everyone seemed to have their own ideas of what it was they wanted to eat, we shared that responsibility, with me thinking of providing the coffee and other non-essentials. On top of all that, I had another very significant function -- that was to pay for the whole deal.

While Lew and I were busy traveling the West Coast looking for a ship, Arnie got Loud-mouth Johnson to buy produce from the local farms where he sometimes worked. Arnie took the food to a custom cannery where everything was processed into standard-sized cans painted with chromate paint. Along with the vegetables, he also canned a deer and some beef.

Everything I owned had to be sold; this was the start of our real serious planning. First I sold my airplane then I told Mac when I left town the houseboat was his for all the help he gave me in getting started in the tavern business. It was just a matter of time until we found the perfect ship.

My plan was to stay at the houseboat until we set sail. However, one day was unusual and almost frightening. The water in the Columbia rose as high as I had ever seen it and we had to let out the lines on the houseboat until the booms sank out of sight. The one-car-at-a-time bridge connecting the mainland to Tomahawk Island, where we were moored, was fast becoming dangerous. Mac and I decided it would be best if we moved off the island, then took turns going out every morning to service the mooring lines.

Van Port sat between Tomahawk and Portland and had built up on the flats. During the war it became the second largest city in Oregon and the largest housing project in the U.S., occupied mostly by employees of the shipyards. The flats would be underwater, save for the thirty-foot high dike which blocked the waters of the Columbia and Willamette Rivers.

On my way to the tavern, after letting out the houseboat mooring lines again, I heard the radio repeat what had become a continuous message: "The U.S. Army Corps of Engineers assures you, the Columbia dike is under no danger of bursting, contrary to concerns voiced by Van Port citizens. The dike is capable of withstanding far more pressure than it is currently under. Residents of Van Port should not panic. There is no cause for concern. I repeat, there is no cause for concern."

As I worked my way into town that Memorial Day, I was thinking about a couple of ships I planned to take a look at, which would suit our needs. Then the announcement crackled across the radio. The dike had given way and people were ordered to immediately evacuate Van Port and all other lowland property behind the dike. Water flooded into the flatland, and the road I was traveling was predicted to soon become a dangerous river. God looked after me again. I got my Cad and me out of the low area, just as Van Port started to flood. Within minutes of my escape, the city was under fifteen feet of water. Two days later the whole city disappeared, never to be rebuilt. Most of the buildings floated down the river and out to sea. Ironically the Portland Speedway disappeared, too. But our houseboat was spared, and it was time to get serious about a ship.

In Hong Kong a shipyard was building Chinese junks to order. The manufacturer shipped the junks into Vancouver, British Columbia and they were advertised in all the West Coast yacht magazines. I decided to take the Greek up on an offer he made to go to the coast of Oregon for a bear hunt. From there we'd drive to Canada and just take a look. This was probably the last trip we would take together for a while.

We spent a day on the coast tromping through the forest, but killing for sport had little attraction, especially in the miserable weather we had.

Then we drove to Astoria and arrived at the 14th Street ferry dock a little before noon. We had a couple of minutes' wait to catch the ferry which would take us across the mouth of the Columbia River into Washington state. The Cad sat on the end of the dock as we walked to the restaurant for a hot cup of coffee. It was 11:55 on 14 April, 1948 when the world underneath us started to move. I wasn't used to a moving *terra firma*. In fact I was quite accustomed to *firma terra firma*. I was speechless as the dock started a slow roll, deliberately nudging my car closer and closer to the edge. As fast as the movement started, it was over. When we got to the car a second rolling motion started, but it was not as bad. Once on board the ferry, I felt safer, and only when we got to the state capital at Olympia did we see the real damage. The roads in town were gridlocked because the fronts of several buildings had tumbled into the street. That was the first time I had ever felt an earthquake and I didn't need any more of nature's wrath.

After looking over the ships in Vancouver, British Columbia, I concluded a Chinese junk had a lot of comfort but it looked to me like it would take the rest of my life to sail around the world in one. They just looked too slow. Although that was the end of any business we wanted to conduct, we didn't want to waste our time.

The Greek and I decided to see if we could scare up a little coozy. There was enough sunshine to put down the top and see if we could attract a couple girls, as we cruised down Main Street. The flashy Cad worked like a charm, luring a couple of bobby-soxers who appeared to be open to most anything. They said they were eighteen and nineteen, which didn't seem too bad. Who really cared about three or four years difference in our ages?

Looking cool, we whipped up our old favorite from Samuel's cabin, a mason jar of grapefruit juice and grain alcohol, guaranteed to corrode the metal lid in a matter of hours. Then we drove to the border with the idea of finding a place to stay back in the states. Fortunately, at the U.S. border the guards did a much better job than we had, of finding out the girl's ages. They were both sixteen. Instantly, we dropped off the girls and all our plans, then fled. We were glad to get out of what could have been a great big mistake.

The next month Lew and I traveled to San Pedro and looked over a ship we had read about. *The Otter* was a 55-foot ketch, a glistening beauty. Built in Portland, Maine, she had sailed around the horn after some drifting around in the Caribbean. She was fast enough; three years earlier she won the Ensenada Race, from Ensenada, Mexico to Hawaii. We could not help notice she was anchored in the harbor alongside actor Sterling Hayden's ship. I had seen Hayden in many movies but still I marveled at his overwhelming stature and manner. When he said *The Otter* was the answer to our dreams, and would whisk us to the South Pacific at a powerful speed, I bought her.

Upon returning to Portland, I sold my Cadillac. Dad bought my bar, even if he did think I had lost my mind. Dad couldn't help ask, "Mel, what are you planning to do when you grow up?" Arnie agreed to stay with Dad for awhile and help him in the bar. Our plan was to have Arnie join us in the fall as we came up the coast to pick up the supplies after our short cruise down the coast. I bought an old truck, loaded it with enough supplies for the cruise, including all the fishing and hunting gear and my sextant and ephemeris. Then Lew and I took off for California.

Freshly back in the water from her inspection and a new coat of paint, we set sail out the harbor for our shakedown cruise along the coast of South America. Lew coached me on every move.

I had read a lot, getting prepared for this trip and knew all the terms. When Lew said, "Unfurl the sails and watch the battens," I knew what he meant. But sailing, not unlike flying or even baseball can't be learned from a book. One has to do it, and maybe even has to make a few mistakes.

Soon I could hit the ball out to center field and we were making good headway. Each day I learned a little more. The ship would have been very comfortable for a crew of six. But two of us could handle her with little difficulty, if nothing happened which was too unusual. Fortunately, nothing unusual happened for awhile.

The Otter was rigged so it could be handled by one person nicely from the cockpit. One person could come about and the only time that person needed help was to change sail. In the good weather we enjoyed, it was no trouble for one of us to get plenty of rest while the other stood watch. I spent many hours just lounging on the deck with the shade of the sail and the breeze of our headway keeping the temperature just right. During the day, we changed off watch whenever the occasion seemed appropriate. At night we kept a regular four-hour watch. With all the dozing I did during the day, four hours was often all the sleep I needed.

As we changed watch at night, it became a ritual to have a new brew of coffee made for the one coming on. Lew needed the coffee to get him going since he was often plagued with violent headaches, something which seemed to worry me more than him. Whenever he awakened we'd talk some and I would give Lew a lesson in shooting a star to find our position.

We ate fish four or five times a week. Arnie had done a good job of putting together a set of gear which included some books which showed what fish we might catch and those that were not good to eat or were poisonous. Most of the catch was small mackerel and bonito, which we learned how to cook every way we could imagine. The canned tomatoes and squash made a great meal too when they were mixed with a little Mexican pepper Lew had picked up in San Pedro. Still, a few days out of port we decided to drop a line to Arnie and have him bring us a cookbook when we joined up later. A little variety would be nice.

One week out, our shot of the sun showed we had crossed the Tropic of Cancer. We started a more easterly course so we could see land as we rounded Cabo San Lucas on the southern tip of Baja, California. Passing close to the shore, the land looked hot and uninviting so we waited until we got inside the Gulf of California to find a place to stop for a few days. With a gentle following wind, we found ourselves approaching the Islas Marias in the southern part of the Gulf in just two days. We decided to lay on the easterly side of the larger of the three islands and take a good swim and get cleaned up. With the anchor out and calm seas, a couple of days of just laying around seemed like paradise found. We were both starting to look like natives, browned and in ragged cut-off dungarees. Lew's idea of sailing into the sunset was looking better every day.

As the sun came up, we pulled anchor. This day we put out all the sail, close to two thousand square feet. Sailing gently down the coast, we stayed just in sight of land. Our plan was to sail into the harbor at Acapulco. The softly flapping sails moved *The Otter* slowly, now. We expected to arrive within a week. Like most things in life, it's not the speed but the steadiness of it all that gets you to where you want to be. In every twenty-four hours time, at just four knots, we made one hundred miles. We couldn't ask for any more than that. The scenery was breathtaking and we relished every moment of it. Rising above the coast was a ridge of mountains which changed color from light gray to blue to red as the sun traveled its course. I told Lew to add a camera to the list for Arnie.

As we sailed into the Acapulco harbor, we chose a moorage area close to a cluster of other ships. That way we could meet other sailors a little easier. By now we had found the international sailing community was in general made up of people like us; most looked like they had money but didn't. Only a few really did have money and they generally had lots of it.

We radioed Customs and made an appointment to clear for entry at the harbor. Three inspectors manned the customs boat. The one who came aboard to conduct the inspection had a fair command of English and seemed good-natured. I had seen him in many south-of-the-border movies at the Roseway theater. He was the heavyset one with the black, slicked-back hair which had a good coating of pomade. He carried a pistol on his side that looked almost too large to use and on his feet he had a pair of well-shined leather riding boots. After looking over our passports and the ship's papers, he gladly took a bottle of grain alcohol when I told him of the magic effects it had on girls. We paid our fees and he was off with a smile on his face. Lew said we had made a friend but I pointed out the ones in the movies always smiled that way just before they shot someone. Our cocktail flag went up the first evening. That was the best way to meet new friends. We hoped at least one of our cocktail guests would reciprocate and invite us over for dinner on their cruiser. It seemed like young men were always welcome on the big yachts. We joked that some sailing aristocrats thought of us young sailors as great catches for their daughters, or at least they treated us that way. I met one young girl under those circumstances though I got the feeling she was right out of an old movie and must never have kissed a guy. Laura seemed so innocent, and so vulnerable and after a few days frolicking on the beach and seeing the town, she invited us to her friend's house on shore for a Spanish dinner. Her friends lived high on a hill overlooking the harbor. From their window I could see *The Otter* slowly rocking back and forth, acting anxious to be put to sea.

Lew and I talked about preparing to leave in two days time. I would write Laura once she got back to her girl's school in Pasadena. She was so tender and young. I could plan on her for the future.

The night before we set sail, Laura took me to her folks' yacht. No one was on board, except a couple men from the crew. She led me to her state room, then she reached into a cabinet and pulled out a bottle of Canadian Club. I had never seen her drink before, but as I got comfortable with the idea, she disappeared through a door saying she wanted to put on something more pleasant. When she returned she was dressed in a sinfully indiscreet, black deck robe and it wasn't long before we were swapping spit and I was thinking of old times in Paris. We rolled onto the bunk in a passionate embrace, with me fully expecting her to spurn my advances at a crucial moment, the price one often pays for seducing a *nice girl*.

She reached for my zipper, deftly sliding it downward with one hand, while protecting my shorts from catching in the metal teeth with the other. I could feel her fingers taunting me, and I could not hold back a second longer; I wanted her. And she wanted me, I was convinced. So I made my move, tearing away our clothing and thrusting my body onto hers, rubbing stick to stick in lustful expectation of creating sparks and then flames.

"Just a minute, I have to put my diaphragm in," she said calmly from beneath my pulsing motions. I drew back in disbelief for a mere second, then obscured my thoughts. My, oh my, this girl had been there before. Here I'd been telling Babe Ruth not to choke the bat.

As we set sail for a southerly course, Lew asked, "You thinking about that young innocent girl you met?" I growled, "Don't be a smart ass."

To really test *The Otter* and our seafaring abilities, we thought we should take a journey which kept us at sea about a month. Later, on our 'round-the-world voyage, we would have to cross the Pacific and we wanted to see if we had it in us. We took on supplies and water which would last us much longer than our month estimate, then set course for the Gulf of Guayaguil in Ecuador on the coast of South America. The sailing part of the trip was expected to be uneventful. The real test was to see how Lew and I did living together for so long in tight quarters.

Three weeks out we crossed the Equator. The Navy particularly, has a ceremony taken quite seriously in celebration of all those who cross the equator. If one lives through the celebration he becomes what's known as a shellback. Lew, having taken part in the ritual while he was in the Navy, played the part of Neptune. We threw over the sea anchor and Lew cooked me up some disgusting fish innards for my meal while he ate the fish, massaging his aching head in silence while he ate. Then it was into the water for me, and I was glad keelhauling had died as a form of naval punishment. Having been initiated into the *Solemn Mysteries of the Ancient Order of the Deep*, I became a shellback at latitude 00.00 and longitude 82.32W. The anchor was lifted and we set sail for Ecuador. Lew and I were still friends, though I was starting to worry seriously about his health.

There was some degree of unrest in Ecuador and clearing Customs became an impossible task. Without looking back a moment, we were on our way north again, planning to pick up Arnie in San Francisco. From there we would sail to Portland together, then load on our four years of supplies. From Portland we would go to Kodiak, Alaska and get in a little hunting, then we would sail down to Hawaii and then to Australia. From Australia we would sail through the Indian Ocean and up to the Suez canal, across the Atlantic, through the Panama Canal then back home. It all seemed like a piece of cake.

With almost three months of sailing *The Otter* under our belt, we started around Conception Point on the California coast. To date, we had not encountered any bad weather. There were some strong breezes, but nothing that ever had us wishing we had another hand on board. Point Conception, though, had a reputation for erratic weather. The Point divides the lower and upper Pacific, which causes some rather unusual conditions. It was here that our Navy had lost a handful of combat ships when the lead ship misread a marker light and all the remaining ships just followed the leader aground. The rusted hulls of the ships were still visible, serving as a reminder of the dangers.

We set sail around the Point in the early evening with more sail than we normally carried at night. Then, as darkness settled in, a real blow started knocking us around, and the winds picked up even more. We fought hard to shorten the sail, then agreed if we had trouble coming about, we had no choice but to run with the wind. All night we ran with the wind. We were hurled around the Channel Islands and the lights on Santa Rosa and Santa Cruz gave us the feeling our ship was going around in circles. Our senses became numbed, taking me back to my days of flight training in the dark, among the hovering dark mountains. We could do nothing, other than keep a seaward heading and in the morning we would pick up headway on our course again. By dawn we were south of the Islands and the blow had mercifully waned.

We put up a little more sail and tried to set the course for Santa Barbara. Although the wind was just a breeze, a thick haze hung low over the water and I couldn't get a fix on our position. Sailing closer to the coast, I hoped a carefully worded question to one of the passing ships would locate us without making us look like a couple of real boobs. We flagged a cruiser and asked how far we were from Santa Barbara. The reply was, "Just around the point, but you are going the wrong way." We made the boob chart anyway.

As we pulled into Santa Barbara, it looked like a tropical paradise. The clean sandy beach was lined with gently swaying palm trees and the weather was soothingly warm. I had been there one time while stationed at Mira Loma, but I had never seen it from the sea. It was indescribably beautiful. My dad's comment crept into my thoughts, "Why do you have to travel all over the world when you haven't seen the United States yet." There was something to be said for that reasoning.

We spent a week in port, replacing a little rigging which got torn in the blow and making some crystal changes in the radio. From there we set sail for San Francisco. We made a long tack out of the harbor with the thought we would carry light sail until we got well around Conception. Our plan was to go on one tack for about two days and then cut back into the bay. That would take us about three days working against the wind. Two days out, we discovered our fresh water tanks had sprung a leak and had taken in bilge water. We set sail for the shore immediately and started drinking the juice out of the canned beans. It's too bad they use so much salt in the canning process, we complained. Thirsty and tired, we limped into Monterey Bay two days later in the middle of the night. There was a fishing strike on then, and the whole fishing fleet was in harbor. We struggled into the Coast Guard dock, crawled to the fire hose and laid our parched faces in the rushing water.

After a couple of days in port working the tank repair problem, we gave up. We loaded on a couple of five gallon cans of water, then set sail for San Francisco where we would fix the tank ourselves. The first night was clear and we traveled the inner lane which the heavy liners used for going up and down the coast. Things were going smoothly until a large cruise ship coming straight for us, did not seem to heed the fact we were under sail. Lew got out the signal light and sent them a message," Give way, we are under sail." A message came back immediately, "Fuck you. We are under power." One has to just put up with the rich.

The sail under the Golden Gate Bridge and into the Saint Francis Yacht Club made the whole voyage worth the trouble. The water was a brilliant deep green and the sky was cloudless as we passed under the massive steel bridge into the gentle harbor. We knew the policy of the Club was to let an out-of-town ship stay moored for two weeks, and the visitor's slip was inviting and open. Once we got *The Otter* docked, we paraded straight to the clubhouse. Our first question to the maitre d' was, "Where can we get some ice cream?" He took one quick look at the two of us ragged creatures and said, "If you don't mind, the service entrance is around the back." The club really had its nose in the air, too much for us. So we went into the city to the YMCA and got a warm shower. Then we moved *The Otter* to Sausalito, a budding, friendly little port on the opposite end of the Golden Gate bridge.

Arnie joined us and we did a little clean up on the ship before setting sail for the north. Early one morning, Arnie left the ship in the darkness, then returned at daybreak with ten gallons of white ship paint and two gallons of varnish. We put a coat of paint on the hull above the water line and made plans to shove off. Sterling Hayden brought his ship into town about the same time, making the headlines for snatching his two kids from the day school where his ex-wife had them enrolled, then sailing out to the Pacific with them. Seems he thought the ways of the wanderer were better for them, and he was smart enough to teach them all they needed to know.

As we sailed out of the harbor, Arnie guided us to a crab-pot float. He reached over the side to pull it up and saw it was loaded with crabs. We took three good-sized crabs and before he replaced the trap Arnie threw in a half-full bottle of whiskey. With our consciences healed we cooked our departure meal as we sailed close to the shore. It looked like it would be a good day for sailing. I was on watch when I spotted a large grey whale spouting not far from us. The massive mammal rolled in our direction and dove straight under our ship. "All hands," I yelled, and Arnie and I thought we were in real trouble. Lew was not so concerned and pointed out that the friendly creature was just rubbing barnacles off his skin on the keel of our ship. Arnie and I froze as the whale made another run on us and then left. His size was what really scared me. He was larger than *The Otter* and could have done what ever he wished with us. But like most sea life he was not out to harm us.

As we sailed up the coast, the wind started to build but the sky was clear and sparkling blue. Storm warnings were out and we decided to sail into port at Coos Bay, Oregon and wait out the weather. We were close to the shore and headed on a tack taking us out to sea. On the reverse tack we planned to go right in across the bar at Coos Bay. As we came about the wind gusted violently and we knew we had to get some sail down, right away. Arnie got on the main winch preparing to reef the main sail, but he did not notice that the main sail track had become fouled, and the sail guide was jammed at the top. With all his brute strength he pulled about two feet of the track off the top of the mast and the sail was jammed up. We were drifting dangerously close to shore as I radioed the Coast Guard. In desperation, Lew threw out two sea anchors to try to hold us in position. Arnie was still trying to undo what he had done. The Coast Guard didn't respond.

I continued to radio for help since the Coast Guard surely had a cutter in harbor which could haul us in. Things were going all in the wrong directions for *The Otter*. We were starting to take water and the auxiliary engine flooded, then stopped. That engine was our last hope for keeping us aligned. As the night enveloped us, I couldn't recall ever being in a situation worse than this while flying. The seas, even more so than the skies, were unforgiving of the uninitiated and the foolhardy.

As despair set in, we saw a faint light flickering on the horizon. We were convinced it was coming in our direction. The light got brighter and brighter and once it was in view, we identified it as a Coast Guard lifeboat. These boats could be battened down and rolled clean over and survive, but the boat hardly looked like it could move *The Otter*.

The lurching craft was manned by a boatswain's mate and a boot. The boot was clinging to the rail, wishing he was anywhere but where he was. The bosun pulled from a hatch, a small monkey's fist connected to a light line, that in turn was connected to a hawser. The waves were breaking over the Coast Guard craft and we lost sight of it several times, though it was but a short distance from us. It didn't look like the boot would be able to get the line so much as close to us. We tried hard to hold a steady course, then we sank into a deep trough, out of sight of everything, struggling to keep our course into the wind. Over the top of the wave came the lifeboat for a fleeting moment. As the Coast Guard craft passed near us, the boot hurled the line at us, giving it all the strength he could muster. It lit on our deck about fifteen feet from Arnie who took a running dive, catching it first then helplessly letting it slide from his hand. The monkey fist snapped across the deck and caught between a belaying pin and a rigging line. Arnie was on top of it, scrambling to get it in his grasp. He clutched it as though it was life itself.

Shortly after we got connected to the Coast Guard boat, we started for the bar at the mouth of the harbor. We knew we weren't home free, not yet. The bar looked even more treacherous than the open sea, and we had work to do. We pumped the bilge and got the auxiliary fired up. Although that little bit of power helped, it was still slow going though, with the winds roaring at ninety miles an hour.

Once we got to the bar, the waves spun clean over the Coast Guard craft and knocked us to the deck. I had never seen waves so monstrous. The three of us huddled and talked about everything that could go wrong, like little boys camping their first night in the dark. The difference was, this was real. Our worst concern was that of losing the tow and broaching. We could feel the mud boiling under us. One of us had to stay on the wheel constantly or we would have gone below and buttoned up the ship. *The Otter* would stand to roll over; with her six-ton lead keel, she would right herself with little difficulty. That was, providing the hull didn't get punctured.

At last we entered the harbor. We were totally exhausted and when the bosun asked if we wanted to be moored at one of the lumber docks I responded in desperation, "As long as it's tied to land." We could feel the storm getting worse and were ready to collapse. The top of the mast was just even with the dock to which we were tied. This docking facility was made for loading ships with eighty feet of freeboard, not sailing craft. Still, we were free from the wrath of the open seas. We all slithered into our bunks wearing new sets of clothes, which were as wet as the ones they replaced. I took the main stateroom which housed the gimbaled dining table. There was no doubt in any of our minds we might have to get up before the night was over. I put my jacket on the table and fell asleep in an instant with the wind roaring like the prop on my Jug on takeoff.

The tail end of the storm was even worse than what we had seen earlier. It blasted through the harbor almost like it was looking for us. There we were hunkered in a corner, wearied and scared. The wall of wind slammed *The Otter* onto her side, forcing the top yardarm against the top of the dock. I woke as the mast snapped at the step, piercing the cabin and the gimbaled table setting close to my bunk, then dropping out the side of the hull. All three of us leapt up with our flashlights in our hands. Our lights danced through the cabin as we surveyed the damage. It was bad; we had to get out immediately. Arnie and I clambered for the hatch, with Lew lagging slightly behind. The ship had been forced under the dock and the top of the structure had collapsed onto the deck.

Reaching the deck, we stepped amongst the rigging that took on the look of *spaghetti* intertwined with all the spars. The mizzen mast was down on the aft deck. Crawling up the collapsed dock was tricky as the wind whipped us around with a one hundred mile an hour force. I grabbed Lew as he lost his balance, one of his headaches had surely seized him. None of us fell; if we had we would have been crushed instantly by the merciless sea.

We walked into the Coast Guard station just as it got light, fighting the wind which forced us to take a thirty-degree lean. Over coffee we realized the palm trees of the Pacific had escaped us for good. I lost *The Otter* without a shred of insurance and was close to being broke. Thanks went to someone for pouring *The Otter's* keel with lead instead of concrete because that was the only thing of value to salvage.

79. Oregon's second largest city, Van Port was lost
to a flood in less than one day.

80. Mel, Arnie Johnson, Jack "Lew" Lewis on board *The Otter*.

81. *The Otter* at anchor in Santa Barbara harbor.

CHAPTER 16

COMING TOGETHER

Dad had sold the Roseway Tavern a short time after we set sail, realizing the real appeal to the customers was a bunch of young guys who would listen to their tales of woe. He was getting too old for that and had too many to tell himself.

Arnie went to work at the Timberline Lodge at Mount Hood as a maintenance man and Lew and I had the great idea the two of us would make good radio announcers. I couldn't come up with a better idea so we enrolled in the Northwest School of Broadcasting. There I met Charley and Gladys Milam who became good friends. Gladys was a jewel, a real conservative girl who knew how to stretch a G.I. school check. She was pretty enough, all right. But if God passed out only so much good looks in this world, Charley got far more than his share. The modeling agency which hired him loved his rugged masculinity, but fortunately Charley was careful not to bore any of the rest of us with that sort of nonsense.

Seeing Charley with Gladys got me thinking about marriage as something one had to do to settle down. Ted married Wheel and Lew was talking about domestic things too, with a stewardess whom he had just met. Maybe it was time to think along those lines and maybe I should see if that girl Genevieve, who the Greek's father always wanted me to meet, was someone I should get to know better. She was still available and had promised to go to lunch with me if the Greek's father went along. Gen was the name everyone called her; "such a nice girl," they always added.

Gen was modestly dressed the day we met, wearing a simple cotton frock and just the right amount of makeup. Light brown hair framed her sturdy face; one which showed conviction. And her personality had just the right amount of vinegar to keep our conversations lively.

After a short while, Gen and I started spending much of our time with the Milams. We had dinner together often. One night, I would bring the Chef Boyardee canned spaghetti and Gen would heat it. The next time Gladys would do the same. With the spaghetti we would have powdered milk, which Gladys perfected by adding just a smidgen of bacon fat. It was really quite tasty and I always told her she had the special touch of the magnificent French chefs at the Carlton in Cannes.

Gladys was resourceful too, understanding the ageless precept of using bread as a filler. Milk was the other oft-used filler, powdered milk that is. She bought it in containers which made twenty gallons; that way the milk cost only about five cents a quart. Altogether, the four of us would eat for less than one dollar and fifty cents. We were pretty proud of that, and I think this is when Gladys and Gen started to plot on how two, namely Gen and I, could eat as cheaply as one. Just a playful thought, they said, though Gen wasn't really all that serious.

After a short time, Lew grew disinterested in the broadcasting school and went to work with Arnie at Timberline Lodge. Charley and I were going to make it to the end, or that's what I said. But I didn't tell anyone how distressed I became one day after listening to some of my simulated broadcasts. Henry Aldridge screeching in his frog-voiced adolescent croak, "Coming Mother!" sounded like music to my ears compared to my recordings. No one would or should have to listen to *that* for long. Then it all came down on me. The twentieth century was half over; life was passing me by. I wasn't a kid anymore and I had to get on with my life. And although I was getting more serious about marrying Gen, my seriousness still exceeded hers, and I knew I would have to do some persuasive courting. This was something I had never done before.

The first time I met Gen's father, I took special note that he had all the looks of a well-built brute. His height added even more to his forcefulness and he acted like the tough Polack he was. Most of his career was spent as a detective on the Chicago police force. When he retired, he moved to the West and took a job as a guard over the Japanese Americans who were interned in a camp in California. I was happy to get a good relationship going with him because I'd been around enough to know this was one of the fundamentals of courting.

I sat and listened to his stories for hours about when he came over from Poland and settled in Chicago, working in the stockyards. He said he always took such a ribbing from the guys because he couldn't speak good English. A few of the hecklers learned their lesson when they tossed a scrap of meat at him. He said that's when they found out he should have probably been a fighter instead of working in the yards. His reputation helped him get onto the police force in the early 20's, he said. In his career with the force, he was in on all the famous or infamous cases, whichever view you accept. The killing of Dillinger in Chicago was his favorite story. That was when the Lady in Red set up Dillinger in front of a Chicago movie house. Gen's dad was involved in the ambush and he always wondered whether it was just a set-up to allow Hoover's G-men to get rid of Dillinger, once and for all. There were no proven charges against Dillinger then, and Dillinger didn't even have the opportunity to pull his pistol.

With her father's blessing and some gentle persuasion, Gen and I were one step from the altar. The clincher was a trip we took to Timberline Lodge at Mount Hood. Lew and Arnie planned the trip meticulously. At the Lodge that weekend, a Hollywood director was shooting a movie with

Rock Hudson and James Stewart, called *Bend of the River.* Lew had gotten to know the director and made arrangements for us to go to the set. Using the director's limousine to take Gen and me to the set on the side of the mountain was a great act which worked like a charm.

Shortly after that, Gen and I married. The whole gang showed up as did all the crowd from skid row. It was something to see all the tavern crowd dressed up in suits of sorts. Hickory and No-Legs Whitey, both had on their artificial legs. I had never seen those two guys on anything but the skateboards on which they rolled around. My brother by this time, had a night club out on the edge of town and he came in style, as my best man.

Charley was all set to go to work at a radio station, but he hadn't passed his test to get his radio telephone license. I had passed mine in about three months. But the instructor at the school, probably after hearing enough of those gravelly tapes of mine, recommended I go east to school to learn more about the up-and-coming field of television. He thought I should study to be an engineer. The school was in Chicago and this suited Gen just fine. There she could be with her friends and relatives. We packed everything we owned in a trailer hitched to our car and drove off for the American Institute.

I approached my studies with just one goal in mind, get through and do good. By now, my life had taken on a certain seriousness. Education, I believed, was the key to making the most of myself and I was determined to get everything I could out of the school. I did homework from the time I got home until I went to bed -- with one goal in mind, to learn as much as I could for the career I was anxious to start. Gen worked and we put my G.I. school checks in the bank.

My grades were flawless. I'd like to think that was because I was so brilliant and worked so hard, but the truth of the matter was, the school tended to grade a little easy. But with those grades and one of my teacher's recommendations I made plans to go on to graduate school.

Cal Tech and M.I.T were the two schools which interested me the most. My first choice was to get into a west coast school, since someone had told me I should go to a school in the area where I wanted to work. Their rationale had to do with becoming a part of the entrenched business world's old boy's network. Alumni tended to stick together, my advisor said, and managers tend to give more consideration to someone from their own alma mater.

Cal Tech accepted about one student from each state into the graduate school of engineering and I just didn't make the cut. At M.I.T, I fared better, probably because by the time I made application I was able to get a letter of recommendation from the technical director at the American Institute, Lee De Forest. He was a world renowned scientist and inventor of the Audion vacuum tube whose work made modern radio possible. The technical community respected his judgment.

Chicago was not a place I found particularly enjoyable to live, but that was not why I was there. I felt the same way about Boston. School was the number one thing on my mind. Getting an education was my sole purpose for being there. The trouble was at M.I.T, I had difficulty staying in the middle of the class, let alone the top. The competition was fierce and the studies became more and more abstract. Not only was that a problem, I missed the west coast. Just into the second semester of my graduate studies, I rationalized that Laplace transforms and Fourier analyses were not the part of engineering I wanted to do anyhow. My thoughts started to focus on leaving.

A recruiter passed through from the Boeing Airplane Company in Seattle and the idea of being close to Portland and working for the company that built the Flying Fortress, and the Stearman I flew in Primary was too much to resist. I accepted the offer, then I took almost all our savings and bought a brand-new Lincoln. We were going home in style. When I called my folks to let them know I was moving only one hundred and fifty miles from them, my dad said, "You seemed to have picked the perfect distance, close enough to borrow money but not close enough to pay it back." If that was an offer, I didn't think I would ever need it again. At last I was on my own.

I'd made a happy landing on very solid ground, at last . . . but everyone knows, no pilot stays on the ground for long.

The changes and trends brought by the Second World War became many of the critical events which marked the twentieth century. Both Japan and Germany are unexpected stories of success built from defeat. In our nation, Washington, D.C. transitioned from a sleepy berg to a major international hub. America entered the war with a national budget of 14 billion, and today the size of our budget is beyond our imagination. We talk about our future and we must ask ourselves how many zeros there are in a trillion dollars.

The industrial revolution rose to a new peak during the forties, as thousands of budding enterprises churned out machines of war. Production has continued to rise ever since and it is this economy which created a demand for workers and which brought women into the work force, giving them their most significant social boost in U.S. history.

From the first call to service during WW II, the government has continued to nudge its way more and more into the lives of American citizens. For the common good, they instituted new programs to meet new goals. As the war wound down America's servicemen benefitted from the single most successful and productive human initiative the government ever undertook, the *G.I. Bill of Rights*. It gave so many of us an opportunity to attain career heights our fathers couldn't dream of and opportunities that have never been as great before or since. Veterans flowed back into civilian life at the rate of one million a month until twelve million had returned to civilian clothes. And despite the opportunities, we had to realize that things would never be as they had been before. For many, it took time to realize those opportunities and the limitations which came with them.

The three years I spent in the service could have been the best or the worst years in my life. I can only say that those years were the most profound and influencing. And least I leave the impression the *Good War* really was *good*, I am acutely aware of the comrades of mine who contributed to the statistics of fifty million deaths, two thirds of which were civilians. They never had the opportunity to benefit from that for which they fought.

Hopefully it was not all for naught. For in this war, I believe America had its last chance to bring everlasting peace through a war fought on foreign soil. However, as Walt Whitman so aptly stated, "But where is what I started for so long ago? And why is it yet unfound?"

EPILOGUE

(discussed in the order in which they appear in the book)

Grandma and Grandpa: Grandpa died in 1955 leaving me with fond memories of stone piles, gopher tails and deep-down love. Grandma passed away three years later. Life for Grandma without Grandpa was purposeless as they had become inseparable over the many years.

Mom: My dear Mom died in September 1989 at the age of 88. Her health was failing, and she lost the desire to fight for her life. I knew that, as I visited her just one month before she passed away. But I remember when she was young and strong. She never grew old in my eyes. And I will miss her. My eyes grew moist as the minister read the following poem by an unknown author at her funeral:

I am standing upon the seashore. A ship at my side spreads her white sails to the morning breeze and starts for the blue ocean. She is an object of beauty and strength and I stand and watch her until at length she is only a ribbon of white cloud just where the sea and sky come to mingle with each other. Then someone at my side says, "There! She's gone." Gone where? Gone from my sight...that is all. She is just as large in mast and hull and spar as she was when she left my side, and just as able to bear her load of living freight...to the place of destination. Her diminished size is in me, not in her and just at the moment when someone at my side says, "There! She's gone!" There are other voices ready to take up the glad shout, "There! She comes!"
And that is dying.

Dad: I woke early one September morning in 1971 to the ring of the telephone. My brother Gord called to tell me our dad had died at the breakfast table that morning. Gone was my backup for all the times I needed help. As much as Dad complained, he was always there. Left now were the good memories. There was not one bad memory I could remember or that I cared to remember. That's the way it should be. I was sorry to see him go.

The family farm: In the summer of 1989, I returned to the farm for the first time in fifty-five years. My cousin Ron Vermeulen and his two sons were harvesting the wheat. Their huge green John Deere swathers crawled boldly across the countryside efficiently spewing out neat rows of cut grain. The grand old barn still stood as the landmark barn of the area next to the farmhouse. Grandma always wanted a farmhouse "rising majestically on the highest point on the property". But today the house lies empty far from the main road, as a castaway remnant of the past. Successful modern-day farmers don't live so far out in the country; they live in the city close to services and friends. Thus the final penalty was paid for the house being built far back on the property on a picturesque hill. I bounced along in a pickup truck, carrying a couple stacks of sandwiches made with bologna and mustard to Ron's two sons, and as I drove off the farm, the descendants of the gophers that I had tried to annihilate with Grandad's single shot .22 rifle for a penny a tail scurried across my path. The stone piles I had built over a half century before, loomed in the distance.

The passing farmhand and the loving trail he left: It was not until my mother passed away that I learned she had a daughter born out of wedlock in 1917. Mom never wanted my brother or me to know of the child and she never breathed a word about her. I suspect Mom put the fear of God in Dad so he too would never reveal her secret about our half sister. That must be why Dad told me shortly before he died, that I had another brother somewhere, and said he couldn't tell me any more. Once I learned of Dorothy, I invited her and her daughter, Doreen to my home. It was a real tear jerker having found a sister on her seventieth birthday, one who reminded me so much of my Mom. How terribly sad it was that it took so long for us to come together.

My brother Gord: After forty years in the tavern and automobile business in Portland, my brother finally settled into retirement and decided he would make sure his car is working even if he is not.

Dorothy Gallager: My mother was cautious in choosing friends, and even more cautious in changing them. Dorothy remained a friend until she died at the age of 70, still telling the embellished story of saving me from the runaway logging train.

R.B. Wesley: R.B. in the early '50s walked out of the past and into my brother's tavern, ordering a short beer. That was the last and only time we have heard from the boy who taught me so much about street smarts.

Streetcars: When streetcars disappeared from Portland in the late '30s and throughout the country in the early '40s, most people thought it was simply a reflection of the changing times. This turned out not to be the case. A corporation, National City Lines, owned by Standard Oil, General Motors, Firestone Tires and Mack Truck conspired to buy up and destroy the nation's streetcar system. In 1947 the conspirators were brought to trial and found guilty.

Miss Crissy: When I returned from the war in '45, I visited Miss Crissy at her home in Portland where she had retired. I joked with her about the times she had rapped my knuckles with her ruler. I remember her pointing out to me that teaching children to count is not as important as teaching them what counts.

Gregory Heights Elementary School: The school building stands today in as good a shape as when I walked its halls. Now Gregory Heights is a middle school and is expanding with the addition of an impressive new wing. The year nineteen hundred and ninety marked the building's sixty-third year. Discipline is still the watchword, although running in the halls and throwing spitballs have been replaced by smoking and doing drugs as the primary offenses which get kids in trouble.

Gregory Heights School store: The school store across the street from Gregory Heights, where I first meet Jack Kendall is now a crack house, a far cry from a place we could buy a lucky bite during recess.

Wesco free writing system: Like many fads, the Wesco free writing system disappeared in a couple of years and Gregory Heights returned to the archaic but uncomplicated Palmer system. To the dismay of any who must decipher my handwriting, I know only the Wesco system. This ornate script, coupled with an unsteady hand and a solid resistance to spelling words the same way twice, created a communication problem throughout my life which I always preferred to overcome with good conversation.

Jack Morton: Mort retired in Oregon and now runs a fence company out of his home. Though he became a better than average golfer, he still says that his best drive down the fairway is in a golf cart.

Marion Morton: Marion and Lionel Beers are still married and are retired in Portland after forty-seven years. That's the proof one can get married at eighteen and make it last. She will forever be my first kiss, which I think more fondly of now than when it happened.

Jack Lewis: Lew died in the mid-sixties of a brain tumor. The headaches he had while sailing were a warning unheeded. My memories will always be of coming around a point on a close haul in a fair breeze, with Lew chiding, "Mel, keep the wind in the sails. What kind of a sailor are you, anyway?"

John Peacheos: The Greek is retired in Portland after a life of driving trucks and overhead cranes. He enjoys traveling to Greece, looking up relatives, and thinking of a foreign life that could have been. He, like me, believes that the Lord will not deduct a day from your life for any day spent fishing.

Clyde Beaty: Mr. Beaty died at the age of eighty-five after dedicating much of his life to the church, shepherding hundreds of children like myself through their childhood journeys. He believed that the world at its worst needed us at our best and he strived hard to make every one of us that way.

Fenton Royal: Red became a successful veterinarian in Portland, and the dogs to this day are delighted to visit his hospital.

Wesley Kocker: Koke lived in the country near Woodburn, Oregon until his untimely death. His wartimes in the submarine encouraged him to spend his few years where there were farm animals, fresh air and peacefulness.

The Paisley's first home on 66th street: My parents paid fifteen hundred dollars for the first house they ever owned. The house has not changed over the years, however, its latest occupants recently paid fifty thousand dollars for the privilege of living there.

Roseway Theater: The Roseway Theater after sixty-three years still serves the neighborhood as well as it did in the past. Gone are the race nights and the giveaways from the movie house. But I recently saw some race-night dishes at an antique auction selling for a hefty twenty-five dollars each.

Okie, Arkie and Tex: Many transients of the crop fields during the Depression remained in the area as times improved. They drove the machinery of the war industries and became the new generation of citizens in the West.

Soap Box Derby: The Derby lives today as a fifty-five year old institution. In 1971 girls were officially permitted to enter the races. Four years later, Karren Stead of Lower Buck Country, Pennsylvania won the Nationals at Akron. Today over twenty-five percent of all the entrants at the national are girls.

Virginia Rogers: Soon after the war I gave blood to Virginia's grandmother. While I waited in the hospital, Virginia and I had a good laugh about the Red Cross girls and how the cold steps finally caught up with me. I never saw Virginia again, but I have faith she lived a good life.

Don Hoff: Until he retired, Don ran his father-in-law's car dealership in Reading, California. He used to tell me he could make my car sound good--simply by quoting me the price of a new one.

Elaine: Elaine was lost to the memories of time. Love at first sight was wisely overthrown by love with insight.

Yaws, Tik Tok, Top Notch, Jim Dandy's Drive-ins: Drive-ins with carhops and hot rods faded into the past. But Jim Dandy's still operates today with ghosts of the past kicking up dust as they peel out for a drag on the edge of town.

Junior Kendall: Junior died at the age of seventy. He always said that being twenty years old was not much better than being seventy years young.

Hot-Rodders: Most of the heavy-footed iron pushers went on to do something else in life which was unrelated to the good times we shared. An exception is Emmy Payne, who runs a combination foundry-machine shop in Portland that only an old hot-rodder would appreciate. Wearing greasy cords and a gow hat, he still reflects our glories past.

Polly Green: I renewed old friendships with Polly when I ran on her while boarding a cross-country flight in the early seventies. The sight of her eighteen year old daughter took me right back to the days of the rumble seat Polly and I carried from her friend's hopped-up Chrysler.

General "Hap" Arnold: Hap died in January, 1950 at his home in southern California, having been instrumental in the formation and development of the Army Air Force. Still today he is the only five star general that the Air Force has ever had.

Santa Ana Army Air Base: After turning out 120,000 bombardiers, navigators and pilots to the training commands, the air base slowly shut down operations after the war. Homes, schools, and shops blanket the area on the fringes of Los Angeles.

Luke Army Air Field, Mira Loma Flight Academy, and Marana Army Air Field: Luke Field still operates as one of the leading training schools of the Air Force. Mira Loma is gone and the field is a privately-owned facility. Marana is still an active airfield used by the Arizona Army National Guard as well as some civilians reportedly engaged in clandestine operations.

Paul Ollerton: Paul retired from the Arizona Air Guard as a General and wiles away his time on a cotton ranch in Casa Grande trying to figure out what the government is going to do in farm subsidy next. He complains to me on a regular basis as if I, as a former member of government, was the one who screwed things up.

Russell Oplinger: Op died in the late '60s, a death surely accelerated by too much demon rum. I will always remember him for the days of wine and roses.

Donald Parry: Parry spent a lifetime serving the Government as a civil servant and week-end Arizona National Guardsman. He now spends his time on the west coast of Mexico; his house powered by a solar power generator and his drinking water trucked in once a week.

D.J. Ross: D.J., living as always in California, retired after spending a lifetime close to the firehouse where he worked most of his career.

Sanford Ross: Starting from the day it was formed, Sandy has been active in the P-47 Pilots Association. After many years he talked me into joining the association and we have had many a night at these reunions re-flying the bombing run on the bridge at Cologne.

Ted Cauthorn: Ted and Wheel married and are still as happy today as the first time I saw them romping on the beach at Seaside, Oregon, when we were home on leave in early '44.

The Jug: The P-47 Pilots Association preserves the memory of this great plane. Also a precious few still fly in the Confederate Air Force. I am proud to have flown the greatest airplane ever built. *La Mort* was only one of the over fifteen thousand that flew in combat.

The Mirabelle Restaurant: The Mirabelle still operates as one of the premier restaurants in London and has, over the years, received more than its share of my hard-earned salary.

Rothschild estate in Paris: My travels to Europe over many years have offered an opportunity to visit many places which bring back fond memories. Particularly delightful was my visit to the American Embassy in Paris. Today the Embassy is in the old Rothschild estate where I spent so many memorable times with the Maquis during the war. I could see Jacques standing there telling me that Annie was on the back porch waiting for me.

Jacques: Though I don't know where Jacques is today, I cherish my memories of a young pilot who appreciated having a worldly friend and comrade at the right time in life.

Annie Simsen: In 1976, I located my old flame Annie, who was living in the outskirts of Paris. As I knocked on her door, I wondered if she would recognize me, or if I would recognize her. A young girl answered the door and I said in English, "Is Annie here?" I could hear the sounds of some shuffling footsteps and muffled French voices, as an elderly lady came to the door. My mind flashed a twinge of recognition, and it lingered. The woman spoke in a very labored English. She said the young girl who came to the door was her granddaughter. It was almost an awkward reunion with Annie, but I left happy that I had found a piece of my past. Too big a gap in time had passed to build an enduring friendship on what we once had, and our cultures had grown too far apart.

Erickson's Saloon: Erickson's still stands with a well-maintained front entrance. Only the memories linger of the rough and tumble loggers from many, many generations gone by who once frequented the famous bar.

Tactical Air Force: Over the years those men who were dedicated to fighting air battles dominated over those dedicated to supporting our nation's ground troops. The Tactical Air Force is no longer prepared to support the Army as it did so well in WWII. The Marine air support of the Marine ground forces is all that remains of what is a much-needed defense element which grew out of the Great War.

Other Comrades from the 390th Fighter Squadron: Maurice "Marty" Martin, Lowell Smitty Smith, John "Doc" Clark, George Wilcox, Emil Bertza, Michael Horgan, Bob Burnes, Pete White, Norman Holt, John Feeney, Bob Brulle, D.C. Johnson, Currie Davis, Marvin Miller, Ray and Jack Kennedy, John Picton, Ross Gibson, Clure Smith, "Dutch" Scholz, Joe Lackey, and Clair Cullinan have all been seen at one time or another at reunions or a gathering of the eagles. More often than not each encounter brings news of the passing of another friend.

Asch, Belgium (Y-29): It is difficult to locate precisely the sight of our former field, though it is clear that it lies beneath what is now a Belgium auto freeway.

Hasselt, Belgium: Hasselt today looks like the town it was in 1944, and Marie's tavern is still operating though it is under new management. Marie is just a fond memory of a loving Belgium girl.

Genk, Belgium: The village of Genk is now a booming town, larger than Hasselt, which once overwhelmed it.

The fine mannered Brits with less than perfect eyesight: While on a visit to England, I had occasion to have lunch with Prime Minister Margaret Thatcher. In talking to her about the fortieth anniversary D-day ceremony, it triggered me to mention the story of my getting shot down by a flight of British Typhoons during the war. Mrs. Thatcher immediately gave a signal to another guest, the British Minister of Defence who was Michael Heseltine at the time. She said to him, "I think you owe this chap an apology for our having shot him down during the Second World War." Mr. Heseltine looked at me and said graciously, "Is that right? I guess we do owe you an apology." My response was admittedly cheeky, "I've waited so long, Mr. Heseltine--I prefer, if it's not inconvenient, to have it in writing." Within a month the apology was delivered by Mr. Roger Harding of the British Embassy. The letter read as if it were written by a cautious lawyer blessed with a clever sense of humor which was unmistakably British: "It has come to my attention that in October 1944, during the so-called Battle of the Bulge, your P-47 was mistakenly shot down by four aircraft which you believed to be RAF Typhoons, attacking out of the sun. While this would say much for the quality of marksmanship and tactical percipience of the Royal Air Force, the pilots' professionalism and enthusiasm were, in this instance, obviously misdirected. I am delighted to be reassured that you suffered neither a hard bump nor hard feelings; we hope to continue to have you in our sights for some time to come!" The letter was such a delightful ending to the real-life saga which was better remembered as a story told.

General James Hollingsworth: Having fought in every war and major police action since WWII, Holly retired as a four star General and now lives in Texas. Our paths crossed many times as I interfaced with the military as an aerospace marketeer. I would complain to him about the outrageous cost of the American war machine and he'd tell anyone who'd listen, and some who wouldn't, that "the cost of our equipment doesn't matter a diddly squat. The only thing that really matters is if you win or lose the war. Winning isn't everything, but losing is nothing."

The 366th Fighter Group: The 366th lives and has fought in every engagement since WWII. It is now based at Mountain Home, Idaho. I was fortunate to have had the opportunity to fly with the 390th squadron in their high-performance F-111s, which they used to support the 1986 raid in Libya.

The cigar-smoking macho image: It took almost twenty years to break my habit of smoking cigars. It began with the encouragement of a well-meaning wartime photographer. I progressed from smoking five-cent White Owls to savoring fifty-cent Dutch Masters. I stopped smoking only after realizing there was little need for me to look any older, and if I continued the habit I might never have to concern myself with how I looked at all.

Genevieve: Genevieve provided me with some fond memories and a great family of kids before our divorce proved her mother was right after all.

Charley and Gladys Milam: After a lifetime in radio announcing, Charley and Gladys settled in Medford, Oregon. Charley says he can tell he is getting old because his feet hurt before he gets out of bed.

Curly's Roseway Tavern and the Roseway crowd: The Roseway tavern is now a bicycle shop and the motley crowd is lost to memories. I can still remember the wisdom of Loud-mouth Johnson's remark, "They better not try to cremate any of these guys when they die or they're liable to blow up the mortuary."

Arnie Johnson: Arnie appeared in my driveway one evening as a white-haired man on a Kawasaki motorcycle. I hadn't seen him in over twenty-five years. We had communicated once when he was in the hospital after a horse rolled on him when he was wrangling in the Blue Mountains of eastern Oregon. He said he'd spent the last twenty years down in Mexico and had been married several times. Just like Arnie, he didn't recall anything about getting divorced. As much as I tried to convince him to stay for a visit, he said he had to keep moving along to get where he was going. He never said where that was, and I'm sure he'll never know.

82. The Gang's reunion in Oregon, 1978. Fenton "Red" Royal, Mel, Wesley "Koke" Kocker, Jack "Mort" Morton, John "the Greek" Peacheos. Friends for all times.

INDEX